Planning for Retail Development

i

Planning for Retail Development

A critical view of the British experience

Clifford Guy

Routledge
Taylor & Francis Group

LONDON AND NEW YORK

First published 2007
by Routledge
2 Park Square, Milton Park, Abingdon, Oxon OX14 4RN

Simultaneously published in the USA and Canada
by Routledge
270 Madison Ave, New York, NY 10016

Routledge is an imprint of the Taylor & Francis Group, an informa business

© 2007 Clifford Guy

Typeset in Galliard by
HWA Text and Data Management, Tunbridge Wells
Printed and bound in Great Britain by
The Cromwell Press, Trowbridge, Wiltshire

British Library Cataloguing in Publication Data
A catalogue record for this book is available from the British Library

Library of Congress Cataloging in Publication Data
Guy, Clifford.
Planning for retail development : a critical view of the British experience /
Clifford Guy.
    p.   cm.
Includes bibliographical references and index.
1. Retail trade–Government policy–Great Britain. 2. Retail trade–Great
Britain–Planning. I. Title.
HF5429.6.G7G893 2006
381′.10941–dc22   2006009107

ISBN10: 0–415–35453–6 (hbk)
ISBN10: 0–203–00122–2 (ebk)

ISBN13: 978–0–415–35453–0 (hbk)
ISBN13: 978–0–203–00122–6 (ebk)

Contents

Acknowledgements

This is a book I have wanted to write for several years. My reading of the endless stream of policy statements and commentaries on retail planning in Britain has suggested that policy is not as coherent or as well founded on research evidence as some would like us to believe. It seems also that a tendency to 're-invent the wheel' shows that past successes and failures of policy are not as widely appreciated as they might be. This book attempts, firstly, to fill a gap in the retailing and planning literatures, by explaining the growth of policy instruments intended to direct retail development in what are seen as socially beneficial ways. Secondly, it attempts a critical appraisal of many of the core objectives and beliefs of policy makers, through examining evidence of the behaviour of retailers and consumers in Britain.

I was fortunate to be awarded a Research Fellowship by the Economic and Social Research Council (reference RES-000-27-0040) which enabled me to escape from routine teaching and administrative duties for two years, in order to prepare this book. I am grateful to Professor Terry Marsden for encouraging me to apply for this award, and all my colleagues at Cardiff University for 'filling in' various duties for me during my absence. I would also like to acknowledge the help of the National Retail Planning Forum, particularly Geoff Steeley and George Nicholson, who took a keen interest in this project and invited me to present some of my findings at the Forum's 10th Anniversary Meeting in November 2005.

Many practitioners and researchers have shown interest in this exercise. Special thanks are due to those who kindly read through draft chapters and suggested factual corrections and improvements in content: Peter M. Jones (Chapter 2); Professor Stephen Crow (Chapters 2 and 5); Michael Bach (Chapter 4); Professor Roger Clarke (Chapter 6); Professor Huw Williams (Chapter 7); Mark Bradshaw (Chapter 8); and Professor Michelle Lowe (Chapter 9). Many other colleagues, including David Bennison, Liz Cannings, Graham Clarke, Gemma David, John England, Chris Goddard, Jonathan Reynolds, Mike Taylor and Neil Wrigley have collaborated in past research exercises or added to my understanding of policy issues. Of course, none of these people or their employing organisations should be held responsible for any opinions expressed in this book.

I would also like to thank the staff of Cardiff University Information Services for their assistance in tracking down obscure material; and applaud the policy of the UK Government and other representative bodies in making reports, statistics and policy statements freely available to researchers through their well-organised websites. Helen Ibbotson and Kate McDevitt at Taylor and Francis have been helpful and efficient.

Finally, as always, my greatest thanks are due to my family for their continued interest and support.

Abbreviations

AMT	Action for Market Towns
AR	Accessible Retail
BCOTR	British Council for Out of Town Retail
BCSC	British Council of Shopping Centres
BITC	Business in the Community
BRC	British Retail Consortium
CABE	Commission for Architecture and the Built Environment
CASA	Centre for Advanced Spatial Analysis
CBHP	CB Hillier Parker
CBRE	CB Richard Ellis
CPRE	Campaign to Protect Rural England
DCPN	Development Control Policy Note
DEFRA	Department of Food and Rural Affairs
DETR	Department of the Environment, Transport and the Regions
DfT	Department for Transport
DoE	Department of the Environment
DoH	Department of Health
DoT	Department of Transport
DTEDC	Distributive Trades Economic Development Council
DTI	Department of Trade and Industry
DTLR	Department of Transport, Local Government and the Regions
ESRC	Economic and Social Research Council
FoE	Friends of the Earth
FTE	Full-time equivalent
GLA	Greater London Authority
IGD	Institute of Grocery Distribution
IMRG	Interactive Media in Retail Group
JPEL	Journal of Planning and Environment Law
LDA	London Development Agency
MHLG	Ministry of Housing and Local Government
NEF	New Economics Foundation
NPPG	National Planning Policy Guidance

NRPF	National Retail Planning Forum
ODPM	Office of the Deputy Prime Minister
OFT	Office of Fair Trading
ORG	Oxford Retail Group
OXIRM	Oxford Institute of Retail Management
PPG	Planning Policy Guidance
PPS	Planning Policy Statement
RTPI	Royal Town Planning Institute
SDD	Scottish Development Department
SEDD	Scottish Executive Development Department
SEU	Social Exclusion Unit
SODD	Scottish Office Development Department
UDP	Unitary Development Plan
URPI	Unit for Retail Planning Information
WO	Welsh Office

Chapter 1
Introduction

This chapter explains the context within which a description and evaluation of retail planning in Britain should take place. It first summarises the purpose of the book, and then discusses the meaning of the term 'retail planning', and explains why most commentators in this area feel retail planning to be necessary. The operation of retail planning and the agencies directly responsible are then discussed briefly. Finally, the topics addressed in forthcoming chapters are introduced.

The aims of this book are:

- To offer a critical history of the development of retail planning policy in Great Britain.[1] Changes in policy are explained with reference to trends in retailing methods and shopping behaviour, and political attitudes to retail development and change.
- To provide a critical view of the basic assumptions which appear to underlie policy. This leads to an evaluation of policy in terms of consistency, effectiveness, and its impacts upon retailer, consumer and town planning interests.
- To relate developments in retail planning policy to other governmental objectives, including the enhancement of productivity, the achievement of sustainable development, and encouragement of urban regeneration and social inclusion.
- To offer views on the most suitable future path of the retail planning system, and the role and content of national level guidance to local authorities and the private sector.

The case for retail planning

Retail planning, the focus of this book, involves the interaction of the private sector (retail property development) with the public sector (the town planning function of central and local government, and occasionally other agencies). It is usually described as part of the process of government regulation of the retail system, although it could be argued that the strategic planning activities of retail organisations, especially concerning new store development, are also part of the retail planning process. The practitioner Bryan Wade (1979: 51) summarised retail planning as

> the planned provision of retail outlets in which the following questions assume critical importance:
> - How much or how many?
> - What type?
> - When?
> - Where?

He went on to note that 'these questions ... cannot be answered in a simple direct manner. The results are the outcome of a complex process of decision making, politics and horse trading' (ibid.).

In discussing the case for retail planning, we should first examine some reasons why it is claimed that public sector intervention is necessary at all in the operation of the retail system.

Boddewyn and Hollander (1972), as summarised by Dawson (1983a), set out five objectives for public policy controls over retailing:

- protecting smaller retailers;
- achieving price stability;
- improving the efficiency of retailing;
- ensuring consumer protection; and
- protecting the environment.

Of these, the first and second have not usually been a specific aim of the UK government, in contrast to some other European countries. The other three objectives have consistently been UK government policy, although the ways in which they have been applied have varied over time.

Davies (1984: 72–5) drew attention to the role of central government in regulating the retail sector, although he also noted that there was 'no special ministry or government department concerned exclusively with the development of the distributive trades ... nor is there a major council or advisory body'. He claimed that this led to a lack of comprehensive monitoring of retailing methods and retail developments, and to a potential for inconsistencies in government policies or even lack of policy in crucial areas.

This type of discussion does not itself justify retail planning as a public sector activity; it can be argued that the retail industry itself can achieve 'the planned provision of retail outlets' in the absence of government regulation, as is broadly the case in parts of North America. Furthermore, any restriction of retail growth and change is likely to impose additional costs upon the retail industry, and hence upon consumers in the form of limited competition or raised prices. Commentators therefore argue that a wider 'public interest' has to be invoked in order to justify intervention through the town and country planning system.

'Public interest' is a much used term in this type of discussion:

> The planning system seeks ... to provide a mechanism for overriding or modifying the operation of the marketplace where it is seen to be against the public interest. What constitutes the public interest is not defined but it is founded on the recognition that land is a scarce resource and its use for private or public sector purposes is of interest to all citizens. Public interest is served if private investment is directed to places and land uses which allow both private and public services to exist and, at the same time, provide benefit to private capital and the general public in a cost effective way. Central and local government, in ensuring adequate provision of these public services, seek to minimise the cost and maximise the benefit to the community.
>
> (DTEDC, 1988: 66)

This largely economic case for planning intervention suggests that retail planning policy should allow the retail sector to grow and change while maintaining a satisfactory level of profitability. Indeed, increasing profitability may itself be within the public interest if it brings wider benefits to national and local economies. However, the public interest also includes non-economic considerations such as the welfare of 'socially excluded' elements of the population, or the need to preserve historic and attractive physical and natural environments.

For example, Thorpe (1974) suggested reasons for the use of planning controls over the retail sector in the UK:

1. The retail case: free market forces need to be carefully controlled in order to prevent the construction of an excessive quantity of shops and to achieve an optimum mix of shop types at the various levels of the retail hierarchy.
2. The urban case: due care needs to be given to planning the distribution of shopping facilities because of the influence they have on complementary land uses, as well as on the overall urban morphology. Town centre vitality is heavily dependent on the complex web of interactions between the diverse central functions.
3. The social planning case: retail planning is necessary in order to ensure equity in shopping provision, such that no socio-economic groups should become disadvantaged.
4. The environmental case: town planners should attempt to separate retailing from non-conforming or incompatible land uses and to minimise the environmental impact of new retail development.

(Thorpe, 1974: as summarised by Ibrahim and McGoldrick, 2003: 22–3)

One of the key questions in retail planning is the extent to which these so-called 'non-economic' matters should override the economic advantages of a particular proposal. Or, to express the professional view of many town planners, the essential question is to what extent the financial goals of retailers and property developers should affect a planner's stance concerning new retail development, where that stance is fundamentally informed by social and environmental criteria. This dilemma is likely to arise frequently, because many planners feel that the economic case for a proposed development is irrelevant when the proposal is being considered by the planning system (Campbell and Henneberry, 2005).

The 'urban case' noted by Thorpe (1974) has been particularly important to most retail planning practitioners:

> A genuine fear among many local authority planners is that the changes in the structure of shopping provision will result in underutilisation of existing facilities … Inherent in this view is the belief that there is a relationship between the retail function of a centre and its other functions to the extent that the success of the latter would be adversely affected if the former were to decline. … planners [also] fear that substantial loss of consumers' expenditure in town and city centres will cause a reduction in the level of services available and in the access provided for the disadvantaged groups of society.
>
> (DTEDC, 1988: 66)

This fear that retail development which takes place outside town centres will have adverse economic and social effects has dominated retail planning practice in Britain, and is a prominent theme in this book.

How retail planning is carried out in Britain

Retail planning takes place in Britain in ways which are rather different from those used in other parts of western Europe (for further details see Davies, 1979; 1995; Guy, 1998a). Retail planning is basically the responsibility of local planning authorities, in two ways. First, in their development plans they specify what appears to them a desirable future spatial pattern of retail development. Second, they decide whether to allow or refuse applications by retailers or property developers to develop new shopping centres or stores, or to provide retail premises in some other way. In this respect the British system is uniquely 'flexible' – each application has to be decided 'on its own merits', although within a framework of policy set out in development plans. Such policy may be criteria-based, indicating where and in what format retail development would normally be acceptable, and/or spatially based, indicating preferred uses for particular areas of land. These latter policies are often referred to as 'zoning', although they are generally more flexible in operation than the rigid zoning policies typical of most of western Europe and North America.

Local planning policies are in theory determined by elected local authority councillors, with advice from officers. Retail policy within development plans is usually fairly clearly specified for proposals of major importance, such as new shopping centres, and increasingly follows central government guidance. This guidance is provided so that local authority planning decisions should respect broader government objectives, and also serves to ensure consistency of policy across the country. If a local authority's development plan is out of date, central government policy in effect takes precedence. However, for minor proposals or for minor details of major proposals (including layout, appearance, etc) development plan policy does not usually give strong guidance, hence details tend to be negotiable between developer and planners:

> where there is an articulated policy which can be clearly applied to a case, development control and appeal decisions tend to abide by it. However, some areas do not have plans, some plans do not cover issues that arise in individual planning applications, and much development control has to rely on unwritten policy and professional skill and judgement.
>
> (Cullingworth and Nadin, 1997: 131)

Local authority councillors also decide on planning applications for new development, after seeking advice from officers. Unsuccessful developers are allowed to appeal to government ministries against refusal or failure to decide upon an application within a prescribed period of time. This shifts the responsibility for decision-making to 'independent' inspectors who conduct public hearings or inquiries into the proposal concerned. Inspectors are expected to make decisions compatible with current government policy, or in important cases, advise government ministers accordingly. In this way, many decisions on proposals for retail development are made more or less directly under central government control.

One key element in decision-making on retail proposals has been the status of factors which are not specifically included in development policies for retail development, but are significant in their own right and are relevant to the proposal or its location. These are usually termed 'other material considerations', and may include matters of design and appearance, or economic outcomes such as employment creation. Before 1991, it appeared that in practice, such considerations were often as important as or more important than development plan policies in determining the outcome of planning appeals. However, in 1991, new legislation held that decisions should be made 'in accordance with the [approved development] plan unless material considerations indicate otherwise'. This gave development plan policies greater weight in the decision process, as long as these policies were held to be 'up to date' and were in accord with central government policy (Cullingworth and Nadin, 1997: 131).

Central government policy itself is in principle devised by government ministers, but in practice the detailed guidance notes which are circulated to local authority planners are drafted by civil servants working in the appropriate Ministry or Department. The content of these guidance notes is generally consistent with broader government policies which relate to retailing and the physical and natural environment, and may also respond to the concerns of various interest groups. These may include organisations who help put the case for retailers and developers; environmental pressure groups; local authorities; and professional town planners as represented by the Royal Town Planning Institute (RTPI) or otherwise. Policy guidance notes are usually issued in draft form to allow interest groups to comment on their content and wording.

The content of this book

This brief review of retail planning and the town planning system in Britain suggests some issues which are explored in later chapters. These include:

- The ways in which a balance between the objectives of retail developers and town planners have been sought, by whom and with what degree of success.
- The degree of success in protecting town centres from what planners and small retailers tend to see as unfair competition.
- The extent to which local authority decision-making on retail applications is controlled by central government policy and practice.
- The extent to which conflicts between different government policies and objectives which affect retail planning have been resolved.
- The ways in which formulation of policy at central and local level have responded to the concerns of interest and pressure groups.

This book examines these and other such issues, using a wide range of academic and professional literature, as well as benefiting from the author's past involvement in case studies and discussions with professionals on all sides. The focus of the book is mainly on public sector policy which relates to the location, size and type of new retail development: methods of retail planning such as sales forecasting or impact analysis are not discussed in depth. Nor is much attention paid to details of design and layout of proposed retail development. These areas have been covered adequately in previous texts such as Birkin *et al.* (2002) and Guy (1994a).

The chapters which follow this introduction fall into two main parts. The first part (Chapters 2 to 5) relate the history of retail planning policy, from the 1960s to the mid-2000s. This history is discussed within a framework of changing trends in retailing and property development, and the growth of new ideas about retail planning purposes and methods. These chapters show how the initiative for planning the location, size and type of new developments has (in effect) swung from the public sector to the private sector, and back again. They also chart the increasing dominance of central government in retail planning.

Chapters 2, 3 and 4 each cover a discrete period of time, over which the essential elements of policy remained roughly constant. In the 1960s and 1970s (Chapter 2), retail planning policy began to emerge, mainly in response to new retail trends which appeared to threaten the prosperity of town centres. In the 1980s (Chapter 3), these trends intensified, supported to some extent by what many saw as an absence of direction from central government. Chapter 4 examines the revival of retail planning from the early 1990s, taking the story up to the time of writing (early 2006). This period has been characterised by a growing belief that government – at central and local levels – should take responsibility for determining the future growth of retail facilities; and also by increasing detail and complexity in central government policy guidance, culminating in Planning Policy Statement Six (ODPM, 2005a) and its Welsh and Scottish equivalents. Chapter 5 examines how a particular issue in retail planning – the assessment of 'need' and 'impact' – has developed over the whole time period covered by this book.

One clear trend over time is for retail planning to become more complex and to represent compromises not just between private and public sector requirements for retail development and change, but also between different government policies and objectives. Chapters 6 to 9 examine critically four of the most important such policies, which relate to competition and productivity; sustainable development and shopping travel; social inclusion; and urban regeneration. These chapters examine the justifications (stated and unstated) for these policies, and the ways in which they have influenced retail planning. Chapter 10 finally explores conflicts between retail planning objectives, as well as reviewing some of the issues raised in earlier chapters. It concludes with some recommendations for future directions for retail planning policy.

Chapter 2
Early days
Retail planning in the 1960s and 1970s

Introduction

This chapter examines the beginnings of what became known as retail planning, during the 1960s and 1970s. At the beginning of this period, there were already firm ideas in place about the proper distribution of retail facilities within urban areas, based loosely upon the academic foundation of central place theory. These notions were severely disrupted by the development of 'new forms of retailing', typified by free-standing large food stores and hypermarkets. A result of this was the first release of 'guidance' from central government ministries to local planning authorities and private sector developers.

This chapter charts the reaction of planning authorities to retail innovation, and also explains changing attitudes to retail development within town centres, which were already the focus of a great deal of developer interest. The chapter then examines ways in which both planning guidance and the policies of local authorities affected the pace of change, especially in the development of hypermarkets and superstores. The tension between planners and developers over 'large new stores' was to some extent relieved by a compromise solution, in the development of a new type of 'district centre'. This use of compromise, plus the tendency for ambiguous or poorly specified areas of policy to be examined through planning inquiries, are typical by-products of the 'flexible' nature of the British planning system, as discussed in Chapter 1.

The hierarchy of centres

Some of the earliest attempts at retail planning involved identification of a central place hierarchy (Davies, 1976), and regulation of new retail development to ensure that the hierarchy was preserved. This was consistent with a wider tradition in town planning, that land uses should be organised spatially under consistent and orderly principles. In a much-used text on planning, Lewis Keeble stated that:

> The objectives of Town Planning ... may be summarised as the provision of the
> right amount of land for each use in the right place and on sites physically suitable

for each use. This includes the proper spatial relationship ... of homes and shopping places of various levels.

(Keeble, 1969: 134)

In practice this led to fairly simple distinctions between town centres, which were the main destinations for comparison shopping, and smaller centres or groups of shops within residential areas, based largely around convenience needs. It was assumed that people would walk, cycle or use public transport to visit their nearest town centre, and would walk or cycle the short distance to the nearest local centre for everyday purchases. However, as many commentators pointed out, this simplistic picture failed to take into account either the ways in which competition between retailers led to more complex criteria for choice of centre, or the increasing accessibility to shopping afforded by use of the private car. Low (1975), in an article criticising what he termed 'centrism', showed how the notion of restricting retail and service development to 'centres' arose from a belief by planners that the empirical regularities identified by geographic researchers such as Berry (1967) were in some way ideal for an urban population. In particular, everyday or convenience needs could be met through 'neighbourhood centres' which through their central location were easily accessible by all those living in a 'neighbourhood'. Other factors influencing shopping destination choice, such as price of goods or car parking facilities, were implicitly ignored, although of course Berry (1967) was fully aware of these criticisms.

Up to the mid-1960s, proposals for major retail development were restricted almost entirely to central areas, except in larger towns and cities, where an intermediate category – usually termed the 'district centre' – was occasionally developed to supply a mixture of convenience goods and comparison goods in areas of suburban residential growth. For example, the Cowley Centre was developed in a suburb of Oxford between 1960 and 1965, and included some 70 shops built around a pedestrian area, and free car parking (Gayler, 1984: 27–8). In design and appearance, it resembled a scaled-down version of the town centres being built at that time in several New Towns.

District centres thus became an integral part of shopping provision in development plans. For example, Liverpool City Council proposed in the early 1960s a hierarchy consisting of (i) city centre; (ii) district centre, with population catchment of around 50,000; (iii) local centre, catchment around 15,000; and (iv), 'local level', catchment around 4,000–5,000 (MHLG, 1967: 28–9). The last of these categories was more commonly termed 'neighbourhood centre', following practice in the early New Towns, where centres were designed to serve neighbourhoods of between 5,000 and 10,000 population.

It was assumed that most people would walk to convenience shopping opportunities, and these were often developed as small 'shopping parades' within new residential areas – a phenomenon clearly seen in New Town design in the 1950s and 1960s (Keeble, 1969: 246–50). Burns (1959), in what might be claimed to be the first British text on retail planning, felt however that everyday shopping provision should be in district centres rather than local centres of under 10 shops, because the latter would not provide all goods required and would not allow competition between shops. He was critical of the 'neighbourhood centre' concept, stating that neighbourhoods (in New Towns and elsewhere) were based around the requirements of primary schools, and that the idea of having a group of shops in the centre of each neighbourhood had been imposed without any consideration of shoppers' preferences or economic reality. Pain (1967) agreed, stating that:

> The future of the neighbourhood centre is uncertain, many of them are too large to be economic. There is a growing tendency … for the bulk of household shopping to be done once a week. The advantages of a great variety of shops and goods in the town centre, coupled with the more social aspect of a family outing by car on Saturday morning, outweigh the more convenient location of neighbourhood centres, and the corner shop is quite adequate for immediate daily necessities …
>
> (Pain, 1967: 8–9)

For convenience of access, Burns (1959) thought that district centres should be supplemented by the modern equivalent of corner shops, either as isolated examples or in very small groups. He did not foresee the development, some ten years later, of large food stores with their own car parking facilities.

Burns tried to base his ideas partly on what he saw as shoppers' needs. For example the corner shop was supported on two grounds – convenience (assuming that everyday items such as food would be bought almost daily and on foot), and as an informal place for social interaction. The traditional corner shop (in its unplanned guise as a converted residential front room) was however criticised for spoiling the 'amenity' of residential areas. Burns also observed that such shops were inefficient and hardly viable in economic terms.

Burns was one of many writers who were very critical of the uncontrolled way in which shopping provision had grown since the late nineteenth century. This meant that there were too many corner shops, and too much retailing along main suburban roads (leading to serious traffic problems and a bad shopping environment). He felt that town planners should be able to control numbers and types of shops to achieve some sort of balance between shopper convenience and choice, economic viability and town planning principles. The latter would include aspects such as visual amenity, the separation of vehicular and pedestrian traffic, and good quality access to shops for goods deliveries and customers.

The attitudes of most town planners to retail provision in the 1960s can be summarised as follows. The central place hierarchy was seen as a good description of the system of retail provision in typical towns and cities, and was a device for ensuring that expansion and modernisation of retail facilities took place in an orderly fashion. The use of private cars for shopping purposes was seen as an increasingly severe problem, one which would require extensive redevelopment of central areas (see below).

It is not clear whether any attempts were made to restrict the floor area of new development in relation to either the position of the centre's place in the hierarchy, or to its population catchment, although methods existed to enable this to be done. In a book intended mainly for an audience of retail companies and property agents, Cox (1968) included a whole chapter on 'estimating shopping provision'. This set out methods which could be used by planning consultants or local authorities 'for towns where population is increasing or real incomes are rising' (Cox, 1968: 146). He explained methods, also dealt with in more detail in the publication *Urban Models in Shopping Studies* (DTEDC, 1970), of calculating sales area requirements for both existing town centres and brand new centres in New Towns or fast-growing suburban areas. It seems likely that such methods were used in planning shopping provision for New Towns (e.g. Diamond and Gibb, 1962), but only rarely by town centre developers or local authority planners.

Early principles of town centre planning

Town centres were the only component of retail planning in which considerable progress had been made since the 1940s, in both academic writing and planning practice. One of the most complete statements of current thinking about the design and function of town centres was to be found in the well-known town planning text by Lewis Keeble. He considered that 'The most important requirements for a town centre are geographical centrality, accessibility for vehicles and pedestrians, ample parking space and a high measure of compactness' (Keeble, 1969: 195). Thus the emphasis was firmly on external access, particularly by car, and internal ease of movement, particularly on foot.

The powers of compulsory purchase bestowed upon local planning authorities in the Town and Country Planning Act of 1944, for 'areas of bad layout and obsolescent development', led to the designation of Comprehensive Development Areas within town centres. Burns (1959) explained in depth how these powers could be used to redevelop town centres, incorporating ring roads, multi-storey car parks and pedestrianised shopping streets, drawing upon his experience in remodelling the central area of Coventry following wartime damage.

Cox (1968) provided a more critical view of the planning system and its policies for retailing, for his intended audience of retailers and property agents. His discussion of town planning policies focused mainly on town centres and included three main issues: 'traffic congestion', 'worn-out buildings' and 'population growth' (Cox, 1968: 135). Taken together these issues supported the case for partial redevelopment of the town centre. In this respect the local planning authority should

> view the problem of town centre redevelopment from the point of view of:
>
> 1. Function: A decision has to be made as to the future size and purpose of a centre. Is the population served by it growing or declining? Will it in the future serve as a primary centre, or is it overshadowed by other centres and its future function limited to a secondary role?
> 2. Layout: If shops are not conveniently located to their markets and to each other, or bus stations, car parks and public buildings are not accessible to the shops, then the layout of the centre is inefficient. Any redevelopment must weld together all these functions of a town centre. This will include offices and entertainment facilities.
> 3. Circulation: Proper circulation of traffic and pedestrians is particularly bound up with layout. Through traffic should be diverted so that it does not interfere with vehicles having business in the town centre. Pedestrians must be able to reach each part of the town centre quickly and efficiently.
> 4. Character: Redevelopment does not mean the wholesale slaughter of an old town centre and its replacement by something entirely different. There should be some continuity; certain old buildings may add to the character of a town and they should be preserved ...
>
> (Cox, 1968: 137; based upon MHLG, 1962: 3)

Cox also stated 'Currently there is much stress on keeping a centre alive at night by introducing entertainment facilities and even housing into a redevelopment' (Cox, 1968: 138). This marked a gradual change in government advice over preceding decades. Following the Second World War, the view had been that 'central areas ... are unsuitable for residential buildings' and 'Permission for other types of development within the [shopping] zone should not be granted on a scale or in places which would endanger the shopping character of the zone or its efficiency for its primary purpose' (Ministry of Town and Country Planning, 1947: paras 88, 102).

Keeble also believed (1969: 203) that 'There seems to me to be little place for residential uses within the town centre ... Noise, traffic and the lack of outdoor space are the most obvious drawbacks'. He disparaged the notion of a 'café society' in British town centres, dismissing such thoughts as:

> a nostalgic yearning for the kind of night life to be found in the centres of continental towns ... [which] are indeed in many ways delightful, but their

availability springs in part from a different pattern of social life, based less firmly upon the home than in Britain, and in part on a kindlier climate.

(Keeble, 1969: 206)

However, one of the Planning Bulletins produced during the 1960s to advise local authorities on town centre renewal noted with approval the incorporation of housing within town centre (re)developments, using mainly examples from the New Towns (MHLG, 1963: Section 4).

Government policy in the 1960s appeared to be that shopping development should be confined largely to town centres, apart from some convenience retailing located within residential areas. This policy was however modified in 1969 with the issuing of advice to local authorities that district centres should be considered for development in towns with central area traffic congestion (MHLG, 1969). These district centres, as suggested by Burns (1959), would serve some 20,000–40,000 people with a mixture of convenience and comparison goods, and might also include leisure and social facilities. As noted above, cities such as Liverpool had already adopted these ideas.

Generally, however, the town planning profession seems to have been little concerned with developments in retailing, and vice versa. For example, an economist's review of trends in the 1960s does not include any mention of town planning amongst 'Government action affecting the distributive trades' (Corner, 1969). A similar review at the end of the 1970s however gave more prominence to town planning policies (Bamfield, 1980).

'New forms of retailing'

In the early 1960s three major trends became established in retailing and shopping behaviour, which have influenced retail development and retail planning policy ever since. These were:

- The growth of self-service retailing, initially in food stores in the 1950s, following much earlier North American innovation. This encouraged the development of more spacious stores, able to display a much wider range of goods.
- The growth of price competition between retail outlets. This derived initially from the abolition of Resale Price Maintenance for most retail goods, in 1963. It enabled retail companies to rapidly expand sales, albeit at a cost to profit margins. Higher sales levels allowed faster growth through development of new stores, and economies of scale in purchasing goods from manufacturers and suppliers. With the simultaneous growth in self-service techniques, a new wave of much larger supermarkets, and eventually other non-food stores, could be developed.

- The growth in the use of cars for shopping. In order to make full advantage of the new wave of large stores, customers needed their own car for taking large quantities of groceries or other goods home. This meant that retail developers now sought car parking facilities, preferably very close to the store, free to the customer and on the same level as the store entrance. Suburban or edge-of-town sites were preferred, because they were closer to where the most affluent customers lived, and land was cheaper and more readily available than in central areas.

The 1960s thus saw major changes in suburban retailing in the US and in parts of continental Europe. These resulted from the opportunities provided by a more affluent and mobile customer base, particularly in the suburbs of the larger cities; and the desire amongst retailers to pursue economies of scale in the form of large and functionally designed stores and shopping malls. Developers started building outside the traditional urban shopping areas, in order to benefit from cheap, large sites readily accessible by car.

The first such development appears to have been the GEM store, which opened in 1964 on a site at West Bridgford, near Nottingham. Although this later became an Asda hypermarket, its original form was more like a department store, with individual departments run by concessionaires. Its sales area was about 80,000 sq.ft. and there were 1,000 car parking spaces (Whysall, 1999).

In the late 1960s and early 1970s, most of the pressure for development outside existing centres came from supermarket operators. They emphasised the advantages of operating large stores built on cheap, accessible suburban land, which would enable shoppers to have a wider choice of items at lower prices and in pleasant, convenient surroundings (e.g. Sainsbury, 1973; Ridgway, 1976). These stores – over 25,000 sq.ft. in sales area – quickly became known as 'superstores', to differentiate them from the larger hypermarkets which included a substantial non-food offer. The main superstore developers were retail companies – particularly Asda in the early days, followed later by Tesco and Sainsbury – whereas hypermarkets (over 50,000 sq.ft. sales area) were associated with the Carrefour and Woolco fascias.[1]

The 1960s also saw the first regional shopping mall proposed in the UK at Haydock Park, Lancashire. This proposal, as with the later Brent Cross scheme (see below), was based upon the North American model and would have included department stores and comparison goods retailing, rather than the supermarkets and community facilities typical of suburban district centres.

At some time during this period a much less reported phenomenon began to take place, although one with important consequences. Large stores selling non-foods – usually furniture, carpets and electrical goods – were established in areas outside existing shopping centres. Typically these early stores either derived from wholesale and mail order businesses which started selling goods direct to the public from the warehouse, or made use of redundant mills, factories, chapels, cinemas, etc.

The 1960s also saw the first examples of integrated, pedestrianised shopping malls in British towns and cities. These were an adaptation of North American community and regional centres (Dawson, 1983b), but developed entirely within central areas, often involving the replacement of existing retailing or mixed land uses. Most town centre schemes at this time were open or partially enclosed 'shopping precincts', anchored around a supermarket or a variety store such as Marks and Spencer. Towards the end of the decade, some larger and fully enclosed schemes began to appear. For further details see Guy (1994a: Chapter 8).

The official reaction to new trends in retailing

During the 1960s, overall control of the town planning system was in the hands of the Ministry of Housing and Local Government (which became the Department of the Environment in 1971), the Welsh Office and the Scottish Office. Policies for the control of retail development were determined by local planning authorities (at that time, county and county borough councils), within parameters set out by central government in the form of Circulars and various statements of 'advice'. The latter generally had the status of 'material considerations' which were to be taken into account by local planning authorities in deciding the outcome of applications for planning consent. Some government publications – for example the Planning Bulletins issued during the 1960s – were intended to assist local planning authorities in their development plan preparation.

As discussed above, there was little progress in formulating planning policy concerning retail development during the 1960s. However, two major issues appeared to concern both retail and public sector interests at this time. The first was the increasing use of cars in towns and cities (Ministry of Transport, 1963), not least for shopping purposes, which was leading to intolerable congestion in central areas and a poor physical environment in those suburban shopping areas which had grown in an uncoordinated way along main radial routes into town centres (Guy, 1994a: Chapter 6).

The second cause for concern was that too many new shops were being built, mainly in town centres. Cox (1968) drew attention to the consequences of developer interest in town centre renewal, which had been fuelled by easy availability of investment funds during the early 1960s (Marriott, 1967) and the pro-redevelopment sentiments of planners. He notes a statement by the Minister of State for the Board of Trade in 1966, indicating that 'planning permission had been granted for new shops which, when added to those already in existence, would cater for a population of 164,000,000' (Cox, 1968: 156). He pointed out that 'we have no national plan in this vital matter' (ibid.: 167). Pain (1967) criticised local authorities for an over-enthusiastic response to government advice such as *Town Centres – Approach to Renewal* (MHLG, 1962):

> This encouragement has resulted in the mass preparation of 'Town Centre Schemes' for towns of every size. Unfortunately, many of these have been prepared without adequate surveys; and ... most of these plans envisage great increases of retail space requirements based on the hope of increasing the shopping catchment area.
>
> (Pain, 1967: 21)

One reason for this overproduction of town centre renewal schemes was that many local authorities were much smaller than has been the norm since the mid-1970s. Relatively small towns were in effect competing with each other to become the main retail centre in their sub-region, and there was no regional or national control over this situation.

Cox (1968) also criticised the MHLG for its 'considered opinion ... that new suburban shopping locations should not be embarked upon until the existing retail facilities in town centres have been redeveloped' (ibid.: 167). Cox, like many other commentators at this time, argued that the increasing proportion of the population who were able to shop by car should be allowed to benefit from modern retailing in accessible locations.

By this time, a planning inquiry had been held into the proposed regional shopping centre at Haydock Park, aided by an impact study commissioned by the developers (Manchester University, 1964). The proposal was initially supported by officers of Lancashire County Council,[2] but refused planning consent by councillors. The appeal was eventually dismissed by the MHLG, on grounds of impact on neighbouring town centres, and traffic considerations (DTEDC, 1971: 65; see also Gayler, 1984: 22–3).

These concerns led to the formation of a working group under the aegis of the Distributive Trades Economic Development Council, one of several councils formed by the new Labour Government in the mid-1960s to create constructive dialogues between industry and government. The working group produced an influential report entitled *The Future Pattern of Shopping* (DTEDC, 1971). This report reinforced the concern about overprovision of shops: on current trends, the amount of new floorspace likely to be built in the 1970s would far exceed the amount which could be justified by forecasts of growth in consumer retail expenditure. The group's 'forecast of where people will shop' is shown in Table 2.1: it suggested that 'corner shops', inner city shopping ribbons and small 'parades' in outer areas would fare the worst in the increasingly competitive environment.

The report recognised the potential for growth in the 'new forms of retailing' discussed above. There was a need for some form of policy guidance: the report

Table 2.1 'Where people will shop'

Areas unlikely to change their share of trade much	(a) Central shopping areas
	(b) Shops in villages and small towns
Areas likely to increase their share of trade	(a) Suburban shopping centres
Areas likely to lose trade	(a) Street corner shops
	(b) Shops in intermediate areas adjacent to town centres
	(c) 'Parades' of the type built in the 1930s
Areas whose performance will depend on the attitude of public authorities	(a) 'Off-centre' stores
	(b) Free-standing superstores
	(c) Out-of-town regional shopping centres

Source: DTEDC (1971: 51)

recommended that central government 'should lay down guidelines stating criteria for their acceptability: such guidance, based on analysis of the financial and social costs involved, would be of great help to all those concerned with developing a high standard of shopping provision' (DTEDC, 1971: 6).

Central government advice on planning specifically for retail development and change was thus issued by the newly created Department of the Environment in 1972, in the first version of Development Control Policy Note 13, and the accompanying Circular 17/72 (DoE/WO, 1972a; 1972b).[3] Its purpose was 'to draw to the attention of local planning authorities retailers and developers the matters which need to be taken into account in dealing with such proposals' (DoE/WO, 1972b: para 1). This sentence introduced two characteristics of government advice notes which have remained to the present day: the 'advice' was supposed to be applicable to both public and private sector interests (although most of the detail seems intended for local authorities); and the tone of the document was mainly educational, explaining carefully the advantages and disadvantages of 'edge-of-town and out-of-town shops and shopping centres', to the shopper, developer and planner. These advantages and disadvantages, as stated in DCPN13, are set out in Table 2.2, although these hardly amount to a full consideration of the 'financial and social costs', as had been argued in *The Future Pattern of Shopping*.

Local authorities were also reminded that 'It is not the function of land use planning to prevent competition between retailers or between methods of retailing nor to preserve existing commercial interests as such' (DoE/WO, 1972b: para 6). This statement has remained, more or less in this form, in government policy advice ever since. Although it signifies an acceptance in government circles of the

Table 2.2 Advantages and disadvantages of edge/out of town shopping

	Advantages	*Disadvantages*
Retailer/ developer	• Easier to secure large sites • Realise economies of scale	• Loss of trade in existing centres
Shopper	• Benefit from increased efficiency of retailing	• Need use of car • Run-down of existing centres
Planner	• Take traffic out of town centres	• Intrusion into countryside • Visual intrusion • Traffic generation • Establishing a precedent for further development

Source: summarised from DoE/WO (1972b)

benefits of retail competition and innovation, the DCPN (like most subsequent statements of government policy) failed to provide any explicit aim of 'developing a high standard of shopping provision', despite the DTEDC's recommendation to this effect.

Circular 17/72 also introduced the 'call-in' option for 'major developments', a characteristic of central government retail policy which has remained in place ever since. This allowed the Secretary of State to decide on planning applications, 'particularly where they involve the conflicting interests of [planning] authorities' (DoE/WO, 1972a: para 6). Planning authorities were 'asked' (in other words, required) 'to inform the Secretary of State of all applications for planning permission for stores or shopping centres of 50,000 sq.ft. or more gross floor area outside existing city, town or district centres' (ibid.). This was added to the power, already available, to call in any applications which 'constitute substantial departures from the development plan' (DoE/WO, 1972a: para 6). An even lower limit, of 20,000 sq.ft., was set in Scotland. The lower limit for informing the English and Welsh Secretaries of State was increased to 100,000 sq.ft. in 1976 (DoE/WO, 1976: para 3), and similarly in Scotland in 1978 (SDD, 1978).

One reason for this move towards central government involvement in retail planning appears to have been that the onset of proposals for off-centre development coincided with what Goss (1973: 84) termed 'a particularly groggy moment for physical planning in Britain, when the old-style development plans are to give place to structure plans not yet formulated'. The latter were not expected to be formally approved by central government until the late 1970s, and were further delayed by local government reorganisation. Thus, accepted policy would have to arise from central government guidance and its response to proposals, as shown through planning inquiry decisions.

In contrast to later documents, this note did not make it clear whether the government favoured any course of action in respect to off-centre developments, other than an implied wish to see consistent and well-informed decision-making by local authorities. The note did no more than set out the criteria which local authorities were expected to use when considering planning applications for edge- or out-of-town retail development, and which planning inspectors would use in making their own recommendations for contested cases.

In hindsight, it is hard to detect from these documents clear advice either 'for' or 'against' large-format or out-of-centre retail development. However, three recommendations which can be construed as 'retail planning' did emerge:

- The development of new district shopping centres, which could include a variety of shopping as well as social facilities, should be preferred to the development of isolated large stores (DoE/WO, 1972b: para 9).
- Local planning authorities were strongly advised to carry out 'shopping studies' which would help them plan the size and location of future retail development (ibid.: para 13).
- Neighbouring local authorities should consult each other over major retail applications, and if necessary carry out 'a joint study' (ibid.: para 15).

Following this release of advice to local planning authorities, it appears that one of the early hypermarket proposals (Carrefour at Chandlers Ford, Eastleigh) was granted planning permission as an 'experiment'. The Secretary of State's decision letter following an appeal against the local planning authority's refusal, stated that '... the particular circumstances of the case may present an unusually favourable opportunity to permit the introduction of a new form of retailing, without the proposal giving rise to serious risk of harmful planning or economic consequences' (DoE/WO, 1976: Annex, p.3).

The DoE then commissioned studies of the actual impact of the Eastleigh hypermarket (DoE, 1976; 1978), presumably with a view to informing future policy. Such studies are discussed in more detail in Chapter 5.

The majority of hypermarket and regional centre proposals during the early to mid-1970s were however refused on appeal or call-in. The Department of the Environment and Welsh Office published a summary of the results of 21 inquiries into shopping centre or hypermarket/superstore proposals (DoE/WO, 1976). Of the 28 separate applications listed in this summary, 21 were refused. The main reasons for refusal were traffic problems created by car travel to the proposed development (eleven instances) and intrusion into proposed green belt or open countryside (eight instances). In six instances the impact of the proposal on either local convenience centres or neighbouring town centres was felt to be a reason for refusal, although not usually the dominant reason. In three instances there was felt to be no need for the proposed store, as there were other new stores already approved in the area. In three instances the application was felt to be premature, in the sense that a structure plan or local plan based upon shopping studies was under preparation.

A second version of DCPN13 was at the same time drafted by the DoE, and issued in 1977, under the title *Large New Stores* (DoE/WO, 1977a), together with a new Circular with the same title (DoE/WO, 1977b). Despite the change in title, the guidance covered much the same ground, but in more detail and with several policy considerations clarified. The main revisions from the 1972 version were:

- The statement about retail competition was revised to read: '... it is not the function of land use planning to prevent *or to stimulate* competition among retailers or among methods of retailing ...' (DoE/WO, 1977a: para 2, emphasis added).

- More detailed advice about shopping policies in structure and local plans was added (ibid.: para 7).

- It was pointed out that new large stores might (or might not) add to overall petrol consumption, but also that this was 'not a reason to discourage this form of development or to discriminate against the use of the car for shopping' (ibid.: para 9).

- A longer statement about the disadvantages of out-of-centre development for shoppers without cars was produced, reinforcing advice that development of large stores within town or district centres would be preferable from this point of view (ibid.: para 10).

- Guidance was given on 'assessment of demand', drawing attention to methods used to 'assess the need for floorspace and the best locations to satisfy new demands' (ibid., para 13). Without recommending any particular method, the advice was to use more complex methods for 'major new development[s] of regional or sub-regional importance' (ibid.: para 14), and 'a less elaborate approach' in less significant cases.

- The statement that 'Proposals for large new stores will involve an assessment of the need for the store – not only in terms of additional floorspace but also of alternative, modern or more convenient shopping facilities – in relation to the planning policies applying to the site and the contribution which the site makes to the policy objectives' (ibid.: para 15) served to reinforce the function of development plans in setting out policies for new retail development, but also introduced the notion that assessment of the need for a store should take place – whether by the applicant or the local authority was not made clear. This issue is considered in more detail in Chapter 5.

In summary, the revised DCPN was much more detailed in its advice. The main issues were presented more clearly, and there was some discussion of methods which local authorities would need to use. Commentators at the time felt that the Note was rather less restrictive on off-centre development than the original version (e.g. Thomas, 1976 who commented on the draft version; Bamfield, 1980). There was no explicit indication that the impact studies at Eastleigh and elsewhere had informed the revision, indeed the impact of large new stores on existing retail facilities took a fairly minor role in the discussion.

Local authority retail planning

At the beginning of the 1970s, local planning authorities were adapting their plan-making procedures from the 'Town Map' and 'County Map' development plans set out in the 1947 Town and Country Planning Act, to the Structure and Local Plans system set out in the 1968 Town and Country Planning Act. Central government gave detailed instructions to local authorities on development plan preparation in the Development Plans Manual (MHLG, 1970): those relating to 'shopping' are summarised in Table 2.3, although policies for shopping did not have to be included at all, as explained in DCPN13 (DoE/WO, 1977a: para 7).

Government attitudes at this time were exemplified in this checklist of policies and proposals which a typical local authority would be expected to consider in its development plan preparation. The list, which predated the first issue of DCPN13, revealed some ambivalence towards new forms of retailing, and was unclear as to responsibilities for retail development. It suggested that 'estimates' were to be made of the 'future needs for more out-of-town centres', but did not include any policies for developing such centres: 'district centres' were suggested instead. More surprisingly, it was not recommended that development control policies specifically relating to 'new forms of retailing' or 'out-of-town centres' should be included.

Otherwise the manual reinforced the notion of the retail hierarchy as a determinant of retail proposals. The illustrative diagram of policies for a fictional county borough shows an area – presumably the town centre – zoned for 'shopping and compatible uses', and three levels of district centre: 'large' (over 12,000 sq.m. gross floor area), 'medium' (8,000–12,000 sq.m.) and 'small' (under 8,000 sq.m.) (MHLG, 1970: Diagram 5d).

Central government clearly believed at this time that local authorities should lead the process of retail development. The counties, in their structure plans, were expected to estimate needs for future development, expressed fairly precisely as additional floorspace, and then allocate this increase to selected town and district centres within the county. Local plans would follow up this process by determining the more precise location and design of new development or redevelopment. A detailed description of the planning process and the methods used is given in Guy

Table 2.3 Central government advice (1970) on structure plan policies for shopping

A. Policies and general proposals	General policy: (e.g.)	• foster growth in town centres • develop district centres • etc.
	Quantity of floorspace at certain future dates	
	Distribution of floorspace	• in main centres • elsewhere
	Criteria and policies for:	• location of new development • local planning & development control • existing development
	Priorities and phasing of planning action	
	Implementation (e.g.)	• promotion and assistance by local authorities • assembly of sites by local authorities • scope of private development
B. Supporting information 1. Survey	Existing situation (e.g.)	• floorspace by centres • turnover by trade and centre • accessibility of centres • prosperity of centres
	Recent trends (e.g.)	• retailing methods • customers' habits • changes in transportation
	Commitments (e.g.)	• new shopping centres • new pedestrian precincts
2. Estimates	Future changes (e.g.)	• increases in expenditure • changes in retailing methods
	Future needs (e.g.)	• more out of town centres • less shops in main centres • more district centres
	Constraints (e.g.)	• access problems • land availability
	Assumptions affecting the above	
	Alternative policies (e.g.)	• strengthening suburban facilities • growth in central area
	Conclusions relating to alternative policies, leading to general proposals	
	Programme for planning action	

Source: summarised from MHLG/WO (1970: 73)

(1980: 100–4). Given this approach to retail planning, which the counties appear to have readily accepted, there was little opportunity offered to the private sector to determine for themselves where (and how) development should take place. In hindsight this entire approach seems misguided, since it should have been clear already from the experience of shopping precinct development that the private sector was accustomed to identifying opportunities and then attempting to 'sell' these to local authorities (Marriott, 1967; Ambrose and Colenutt, 1975). Indeed, earlier advice on town centre renewal had included pro-developer statements, such as:

> Local authorities receive a steady stream of applications for permission to redevelop individual buildings or small groups of buildings in the town centre. These proposals are the life-blood of renewal and are to be welcomed, provided they do not prejudice essential long-term objectives. Some authorities may be tempted to impose a veto on all proposals of this kind in the hope that comprehensive redevelopment of the town centre as a whole may some day be possible. But this is seldom, if ever, practicable.
>
> (MHLG, 1962: para 44)

It is not clear why the Development Plan Manual gave such prominence to local authorities in the retail development process. It may be that this advice emanated from those planners within the Ministry who enthusiastically supported the ideas about 'rational planning' which had recently been promoted in texts such as McLoughlin (1969), whereas earlier advice (produced elsewhere in the Ministry) appears to have been grounded in a practical understanding of the problems and potentials of town centre renewal.

This method of retail planning – involving estimation of future retail needs, and determining their location – was opposed by private sector interests. They argued that the forecasts of increases in demand for retail floorspace were too conservative, and that no attention was paid to the poor quality of much of the existing retailing (Thorpe, 1975; Thorpe *et al.*, 1976). They also argued, as they had done throughout the 1960s, that the increasing use of cars for both convenience and comparison shopping required more radical thinking amongst planners. If car access and parking could not be improved in central areas, then there was a strong case for allowing a much greater amount of off-centre development, preferably edge-of-town in order to maximise access from the rapidly growing motorway system (see for example statements by retailers: Sainsbury, 1973; McLaurin, 1976; Ridgway, 1976).

The evidence is, however, that most if not all professional planners were opposed in principle to the development of free-standing large stores and shopping centres. The anonymous columnist 'Pragma' wrote:

Town planning legislation is a curious and unbalanced mixture: carefully spelt-out requirements and constraints are combined with a virtual carte-blanche that allows planners to formulate their own interpretations of the spirit of the legislation ... Planners, on the other hand, have their own motivations – their personal psychologies which can be reflected to varying degrees in their approaches to planning and in their interpretations of both legislation and policies ... The phenomenon of the British planner's whole-hearted resistance to hypermarkets and out-of-town shopping centres illustrates my point. Planners almost to a man [*sic*] have set their hearts against such a development.

(Anon., 1972)

Further confirmation of this generally hostile attitude towards 'new forms of retailing' may be found in empirical research carried out later in the decade: see, for example, Thorpe *et al.* (1976); Sumner and Davies (1978); Gayler (1984).

'Pragma' then went on to suggest reasons for this hostile attitude. The first three – the effects on other shopping centres, on traffic and on 'local amenities' (i.e. open land and countryside) were to become familiar in DCPN13 and reports of planning inquiries. The fourth reason – 'current planning policies are likely to be distorted by such a proposal' – seemed to be 'a more dangerous motivation' (ibid.). Existing development plan policies were based upon a belief in the town centre rather than upon an understanding of 'present and potential trends': 'Under current legislation there is no authority for a planner to intervene in the competitive working of the retail market. Yet he insists on taking the commercial effects on existing shopping centres into account in his grounds for refusal' (ibid.).

This last point relates to the contemporary advice from the DoE/WO (1972b: para 6) that 'It is not the function of land use planning to prevent competition between retailers or between methods of retailing nor to preserve existing commercial interests as such'. It quickly became clear that this was to be interpreted in a narrow sense. Competition between one retailer and another was not a relevant concern for town planners, but trading impact upon any existing shopping centre was relevant (or so it appeared from decisions made by Secretaries of State: see Lee and Kent, 1976; 1978; Gibbs, 1981). This issue was not clarified by the government until 1985 (see Chapter 3).

A review of current approved and draft Structure Plan policies in England and Wales led Thorpe (1975) to draw the following conclusions:

(a) [Planners believe that] Demand for shops does not necessarily indicate there is a need for them. This presents a would-be developer of new premises with almost an impossible case to prove and in so doing will deny consumer demand and slow competitive innovations.

(b) [Planners believe that] Advantages gained by one group necessarily lead to disadvantages for others. ... It implies a zero-sum game whereas retailing evolution has usually demonstrated rapid adjustments by existing traders to innovations ...

(c) Policies are more likely to be influenced by the fear of what may happen rather than any reasonable balance of fact.

> (summary taken from Thorpe *et al.*, 1976: 24)

Summing up the experience of Structure Plans in the 1970s, Ross Davies claimed that:

> by and large the example specifications laid down in the manual for retail and commercial policies [i.e. MHLG (1970)] have been quite faithfully followed. This means that ... [the policies] remain rooted in physical and locational concerns. The emphasis is placed on examining the existing stock of resources and then adjudicating what corrective action needs to be taken to reduce any spatial imbalances found. There is no reference to how the distribution system can be helped to become more efficient or consumers provided with a wider choice and cheaper range of shopping provisions. Nor is there consideration for the employment prospects afforded by new stores or the social problems that may accompany the decline of small shops. This lack of socio-economic perspective is not only disappointing but seems at variance with the wider stated intention for Structure Plans.
>
> (Davies, 1984: 90)

Development outcomes

This section examines ways in which retail development was influenced by the retail planning pronouncements of central government, the early Structure Plan policies and decision made by inspectors and Secretaries of State following planning inquiries.

Shopping 'precincts' were developed in many town centres, from about 1963 onwards, peaking in the early 1970s. These were consistent with retail planning policy for central areas, and contributed to the 'modernisation' which was sought by central government. Many of the new precincts were part of wider plans for improving car access and replacing 'worn-out' Victorian development or war-time bomb-damaged sites. In some cases the shopping precinct developer provided car parking and/or other facilities for the town centre. This movement came to a halt in about 1973, due to the 'property slump' and a consequent shortage of investment funds (see Guy, 1980: 120–5). By this time, it was also clear that not every town centre precinct would be successful: several commentators including

Marcus (1973) and Thomas (1976) drew attention to precincts which stood largely unoccupied, because of poor location, or poor design, or reliance upon an inappropriate anchor store such as a supermarket. Clearly, the warnings of Pain (1967), Cox (1968) and the DTEDC (1971) concerning overprovision of shops had not been heeded.

These developments also met increasing popular opposition during the 1970s. Many town centres were expanded and modernised, but often at a cost to those features of the town centre which local people valued the most. Important historic buildings were lost; ancient street patterns were replaced by privatised spaces which were closed to pedestrians at night. Old patterns of mixed land uses (including small-scale wholesale and manufacturing) were destroyed, and town centres were isolated from their residential hinterlands by urban motorways, ring roads, bus stations and car parks (Evans, 1997: 116–21). Independent retailers whose premises were demolished in the course of redevelopment were unable to pay the high rents demanded in the new precincts (Thorncroft, 1976).

The 1970s also saw the beginnings of out-of-centre development, largely in the form of hypermarkets and food superstores, with some retail warehouses towards the end of the period. At the very beginning of the 1970s the UK possessed only 6 superstores, compared with 368 in Germany and 73 in France (DTEDC, 1971: 90). However the development of superstores accelerated during the 1970s. After 1972, the number of stores opened each year jumped from around 5–10 to around 15–25 (Jones, 1978: Table A). Much of this early development was opportunistic, finding sites where planning permission for retail was easy to get (Guy, 1988). For example, the first hypermarket in Britain – at Caerphilly, south Wales – took advantage of an unclear 'commercial' land use allocation for a site about 1 km from the centre of the town.

Many proposals were made in the latter half of the decade for hypermarkets and superstores in off-centre locations, resulting in about 60 planning inquiries, some of which considered several schemes at the same time (Couper and Barker, 1981: 631). Out of 47 proposals reviewed by Lee and Kent (1978), only 24 per cent were allowed by Secretaries of State.

An increasing number of superstores were however developed as the hub of new district centres in residential areas. These were suggested by the grocery retailer Asda, in a paper designed to appeal to planners who, with government support, were keen to establish district centres, either in new suburban expansions or in redeveloped inner city areas. By 1976, 21 out of a total of 64 Asda stores were built or planned within district centres (Ridgway, 1976). Asda used to refer to this model as the 'Superstore + 6', meaning that a token six shops had to be added to the superstore in order for it to become a district centre.[4] Many such examples were depicted in the URPI (1977) report. These developments were generally organised by local authorities, using powers of compulsory purchase where necessary (Guy, 1994a: 147–8). However, the grocery retailers saw this as an opportunity to develop superstores with local authority support, thus saving time and expense compared with the more uncertain process of developing an out-of-centre store, usually with opposition from the local authority concerned. And the local authorities found that, in order to get district centres developed at all, they were obliged to allow the superstore as the main retail focus. This meant that the size of the centre, and its catchment population, would probably be rather larger than originally intended. For example, district centre development in Leeds was dominated by developer requirements:

> It will be noted that the retail sales area of the completed scheme [at Holt Park Village Centre] exceeded the proposed content by 20,000 ft². A large part of the increase is attributable to the final size of the superstore, though this represents nothing more than a response by the Private Developer to and a recognition by the Local Planning Authority of emerging trends towards much larger superstore type developments. It is, perhaps, fair to say that any lack of flexibility on the Local Authority's part at this stage might well have jeopardised the completion of the scheme.
>
> (Finney and Robinson, 1976: para 2.8)

Another case study, of Swindon, showed how the local authority and private developers could work together to produce an outcome acceptable to both sides – in this case, a district centre anchored by a Carrefour hypermarket (Blythe, 1982).

Evidence began to appear that the trading impact of hypermarkets and superstores was not as serious as commentators such as Pickering (1972) and Hillman (1973) had warned. Empirical studies of stores at Caerphilly (Lee *et al.*, 1973; Lee and Kent, 1975), Eastleigh (DoE, 1976; 1978), and several stores examined by Thorpe *et al.* (1976) and Evely (1980), all demonstrated that these stores had large catchment areas, diverted expenditure largely from other large stores where these existed, and took little trade away from independent food stores.

Retail warehouses grew rapidly in numbers during the late 1970s. By 1981, there were over 1,100 such stores, almost entirely in three categories which became known as 'bulky goods': DIY and home improvement; furniture and carpets; and electrical goods (URPI, 1982). According to Jones (1984: 44), the majority of these stores were located outside existing town or district shopping centres. There were three possible reasons for this situation, which would normally be contrary to accepted planning policy:

- Local planning authorities gave consent for what they thought was a storage warehouse development, not realising its retail nature.[5]
- Planning policy allowed off-centre development of large new stores, provided that these were for 'bulky goods' only.
- A refusal was overturned by the Secretary of State, following a planning inquiry.

Planning policies which allowed retail warehouse development subject to listed criteria began to attract interest around the end of the 1970s. Following representations by the retailers involved, some local authorities accepted that 'bulky goods' retailing was unsuited to town centres, because of its need for access by car, and that this type of retailing was growing rapidly and hence posed little competitive threat to town centres. Gibbs (1981) showed that planning inspectors and Secretaries of State were much more sympathetic to the needs of retail warehouse operators than they were towards large food store retailers: some 52 per cent of the 49 proposals reviewed were allowed.

Progress on regional shopping centres and other major developments outside conventional locations remained slow. The only major scheme of this nature approved during the period was the Brent Cross regional shopping centre in north-west London. This scheme was first proposed in 1965 by the property developer Hammerson at a site used for allotments and playing fields, but with excellent access from several major highways. The proposal was agreed with the local planning authority, not surprisingly as they owned most of the site, but appears also to have been accepted in principle by planners at the Greater London Council as it filled in a 'strategic gap' in the provision of large town centres in outer London. Opposition arose from four neighbouring London Boroughs who feared the results of trading impact upon their town and district centres. The proposal was called in for determination by the DoE and planning permission was eventually granted in 1970 (for more details see Blake, 1976).

It has also been argued (Guy, 1994b) that some of the central shopping developments in New Towns were the equivalent of regional shopping centres, notably Central Milton Keynes (opened in 1979). This fully enclosed centre was described by Mackie (1980) as 'one of the largest covered shopping developments in Europe, with probably the most modern and comprehensive range of shops and services ever assembled under one roof in this country', well in excess of the requirements of a population of some 100,000.

In all of these developments a pattern was emerging, of developers showing preference for a limited range of retail schemes, and building these in circumstances where there was a need for new retailing (usually because of population growth), instead of the more modest schemes which local authority planners tended to favour. However, many other potential schemes were not built during this period, because of opposition from local planning authorities and/or central government:

> Britain stands virtually alone amongst the westernised countries of the world in its
> heavily restrictive planning controls over the decentralisation of retail trade. ... No-
> one, of course, would wish to advocate a repetition of the mistakes of uncontrolled
> expansion too frequently experienced in North America over the last two decades,
> and there is a clear responsibility towards preserving the relative economic health
> of the central areas of our cities. There is a strong case, however, for a more
> enlightened planning policy particularly towards the convenience trades.
>
> (Davies, 1976: 193)

Conclusions

Although this chapter has considered the two decades from about 1960, there
are sharp differences between them so far as retail planning is concerned. In the
1960s, retail planning was uncontroversial, and limited in its impact upon retail
development and change. The focus of attention in retail planning was very largely
on the supposed need for large-scale redevelopment of central areas, and the role
which property developers and local authorities could play in this process. Thus,
almost all major development took place in town centres, and suburban shopping
was small scale and based upon the principle of serving surrounding residential areas
for everyday needs. Indeed, it was argued later that the 1960s saw an anomalous
development of food stores (mainly supermarkets) within central areas, rather than
in the suburbs which were more accessible to shoppers (Thorncroft, 1976).

From the end of the 1960s onwards, the source of concern amongst planning
and property interests turned away from town centres, towards what became known
as 'new forms of retailing', 'large new stores', 'out-of-town shopping', and other
such terms. Large stores and centres, proposed on cheap suburban land with good
access for the private car, became the new focus of attention for developers and
planners. Specific government advice on retail planning was issued for the first time.
It dealt almost exclusively with new forms of retailing, although earlier guidance on
town and district centre planning still remained in force. The issuing of DCPN13
took place at the same time as a requirement to notify Secretaries of State about
retail proposals above a certain size: thus, decisions on such developments began
to be made centrally rather than locally.

Writing at the end of this period, Ross Davies summarised the position as
follows:

> The chief question addressed by central government has been whether to continue
> concentrating new large investments in existing places or to encourage a more
> dispersed pattern of resources particularly into suburban localities ... the point

of emphasis in the planning approach has been on establishing a set of land use controls rather than formulating some wider socio-economic goals.

(Davies, 1984: 2)

This change of emphasis also marked a move away from *active* planning, whereby in the 1960s planners were expected to initiate and plan in detail 'improvements' to central areas, to *reactive* planning in the 1970s, whereby planners were told how to treat pressures for growth initiated by the private sector (Davies, 1984: 75–6).

While retail planning was thus moving up the agenda for the planning profession, a greater diversity of views became apparent. For the first time, there was a conflict of interest between retail developers and local authorities, but local authorities were also inconsistent in their approach to new forms of retailing. Some were minded to allow development, others were implacably opposed. A third option – using superstores to anchor new district centres – quickly became evident.

A set of methods which could be used for forecasting retail sales and examining the trading impacts of new development were refined in the 1960s and much used in planning inquiries in the 1970s. However, practitioners found it difficult to come up with consistent forecasts, and scepticism quickly resulted amongst planning inspectors and government officials. This led to replacement of complex mathematical models by simpler methods upon which all parties at an inquiry could agree (Couper and Barker, 1981: 651). It was also the case that the sophisticated forecasts of retail growth in the preparation of some structure plans and sub-regional studies were often ignored in the process of determining planning policy (Davies, 1977: 42).

Three questions, largely unvoiced at that time, need examining. First, who or what was retail planning for? The view of Burns (1959) that the needs of the shopper were to form the basis for designing a set of shopping opportunities in an urban area seems to have become subordinated to a rather woolly mixture of urban design principles, notions of urban containment, and concerns over traffic flow. Towards the end of the 1970s, concern for the needs of the shopper with limited access to private car travel began to emerge as a major theme in retail planning, but other social issues were ignored. For example, as Bowlby (1984) later pointed out, the vital social trend of increasing female participation in the labour force, and hence the decreasing utility of local or neighbourhood shopping, brought no response in planning guidance (although a clear response from some retailers).

A second area of uncertainty was over who should 'lead' the process of retail planning. In hindsight, two broad options were available. The first was that planners, at central and local level, should determine the future location, size and type of retail facilities, restricting private developers essentially to providing these facilities. This approach characterised some European countries, particularly Germany (Dischkoff, 1979). The second option was that private developers should be allowed to determine the location, size and type of new facilities, subject to some control by planners so as to avoid detrimental effects to the environment generally. This approach characterised France and some other countries, prior to the mid-1970s. This choice between public sector- and private sector-led development was however never presented as a matter for public debate: most of the discussion in planning journals at that time clearly favoured the first alternative. We shall see in the next chapter that in the 1980s, government advice swung towards the second alternative – of giving the private sector responsibility for retail provision. This led to major problems for local authorities which had by this time prepared development plans and were assuming that these could regulate the supply of future retail floorspace.

A third area of uncertainty lay in the relationship between two key ideas in British planning thought – 'flexibility' and 'consistency'. 'Flexibility' is a basic characteristic of development control, allowing local planning authorities considerable discretion over their treatment of planning applications, and differentiating British town planning from most other such systems (Booth, 2003). 'Consistency' is a quality sought by central government, on the basis that the treatment of planning applications should not vary markedly over time and space.

Finally, retail planning can be criticised for concentrating too much on one issue – the 'new forms of retailing' debate. Other problems, such as the decline of inner city retailing and 1930s shopping parades, as forecast by DTEDC (1971), were neglected in government advice and local authority planning:

> The monopolistic powers of the planning authorities have so far tended to mitigate against the smaller, marginal businessman and support the claims of the larger organisations. There is no argument here that the weaker elements of the commercial system should be supported in perpetuity, but more scope in new sites must be offered in the future in order to give them a fair chance for survival.
>
> (Davies, 1977: 57)

Lock (1976) also drew attention to the detrimental (and usually accidental) effects of planning policies upon the 'small shop'.

Unfortunately perhaps, planning policies continued to be dominated by debates about the most suitable location for 'new forms of retailing', as Chapters 3 and 4 will show.

Chapter 3
A free for all?
Retail planning 1980–90

Introduction

This chapter examines the development of retail planning during the 1980s. Throughout this period a Conservative government was in control: this itself affected policy formulation, in contrast to the 1960s and 1970s when the political parties seemed to be in broad agreement over retail planning. The period has sometimes been regarded as a 'free-for-all' in which earlier principles of conserving the retail hierarchy were abandoned, and retail developers were allowed to build whatever and wherever they wished. The evidence reviewed in this chapter shows a more complex picture. In comparison with the preceding and following periods, developers were given much more freedom to build new stores and centres in locations chosen by themselves. However, some previously agreed elements of retail planning remained in force, and many proposals for large new developments were rejected by the planning system.

The account of the main elements of retail planning and its effects during this period is prefaced by a more general discussion of retail development trends, and firstly, a brief summary of changes in political approaches to local government and planning which marked the arrival of a long period of Conservative government.

New government attitudes to town planning and commercial development

The Conservative Government under Margaret Thatcher was first elected in 1979. It saw the town planning system as a hindrance to economic development: the road to economic success lay in speeding up and simplifying the planning system. This was part of a wider agenda which sought to reduce the powers of local authorities, particularly Labour councils in metropolitan areas (Thornley, 1991).

In 1980 the Local Government, Planning and Land Act 'streamlined' the planning system by simplifying procedures for plan preparation and approval, and by making local plans less dependent upon structure plans. The key purpose of development plans was now to provide an orderly and straightforward framework for property development:

The end-product of the plan-making process should be a clear and concise statement of the policy framework for development ... such a statement must be up-to-date and easy to grasp and interpret.

(DoE/WO, 1981: para 2)

By this time, structure plans had been drawn up and approved for most of England and Wales. These were criticised for 'over-elaboration', particularly at the survey stage (DoE/WO, 1981: para 8). Local planning authorities were instructed to keep new survey work 'to the minimum necessary' (ibid.).

The Act allowed local authorities to adopt a local plan in advance of the approval of the relevant structure plan, although this procedure itself had to be approved by the Secretary of State. Local plans were still expected to be in 'conformity' with the structure plan, but the Town and Country Planning Act of 1971 was 'amended to provide that where there is a conflict between the provisions of an adopted or approved local plan and the provisions of an approved structure plan, then the local plan shall prevail' (DoE/WO, 1981: Annex, para 21).

In these ways, the role of the counties in strategic planning was weakened. Proposals for development within a sub-region were less likely to be considered from a perspective which took into account the needs of the area as a whole. In 1986, the then Secretary of State for the Environment, Nicholas Ridley, announced that structure plans were to be abolished, and although this threat was not carried out at that time, county planners felt that their status in the planning system was being marginalised.

A final stage in the demotion of sub-regional planning was the abolition, also in 1986, of the Greater London Council and the six Metropolitan County Councils in England. While arrangements were set up to co-ordinate planning policies within these areas, the resulting bodies had no statutory authority, and in practice the London Boroughs or district councils could pursue policies almost independently of one another. In particular, districts could compete for major new developments without any overall sub-regional control.

The government also sought to encourage development in areas of economic decline, through the creation of Enterprise Zones and Urban Development Corporations. Enterprise Zones were designated in worked-out mining or industrial areas where the property market could not be expected on its own to create new industrial or commercial development. A combination of financial incentives and relaxed planning powers were intended to overcome the barriers to property development (Thornley, 1991: Chapter 9). The Urban Development Corporations were appointed in parts of the larger cities and conurbations, to carry out planning and development functions similar to those already employed in the New Towns. They were unelected bodies with a limited time span, whose purpose was essentially to take over the planning powers from local government, with a view to making land available for economic development (Imrie and Thomas,

1999). Thus, local planning authorities lost overall control over development in several urban areas.

More generally, the government was concerned that town planning policies were inhibiting economic growth and the creation of jobs. At an early stage local planning authorities were told that they should encourage new development of industry and commerce:

> Development control must avoid placing unjustified obstacles in the way of any development especially if it is for industry, commerce, housing … Local planning authorities are asked therefore to pay greater regard to time and efficiency; to adopt a more positive attitude to planning applications; to facilitate development; and always to grant planning permission, having regard to all material considerations, unless there are sound and clear cut reasons for refusal.
>
> (DoE/WO, 1980: para 3)

This was widely interpreted as shifting the responsibility for determining planning applications: it appeared that, instead of the developer having to justify the proposal, the onus was now on the local authority to show why it should be refused. Thornley (1991: 147–51), in a summary of Circular 22/80 and its impact upon appeal decisions, did not make this specific point, but found that the interests of business were given greater weight, and 'design matters' were given less weight. The overall effect was to reduce the influence of local authorities (and local interests generally) in decisions over controversial planning applications, and pay more attention to the stated requirements of businesses and the property market.

This was followed in 1985 by advice that:

> there is always a presumption in favour of allowing applications for development having regard to all material considerations, unless that development would cause demonstrable harm to interests of acknowledged importance.
>
> (DoE/WO, 1985: para 3)

Three key questions emerged from this statement: what constituted 'material considerations', when did 'harm' become 'demonstrable' and what 'interests' were of 'acknowledged importance'? The answers to these questions were not provided in any official guidance. Instead, they had to be sought by indirect means, through analysis of the Secretary of State's decisions on development proposals brought to appeal or called in.[1]

The 1980s were thus a period in which central government adopted a stance favourable to private property developers, and manipulated the planning system to ensure that development took place in many cases where local authorities might not be compliant. The system of strategic planning, set up under the 1968

Town and Country Planning Act, was in effect dismantled, to be replaced by a more reactive and less well co-ordinated approach, which had to argue a case for intervention where private sector development would appear to be harmful to the wider public interest.

Retail development trends

The period was marked by a rapid expansion of retail development of all types, including an important innovation – the retail park. Much of this expansion was in the form of large stores in off-centre locations, and pressure also grew for the development of large regional shopping centres in edge-of-town and suburban locations.[2] Redevelopment and expansion within town centres also continued to take place.

Retail innovation and expansion was fuelled primarily by a major boom in consumer retail expenditure in the mid-to-late 1980s, following a deep economic recession. The rapidly growing demand for clothing and personal goods brought pressure on town centres, which had failed to continue to grow in retail floorspace terms since the collapse of the property market in the mid-1970s. 'High street' rents soared, and many retailers began to seek more radical ways to expand. In so doing they were simply following trends towards out-of-centre shopping, already well established in North America, and (to a lesser extent) in several continental European countries.

The 1980s were also characterised by the aggressive expansion of several leading retailers in food and household goods, partly through new store development and partly through acquisition of other firms (particularly the growth of Argyll Stores [later to become Safeway], Gateway and Kingfisher). These retailers operated on principles of high sales volume and low margins, and hence required large stores in low-cost locations in order to benefit from economies of scale. After about 1986, the 'race for space' between leading food multiples intensified, with Tesco, Sainsbury and Safeway competing for good quality suburban locations, and paying prices of up to £2–3 million per acre for the land required (Wrigley, 1991; 1992).

There was thus a rapid growth of food superstores, and a rather slower growth of hypermarkets. This was accompanied by the closure of small supermarkets in town and district centres (for example in Cardiff, 14 small supermarkets closed between 1982 and 1986: see Guy, 1996b), and of small specialist food stores.

Non-food retail warehouse stores also grew rapidly in number, mainly selling bulky goods such as DIY supplies and furniture, but also beginning to sell 'high street' goods such as toys and sports wear. New companies such as B and Q, Texas, and Queensway specialised in off-centre large stores, although the first two of these were later acquired by longer-established retailers. By 1987 it was estimated that there were over 1,300 retail warehouses in the UK (Lee Donaldson, 1987: 13).

The 1980s were also the start of the retail park boom, following evidence that clusters of retail warehouses brought some advantage to customers and traders (Guy, 1994a: 158–62; Guy, 2000). A definition of a retail park comprising at least three retail warehouses and a total gross area of at least 50,000 sq.ft. was formulated by the property consultants Hillier Parker and quickly became accepted generally. Most retail parks were developed within urban areas but outside existing shopping areas, typically on unused land intended originally for industry or warehousing. By 1993, about 235 retail parks had been completed (Guy, 1994a: 159).

The first signs that 'high street' comparison goods were beginning to be sold in off-centre locations were reported in a famous article by Schiller (1986). He associated this 'third wave of decentralisation' with retail parks and the 'retail strips' more typical of North American cities, and also with regional shopping centres which attempted to serve the full range of comparison shopping within an easily accessible suburban shopping mall, again in the North American style.

Such developments were stimulated by the consumer spending boom and the shortage of space in town centres. There was a flood of applications for regional shopping centres in the mid-1980s: at one time around 60 separate proposals had been made (Guy, 1994b). These proposed centres were to be anchored by at least two department stores, and included many smaller shops in an enclosed, climate-controlled environment. They were located away from existing town centres, some in open countryside on the edge of urban areas, others on formerly industrial or vacant sites within urban areas. They would offer several thousand free car parking spaces, which would make them powerful competitors with conventional town centres.

Retail developments within town centres also continued to take place, with fully enclosed and climate-controlled schemes similar to North American regional centres appearing in several larger towns and cities. These offered a much higher standard of internal design, comfort and security than the typical 'shopping precincts' of the 1960s and early 1970s (Scott, 1989). More commonly, smaller partly-enclosed schemes, often anchored by supermarkets, continued to be built.

Within many town centres, service uses started to grow more quickly than retail, often seeking to acquire premises in prime retail positions. Building societies and estate agents were prominent in this trend during the late 1970s, and fast-food outlets and amusement centres during the early 1980s (Kirby and Holf, 1986).

Government advice on retail planning

In England and Wales, DCPN13 (DoE/WO, 1977a; see Chapter 2) remained the source of official guidance to local authorities and developers until 1988. The government's attitude to large store and off-centre development did, however, change after 1979, in line with the principles discussed above of allowing more freedom to property developers and restricting the influence of local government. Central government policy had, more than ever, to be assessed through analysis of appeal and call-in decisions. It became clear that for most large store proposals (superstores and retail warehouses), it was difficult for local authorities to demonstrate 'harm' to 'interests of acknowledged importance' which would override the case in favour of the development. There was a tendency to allow development in spite of structure plan or local plan policy (especially where the structure plan was not yet approved).

Following general principles at that time, the development plan (structure and/or local plan) was given the status of a 'material consideration', thus being no more (or less) important, in principle, than any other consideration, when a proposal was being considered. In this way the supposed advantages of a proposed scheme, and lack of demonstrable harm, could be judged by a planning inspector or the Secretary of State to outweigh the proposal's inconsistency with the development plan. This was bound to happen in many cases where development plans were prepared according to principles set out in the Development Plans Manual (MHLG, 1970; see Chapter 2). These had emphasised the importance of the retail hierarchy, a concept which fitted uneasily with the desires of retailers to develop outside existing retail areas.

As there was to be no official revision of retail planning policy until 1988 (in Scotland, 1986), the attitude of central government had increasingly to be judged from analyses of inspectors' or Secretaries of States' decisions on appeal or called-in cases.[3] Indeed, it was claimed at the time that 'the superstore appeal process has been largely instrumental in shaping central government planning policy on this topic' (Lee Donaldson, 1991: 12). In other words, a kind of 'case law' was built up through consideration of successive appeal cases, which the civil servants were eventually to use in drawing up planning guidance.

In their reviews of decisions on superstore proposals, Lee Donaldson (1986a; 1991) identified the main reasons for dismissal, as 'land use', 'shopping' and 'traffic'. These are outlined in Table 3.1.

Over the period between 1970 and 1990, about 40 per cent of the 315 superstore appeals were upheld, the proportion increasing to 50 per cent or more between 1986 and 1989 (Lee Donaldson, 1991: 36). The main reasons for allowing proposals were that the developer had demonstrated a need for the scheme, which in the inspector's judgement outweighed the scheme's disadvantages; or that there was simply no serious objection to the scheme on any of the grounds outlined above (ibid.: 38). The meaning of 'need' and its changing interpretation over the years are discussed further in Chapter 5.

Table 3.1 Main reasons for dismissal of superstore proposals in 1980s

Reason	Explanation	How Important?	Cases (n=188)
Land use – environment	Need to protect Green Belt and open countryside	Very important – often the determining factor	75
Land use – supply	Need to protect land designated for other purposes (usually industrial)	Important if evidence of shortage of industrial land, or site suited to 'high tech' industry	21
Impact – shopping	Severe trading impact upon existing town or district centres	Important if loss of sales substantial, or if existing centre is trading poorly	48
Impact – policy	Need to retain priority for retail development supported by local authority	Important only if firm proposal for superstore elsewhere (e.g. district centre)	22
Traffic – access	Unsatisfactory access to site	Rarely important (usually mitigated by Section 52 agreement)[1]	7
Traffic – network	Proposal would cause congestion	Rarely important	7
Other objections / mixed			11

Source: based upon Lee Donaldson (1991)
1 Agreements made under Section 52 of the Town and Country Planning Act, 1971, obliged developers to provide external facilities which were in some way related to the main development, for public benefit.

A similar analysis of a smaller sample of 50 retail warehouse appeals shows that the main objections to the proposals were related to land supply for industry, and the impact of the proposal on the trading performance of existing town centres (Lee Donaldson, 1987). Since about 80 per cent of these proposals were in land zoned for industry, the question of development in open countryside hardly ever arose. An earlier analysis of a larger sample of appeals drew similar conclusions (Gibbs, 1986). Lee Donaldson (1987: 11) concluded that the results of the appeal process did not help government departments much in their attempts to formulate general guidelines. In many cases schemes were allowed by inspectors simply because the local authority was unable to mount convincing objections, and schemes varied a great deal in type of retailing, size and location.

Analysis of appeals and call-ins for the relatively few regional shopping centre proposals which reached this stage shows that, as with superstores, land use considerations were important. It became clear that proposals located in Green Belts or countryside not scheduled for urban development were unlikely to succeed (Lee Donaldson, 1986b). Surprisingly, impact upon existing town centres appeared a less important concern in deciding outcomes, despite the colossal amount of time and effort undergone by planning consultants in preparing impact studies and presenting and defending them at public inquiries (Norris, 1990).

Commentators during the early 1980s (e.g. Wade, 1985) complained that the government was allowing retail planning to drift: neither the local authorities nor the developers felt they were being offered consistent support and guidance, at a time when the pace of change was faster than ever before. Questions of transparency and consistency in decision-making arose. It also seemed that the 1970s policy of improving district centres for convenience shopping (see Chapter 2) was not being supported by central government, which accepted instead that food superstores built off-centre would serve the same purpose.

The only government statement relating to retail planning which appeared during the early 1980s was a single paragraph in advice to county councils on structure planning:

> Policies and proposals for shopping should include a broad guide to floorspace provision. They should take full account of current trends in retailing, like the establishment of large stores away from existing centres, retail warehouses and garden centres. Authorities will wish to avoid substantial overprovision of shopping facilities and take account of the likely impact of new development on the continuing viability of established town centres. Policies and proposals should neither seek to regulate competition between retailers, nor to stifle the evolution of new forms of retail provision. Policies in structure plans relating to large new shopping developments should be based on a careful consideration of the need for convenient access to adequate shopping facilities for all sections of the population, the requirements of the retail industry, the effects on existing shopping centres and the relief of traffic congestion.
>
> (DoE/WO, 1984: para 4.22)

This advice reinforced DCPN13 regarding the role of counties in planning future floorspace requirements, although the inclusion of phrases like '*broad* guide to floorspace' and 'avoid *substantial* overprovision of shopping facilities' (my emphases) indicated a sceptical view of the need for precise and detailed analyses.

The guidance also confirmed that plans should continue to consider the trading impact of new facilities, and the need to ensure adequate and convenient access for all shoppers.

A Parliamentary statement of 1985 attempted to clarify government policy on the question of impacts of new developments upon existing centres, and introduced the term 'vitality and viability' (although this term was not defined). This statement included the following:

> it is not the function of the planning system to inhibit competition among retailers or among methods of retailing, nor to preserve existing commercial interests as such; it must take into account the benefits to the public which flow from new developments in the distributive and retailing fields. The public needs a wide range of shopping facilities and benefits from competition between them. Local planning authorities must take full account of these various needs, both in framing structure and local plans and in dealing with applications for new shopping developments of all types.
>
> Since commercial competition as such is not a land-use planning consideration, the possible effects of a proposed major retail development on existing retailers is not in this sense a relevant factor in deciding planning applications and appeals. It will be necessary, however, to take account in exceptional circumstances of the cumulative effects of other recent and proposed large scale retail developments in the locality and to consider whether they are on such a scale and of a kind that they could seriously affect the vitality and viability of a nearby town centre *as a whole* – for example, whether they seem likely to result in a significant increase in vacant properties, or a marked reduction in the range of services the town centre provides, such as could lead to its general physical deterioration and to the detriment of its future place in the economic and social life of the community. Town centres need to maintain their diversity and activity if they are to retain their vitality, but the range and variety of shops and services will change, as they have always done, in response to changing conditions.
>
> (DoE/WO, 1988a: para 7)

The statement also recognised that agreed town centre schemes should be protected from off-centre rivals. However, the statement (later to be included *verbatim* in PPG6, see below) was widely regarded as downplaying the need for impact studies in routine cases such as food superstores.

In 1986, new official advice was issued in Scotland (SDD, 1986). This established as one of the main criteria for retail planning policy, that 'There is a national interest in ensuring that consumers have access to a wide range of shopping facilities and are able to benefit both from new forms and methods of retailing and from competition among retailers' (SDD, 1986: para 1). After setting out some of the advantages of retail parks and 'shopping complexes',[4] the Guideline continued:

> These changes do not mean that the policies underlying the 1978 Guidelines need to be abandoned. City and town centres retain many natural advantages as shopping locations and shops make a major contribution to their character. Many have been the subject of major public and private investment. Wherever opportunities exist planning authorities should support the provision of sites for major new retail development in or adjacent to existing centres.
>
> (SDD, 1986: para 6)

However, it went on to emphasise that

> Some types of retail development are unlikely to be capable of being accommodated in existing centres because of the space, access or surroundings which are required if they are to be successful and meet consumers' needs.
>
> (ibid.: para 7)

This gave the signal that local authorities' policies should accept the need for off-centre development. The potential trading impact was a valid criterion when judging specific proposals, but 'the protection of the commercial interests of existing individual retailers is not a land use planning consideration' (ibid.: para 7). This of course repeated earlier advice. Local authorities should however 'take account of the likely longer-term effects of new off-centre developments on the vitality and viability of existing centres and a judgement has to be made in the light of the prospects for each individual centre' (ibid.). This wording was very close to that used in the Parliamentary statement of 1985 (see above). The Guidance also suggested that 'the provision of an impact statement by developers which indicates the likely effect on spending patterns in nearby existing centres and traffic in the vicinity of the development will help planning authorities in their assessment of applications' (ibid.).

Although this advice appeared mainly to address the control of retail development by local authorities, it also instructed regional councils to review their structure plan policies, and 'determine the extent and general location of opportunities for the development of new forms of shopping, including ... shopping complexes ... [and] retail warehouses or retail parks selling durable goods'. District councils should in their local plan preparation add detail to the 'opportunities', and 'contain policies and measures for improving the environmental quality of existing city and town centres' (ibid.: paras 8, 10).

Thus the SDD clearly believed that local authorities should continue to take a major role in determining the future size and location of retail development, so long as they were aware of the advantages to the consumer of large stores and off-centre growth. It also supported local authority attempts to maintain and enhance town centres.

Finally, the SDD raised the lower limit for referral of development proposals to the Secretary of State to 40,000 sq.m. In the same year the lower limit in England and Wales was raised to 250,000 sq.ft. (23,325 sq.m.) (DoE/WO, 1986). These amendments gave a clear signal that developments below these limits (which would include hypermarkets and most retail parks) were not considered to be of strategic importance.

In England and Wales the impression grew amongst commentators (and also developers, as shown later in this chapter) that central government was favourably disposed towards large-scale retailing in out-of-centre locations. This was exacerbated by a comment by Secretary of State Nicholas Ridley that 'It [out-of-town shopping] is a bigger force than I. ... I don't think it can be stopped with the powers that the government has' (reported in Anon, 1987).

The Scottish Guidance was however followed in January 1988 by the first version of Planning Policy Guidance 6, Major Retail Development, which was to apply in England and Wales (DoE/WO, 1988a). The Planning Policy Guidance series (PPGs) were created around this time to replace Circulars and Development Control Policy Notes with 'concise and practical guidance on planning policies', intended both for local planning authorities and private developers. The Guidance, usually known as PPG6, reproduced in full the Parliamentary statement of 1985 noted above. It drew attention to 'trends towards larger shops', but also noted the need for smaller shops to continue in business, especially for those consumers who did not have the use of a car.

In contrast to the Scottish Guidance, PPG6 did not require local authorities to suggest locations for major new development when preparing structure and local plans. It merely advised that policies should be consistent with 'general principles' set out in the 1985 Statement, and continued:

> When preparing plans it will be appropriate for local planning authorities to take account of forecasts of retail expenditure over the plan period and the possible implications of these forecasts for the location of different types of retail development. However, policies should not attempt to prescribe rigid floorspace limits for new retail development, either overall or in specified locations, since this would impair the ability of developers, retailers and the planning authority to respond to changing market conditions and the demand of customers.
>
> (DoE/WO, 1988a: para 8)

In keeping with this view, previously issued advice that '[local] authorities will wish to avoid substantial overprovision of shopping facilities' (DoE/WO, 1984: para 4.22) was officially withdrawn.

The guidance also considered various types of retail development [...] is summarised in Table 3.2.

The Guidance thus implied a very simple approach to the considera[...] major retail development proposals by local authorities. The impact of 'm[...] developments of over 100,000 sq.ft. (which would include most retail parks) up[...] both existing centres and traffic flows could be a relevant issue, but the impact of free-standing large new stores was apparently not. The 'cumulative impact' of several proposals was however a matter which could be of concern.

Table 3.2 Advice in PPG6 (1988) concerning types of retail development

Type of Development	Advantages	Criteria for considering development proposals
Town centre modernisation and refurbishment	• Can bring about environmental improvements • Can regenerate inner cities • Can make existing centres more attractive to shoppers	
Major out-of-town developments (over 100,000 sq.ft.)	• Can assist reclamation of derelict land	• Not allowed in Green Belts • Not generally acceptable in open countryside • Effects of proposal (and cumulatively with other proposals) on town centre vitality and viability • Road traffic implications
Large modern retail stores (of up to 100,000 sq.ft.)	• Meet consumer demand for convenient car-borne weekly household shopping • Take car-borne shopping out of town centres • Can use derelict sites, provide environmental gain and new employment opportunities	• Not in land allocated for industrial purposes where there is heavy demand for this

Source: based upon DoE/WO (1988a): paras 13–20

criticised by town planning interests and local
...nd Howard, 1989: 19). For example the Royal
...t it was 'clearly undesirable that market forces,
...ual local authorities not necessarily concerned
...mine the location of these highly significant
...The advice that detailed forecasts of retail
...amount of new retail development, were
...rt's report *Planning for Shopping into the 21st*
...o: 52). A later survey of local authority planners found 'a
...cal of confusion and uncertainty ... Planning authorities felt [PPG6] gave
insufficient detail and guidance' (BDP Planning, 1992: 112).

Differences between PPG6 and the Scottish advice (SDD, 1986) should be
noted. The latter stressed the role of local authorities in maintaining and enhancing
town centres, and also required regional councils to plan the future pattern of new
large stores and centres; but PPG6 did not present any such advice to county or
district planners in England and Wales.

The advice in PPG6 led to some changes in the criteria used to determine
the fate of appeals against planning refusals. In the case of superstores, the local
planning authorities' position was substantially weakened. Forecasts of floorspace
requirements, and arguments that there was no spare capacity for a large new
store became redundant. The trading impact of a new store, taken in isolation,
was irrelevant, although the cumulative impact of several proposals could still be
significant (Lee Donaldson, 1991: 8, 24). In the case of regional shopping centres,
impact was a valid consideration, but local authorities could not legitimately argue
that there was adequate provision of shopping in an area and hence no need for
a new development.

Local authority retail planning

In the early 1980s, county structure plans were concerned with a wide range
of issues. Burt *et al.* (1983), in a review of retail policies in English and Welsh
structure plans, classified these as firstly, 'issues directly dependent upon structural
change', including large new store proposals and loss of local shops; and secondly,
'issues relating to the impact of these changes on existing urban planning policy',
including the maintenance of the retail hierarchy, traffic management and inner
city regeneration (Burt *et al.*, 1983: 11). From their analysis they distinguished
12 types of policy, which are shown in Table 3.3.

From this survey it appeared that 'few authorities have a comprehensive view
of retail planning with most perceiving two or three key issues and responding
accordingly ... there is evidence of authorities responding to problems rather than
acting in advance and initiating change to avert problems arising' (ibid.).

Table 3.3 Retail planning policies in English and Welsh structure plans in the early 1980s

Policy area	Number of structure plans		
	With policies on this topic	Without policies on this topic	No response or not applicable
Control or encouragement of hypermarkets and superstores	55	3	
Maintenance of an existing retail hierarchy	50	7	1
Local shop provision	46	12	
Retailing from industrial units	44	14	
Control or encouragement of large comparison goods stores	36	22	
Expansion of retail floorspace for certain levels of the hierarchy	30	25	3
Provision of car parking for consumers	29	29	
Inner city regeneration through retail investment	25	20	13
Servicing of shops in established shopping districts	15	43	
Quasi-retail activity in retail districts	7	51	
Mobile shops	5	51	2
Shopping centres in refurbished historical buildings	5	53	

Source: Burt *et al.* (1983)

A subsequent survey of structure plan policies in the Scottish regions showed similar results (Sparks and Aitken, 1986). All plans except one included policies which attempted to maintain the existing retail hierarchy. These were usually allied to policies which forbade or restricted development of off-centre stores over a specified size limit. One difference compared with typical English or Welsh structure plans was however that food superstores and retail warehouses were usually considered together under a 'large stores' heading. This reflected earlier advice from the Scottish Office to this effect (SDD, 1978).

It is clear that local authorities generally adhered to the principle that retail development should take place in accordance with the hierarchy of centres. This meant that development outside existing retail areas was either completely forbidden, or was allowed in certain circumstances, subject to restrictions on size and the nature of goods sold. Burt *et al.* (1983: 12) found that about one-third of structure plans in England and Wales had policies totally prohibiting hypermarkets, one-third restricted development to certain specific sites, and one-third treated each application on its merits, although 'some observers might argue that this latter approach is not a policy at all' (ibid.). Policies restricting development have elsewhere been classified as site-specific or criteria-based. Site-specific policies have been termed 'firm allocations of land for the most common forms of development' (Crow *et al.*, 1997: 34), and allow development of a particular type in a particular area. An appropriate example here was a policy of the former South Glamorgan County Council in the early 1980s to allow development of do-it-yourself (DIY) stores in three areas of Cardiff (Jones, 1983: 15; Guy, 1998b: 299–300). Criteria-based policies were more common, giving 'guidance to decisions about less common and unexpected forms of development' (Crow *et al.*, 1997: 34). These allow development under certain specified conditions, which could in practice be very restrictive. So far as retail development was concerned, such conditions related mainly to trading impact, traffic generation and potential alternative uses for the land concerned. These matters also affected decisions by Secretaries of State following planning inquiries (see below).

Despite increasing evidence that central government was sceptical of forward planning of retailing, local authorities were still following Development Plans Manual (MHLG, 1970) advice in estimating future requirements for new retail floorspace. A survey carried out by the RTPI Working Party found that about three-quarters of the 200 largest district councils in England and Wales had carried out 'shopping studies', and almost all had identified a need for additional floorspace, often over 250,000 sq.ft. The districts had also specified sites for new development, of which three-quarters were in or on the edge of town centres. Only a quarter had identified sites in district centres, and a quarter had specified opportunities for retail parks (RTPI, 1988: 40). A later survey carried out for a literature review commissioned by the DoE found that structure planning authorities were still attempting to 'project the likely supply and demand for retail floorspace over specified periods. This [*sic*] data was then translated into clarification of [shopping centre] hierarchies which had been designated, [and] to which retail development should be steered' (BDP Planning, 1992: 111).

Local planning authorities were however in a difficult position. They had prepared structure plan policies according to the Development Plans Manual, which recommended adherence to the hierarchy of centres, and the building of new centres to serve areas of population growth. However, the Manual did not clearly advocate policies for dealing with new forms of retailing. Proposals for off-centre development would violate the main principles of retail planning, and would also take up much of the floor space additions which local authorities were instructed to plan for town centre growth. This led to attempts to shoe-horn new types of large store into town centres. These ideas were however criticised by the retail trade as adding to costs, and by other planners as introducing unpleasant 'big box' built forms and large car parks into historic environments. Thus began a lasting debate in retail planning (see Chapters 6 and 9).

As the 1980s progressed, retail planners became more and more despondent. The structure plan policies approved in the early 1980s were clearly out of date, given the pace of retail innovation and growth, and were often ignored by inspectors in appeal decisions, on these grounds. In any case, development plan policies were only one of several possible 'material considerations', and central government appeared to claim that the advantages to shoppers of new large-scale developments were sufficient to over-ride the established planning principles of adherence to a retail hierarchy. The report of a Working Party of the RTPI complained that:

> It is thus, perhaps, inevitable and it is certainly true, that the challenge offered by the restructuring of the distribution of retail facilities, which is taking place is not being well handled by the planning system at any level. The District level has horizons too close to be able to appreciate the wider distribution of facilities; the role of the Structure Plan does not include the sort of prescriptive planning which may be needed, and the Government appears increasingly to take the view that the market should decide questions of location and distribution.
>
> (RTPI, 1988: 49)

The cancellation of the 1981 and subsequent Censuses of Distribution, on grounds of economy, made both forward planning and impact assessment particularly difficult for local authorities (Wade, 1983a; Dawson and Sparks, 1986; Guy, 1992).

One result of the uncertainty over retail planning principles was the partial breakdown of sub-regional co-ordination, particularly in the metropolitan county areas after these counties were abolished in 1986. Suburban districts started to allow large-scale developments in order to recapture some of the expenditure leaving the area, to kick-start other economic development and to increase business rate revenue. An example is provided by the chaotic situation arising from various off-centre proposals in the former Greater Manchester area in the late 1980s, where several proposals were supported by the local authority in which the proposal lay, but opposed by every other local authority in the area (see Stocks, 1989 and Evers, 2004: 170–6 for further details). Among these was a proposal for a regional shopping centre at Dumplington, which was vigorously opposed by a consortium of local authorities, but was eventually allowed by the Secretary of State and opened as the Trafford Centre in 1998.

Another example was in the West Midlands, where Sandwell Metropolitan Borough Council approved the development of a regional shopping centre and associated leisure facilities, despite the imminent completion of another regional centre at Merry Hill, some 12 km distant. The Sandwell Mall would have in effect become the town centre for Sandwell, an area without large existing town centres. The RTPI mentioned this scheme specifically as one that should have been called in for determination by the Secretary of State (Planner, 1988; RTPI, 1988: 53).

Faced with the rapid growth in 'new forms of retailing', and the ambivalent attitude of central government, a consensus view amongst planners was set out in the RTPI (1988) report. This recommended that local authorities should:

- Carry out joint studies at subregional level to identify the likely retail floorspace required in the sub region up until the year 2000.
- Identify the likely retail floorspace required in their authority up until the year 2000 and assess where the identified floorspace can be located. In particular, they should take careful note of the environmental impact of additional shopping floorspace on established shopping centres, accepting that where necessary desirable floorspace excess to capacity will have to be located outside established centres.
- Consider the commercial realities of retailing and the need to accommodate new retail concepts and formats as failures to do so will simply result in a fossilised pattern of retailing unsuited to the requirements of retailers or the shopping public.
- Identify potential retail sites with access in their local plans as ad hoc provision does not meet the needs of the disadvantaged. Wherever possible accessible locations in or near population centres or the distribution network should be considered in preference to remote sites.

(RTPI, 1988: 61–2)

These recommendations thus recognised the case for development of new retail formats, in off-centre locations where appropriate, but aimed to set this within a planned framework which would protect the status of existing centres and as far as possible protect the interests of those who found access to new off-centre retailing difficult. However, much of this was contrary to central government advice (in England and Wales at least), which as we have seen recommended an essentially non-interventionist stance, and indicated that retail development proposals should be 'judged on their own merits' rather than in the context of retail planning at sub-regional and local levels.

The introduction of PPG6 in 1988, as noted above, caused further concern amongst local authority planners. Not only were the foundations of planning policy, including the maintenance of the hierarchy of centres, deemed unimportant; the new guidance was too vague to be useful:

> Few authorities knew how or what to assess as a measure of vitality and viability and no checklist of factors was provided in PPG6 to assist in definition of these terms. Furthermore PPG6 did nothing to explore or amplify these issues. … Many [local authorities] were worried about the physical decline in their town centres but they were unable to describe precisely how or why they were declining. Most authorities, however considered that out of town shopping trends were responsible in some way.
>
> (BDP Planning, 1992: 112)

Perhaps the most positive aspects of local authority retail planning were seen in town centres. As noted above, most district councils favoured expansion of retailing in town centres and some had designated sites for this purpose. Compared with the conflicts over off-centre retailing, there were few controversies regarding town centre developments.

One fairly pervasive planning problem within town centres was the continuing pressure for non-retail 'service' uses such as building society offices, amusement centres and fast-food outlets. Over much of the period, there was uncertainty amongst planners as to whether a change of use from a shop to a service use was in legal terms 'material', because the Use Class 1 ('Shops') could include 'any other purpose appropriate to a shopping area' (Kirby and Holf, 1986: 28). In a survey of 261 local planning authorities in England and Wales, about three-quarters agreed that non-retail growth was a cause for concern. About 85 per cent of the authorities in this survey had formulated planning policies relating to non-retail uses, of which half had policies controlling through some kind of quota system (ibid.: 29). Typically it was felt that the proportion of retail uses in prime parts of shopping centres should be at least two-thirds.

In 1987, the Use Classes Order was amended, the new Class A1 being shops, A2 financial and professional services and A3 food and drink (for consumption on the premises or hot food take away). It is not clear whether this eased the problems faced by local authorities in attempting to control service growth.

Councils were also becoming aware of the poor physical environment in many town centres, often exacerbated by the comprehensive renewal carried out in earlier decades. Jones (1989) explained how competition from out-of-centre developments was leading to better quality enclosed shopping schemes within town centres, and also attempts to improve the pedestrian environment in traditional shopping streets. Town centre management, first suggested for the UK in 1980 (Spriddell, 1980) was beginning to take hold.

Development outcomes in relation to planning policy

This section reviews the pace and location of retail developments in the 1980s. Explanations include the effects (where evident) of retail planning policy at central and local levels. We first examine the expectations of retail developers and their attitudes towards retail planning.

From the developer's point of view, development plans could potentially be valuable as providing 'a clear framework that contributed to a sense of certainty in the market place. They provided a set of ground rules which, whether appropriate or not, gave investors, developers and retailers confidence for their own long-term planning and investment programmes' (ORG, 1989: para 1.2). However, the plans of the early 1980s were criticised by the private sector on the following grounds:

- An over-emphasis on analysis of the existing retail system without much attention to the dynamics of change.
- Forecasts of future retail floorspace provision from past trends which would not necessarily be sustained.
- Reliance on historic data, including the 1971 Census of Distribution, in making decisions on development proposals.
- Restrictive and inflexible policies which could not be easily adapted to rapidly changing retail pressures.

(ORG, 1989: para 1.1)

Lord Sainsbury (1989a) identified what he saw as key shortcomings in local authority planning. These were:

- A lack of understanding of the needs of commerce and the development industry.
- That local authorities were putting forward policies and making decisions which ignored central government policy.
- That development plans were too idealistic and inflexible.
- That planning control was slow and inefficient; and
- That planners were too much concerned with the appearance of new buildings rather than wider urban design concerns.

These views were widely held, but there was disagreement amongst private sector interests about basic retail planning objectives. Whilst food and 'bulky goods' retailers favoured relaxation of planning restrictions and constantly emphasised the advantages to consumers of free competition, 'high street' retailers called for clearer government guidelines and supported the strategic planning role of the counties (e.g. Hampson, 1987; Henley Centre, 1988).

As noted above, central government was often ready to override 'restrictive and inflexible policies' (Sainsbury, 1989a) in allowing appeals against refusals of planning consent. It seems also that local authorities, faced with the likelihood of appeals being allowed, often felt obliged to give consent to applications for schemes which were contrary to development plan policies (for examples see Guy, 1988).

As a result of development pressures and the increasingly liberal attitude of both central and local government, the amount of off-centre retailing expanded enormously during the 1980s. From a base of about 5 per cent in 1980, off-centre sales rose to 17 per cent of all sales in 1991, according to Verdict Research (BDP Planning, 1992: 20).

Food superstores

These were the focus of much of the 1980s debate over retail planning. Although the multiples continued to develop smaller stores in town and suburban centres, the number of superstores rose increasingly rapidly until about 1992. The increasing rate of store development coincided with a greater acceptance of superstore development amongst planners, as noted above. The Chairman of Asda commented in 1984 on 'the relative scarcity of superstore sites when compared with demand', but claimed that because of increasing acceptance by planning authorities, 'the pace of superstore development should therefore increase' (Asda, 1984: 9; cited in Price, 1985: 379).

The proportion of superstores built in 'purpose-built shopping centres' (i.e. district centres) declined between 1980 (25 per cent) and 1987 (12 per cent), whereas the proportion at 'edge-of-town/free-standing' sites rose from 25 per cent in 1980 to 41 per cent in 1981 and 58 per cent in 1987 (IGD, 1989: 120). Thorpe (1991: 359–60) found that in the case of Tesco, the majority of superstores opened before 1983–4 were in town centres or new centres, but thereafter the proportion dropped below 30 per cent in each year to 1988–9.

It should be noted that only about one in every six superstores built up to 1990 were the result of successful appeals (Lee Donaldson, 1991: 11). Davies and Sparks (1989: 77) estimated that between 52 per cent and 77 per cent of applications for superstores were approved by planning authorities each year between 1980 and 1986. These two sets of findings suggest that many superstores were built in off-centre locations, having gained approval from the local planning authority, even though this was likely to be contrary to Structure Plan policy. Davies and Sparks (1989: 83) also show that during this period, rejection rates were highest in southern Britain (South-East, South-West, and East Anglia regions) and in Scotland. This established the now familiar belief that permission could be obtained more easily in areas of economic weakness: Thorpe (1991: 358) suggested that 'areas suffering from high unemployment rates afforded retailers with low land costs and policies favourable to any form of development', and 'in affluent areas out-of-centre development may well have been resisted because of the shortage of development land and the pressure on such land for housing and genuine employment creating activity' (ibid.). This theme is examined in more detail in Chapter 9.

It is likely that food superstores also formed the anchors for the district centres built during this period. The definitive list of shopping centres published by Hillier Parker (1987: 3–4) noted 38 district centres, of which 25 were developed by food retailers. Their average size was 8,789 sq.m. (gross). In the following two years a further 13 such centres were opened (Hillier Parker, 1989a: 8).

At the end of this period, a number of factors including a consumer spending recession, saturation in some local markets and difficulties over raising capital for new food store development took effect in slowing down rates of development (Wrigley, 1991; 1992; 1994).

Retail warehouses

Construction accelerated rapidly and there were over 1,300 such stores by 1987 (Lee Donaldson, 1987: 13). These were less affected by planning policy constraints than were superstores: they required smaller sites, and were likely to entail smaller trading and traffic impacts because of their low sales density. It seems that many planners realised that the design and access requirements of 'bulky goods' retail warehouses made them unsuited to a town centre location. Most planning applications were for development on industrial land (about 80 per cent of the sample of appeal cases examined by Lee Donaldson, 1987), so that traffic and amenity questions were of little relevance. These arguments were generally supported by inspectors at planning inquiries, with the result that many appeals were allowed, including 60 per cent of the Lee Donaldson (1987) sample and 53 per cent of the larger sample examined by Gibbs (1986).[5] It appears generally that the local authorities found it difficult to convince inspectors that there were sufficient planning objections to the proposed schemes. Gibbs (1986: 4) found that a higher proportion of DIY warehouse applications were allowed than for other categories, reflecting the greater likelihood of trading impact arising from other stores selling electrical goods or household furnishings, for example.

Where retail warehouse applications were approved or allowed, they were often made subject to conditions which restricted the nature of goods which could be sold (Guy, 1998c). These attempted to prevent 'high street' comparison goods such as clothing and footwear, and also food, being sold from off-centre locations.

Retail parks

Development also accelerated in the mid-1980s along with the consumer spending boom (Table 3.4). In 1990 rates of development began to decrease, due probably to the economic recession and problems facing some of the main retailers and developers involved. There has been no published analysis of the planning reaction to retail park proposals in the 1980s, but it is unlikely that the slowdown in development after 1989 was due to changes in government policy.

Most of the retail parks developed in the 1980s were relatively small in size, typically between 8,500 and 15,000 sq.m. gross area (Hillier Parker, 1989b: 5). Most were developed within urban areas rather than edge-of-town, and sometimes close to town centres. Sites were typically 'on industrial land, such as old goods yards, timber and builders yards, and old factory sites' (ibid.). The same source (ibid.: 6) noted that compared with similar developments in other countries, retail parks lacked small shops: this was due partly to conditions attached to planning consents which prohibited shop units of below a certain size, for example 1,000 sq.m.

Town centre schemes

These also increased substantially in number during the late 1980s (Table 3.5). The average size of development, at around 10,000–15,000 sq.m., was rather smaller than the typical town centre scheme of the previous development peak in the early 1970s. The comprehensive renewal ethos of the 1970s had by now been replaced by a greater awareness of need to preserve built environments and 'character' of historic town centres (RTPI, 1988: 42). Some town centre schemes, such as The

Table 3.4 Retail park openings, 1982–90

Year	Number of schemes	Floor area (sq.m.)
1982	1	8,640
1983	3	28,428
1984	0	0
1985	5	51,468
1986	8	82,590
1987	31	361,670
1988	55	614,923
1989	71	753,441
1990	40	459,218

Source: Hillier Parker (1991a)

Table 3.5 Town centre shopping schemes opened 1982–90

Year	Number of schemes	Floor area (sq.m.)
1982	16	190,265
1983	15	233,000
1984	23	239,039
1985	18	172,706
1986	25	181,160
1987	29	325,252
1988	27	273,320
1989	33	427,074
1990	37	481,979

Source: Hillier Parker (1991b: 4)

Lanes in Carlisle, were praised for their integration into the historic fabric (Scott, 1989). Local authorities also helped to improve town centres through introducing pedestrianisation schemes, of which some 155 were carried out between 1981 and 1987 (DTEDC, 1988: 28).

Regional shopping centres

Despite the amount of controversy and concern raised by the large number of applications for large out-of-centre shopping malls in the mid-1980s,[6] less than fifteen were built or received planning consent during this period. These are listed in Table 3.6. During most of the 1980s, the amount of floorspace under construction or with planning permission in town centres well exceeded that in out-of-centre locations (DTEDC, 1988: 52). Only in 1986 was more shopping centre space (excluding retail parks) developed out of centre (Hillier Parker, 1991b: 4).

In hindsight, it is clear that the 'threat' from regional centres was much less than appeared at the time. Several proposals were simply alternatives to one another, and would not be economically viable were they all to be developed. Some proposals seem to have been little more than opportunistic attempts to increase land value in unpromising vacant or polluted sites which happened to be close to motorway intersections.

The 1986 and 1988 policy guidance in effect ruled out most of the out-of-centre proposals which had progressed as far as a public inquiry, in contrast to the situation with superstores and retail warehouses. Of the 24 schemes which were at appeal or awaiting a decision (Davies and Howard, 1989: 14), only three were eventually allowed. The main reasons for dismissal were the potential loss of Green Belt land; traffic problems; loss of important industrial sites; and unacceptable

Table 3.6 Regional shopping centres approved up to 1992

Name of scheme	Location	Date approved/ allowed	Nature of planning consent	Eventual outcome	Date opened
Brent Cross	London		All	RSC	1976
Metro Centre	Gateshead		EZ	RSC	1986
Merry Hill	Dudley		EZ	RSC	1989
Lakeside	Thurrock	1987	All	RSC	1990
Meadowhall	Sheffield		App	RSC	1990
White Rose	Leeds	1989	All	RSC	1997
Cribb's Causeway	Bristol	1991	All	RSC	1998
Trafford Centre	Manchester	1995*	All	RSC	1998
Blue Water	Dartford	1990	All	RSC	1999
Braehead	Glasgow	1990	All	RSC	1999
Parkgate	Rotherham		EZ	Non-retail	
Sandwell Mall	Sandwell		App	Non-retail	
The Royals	London		App (UDC)	Non-retail	
Cheshire Oaks	Ellesmere Port	1990	App	Outlet centre	

Source: Davies and Howard (1989: 13–15); URPI (1990); BDP Planning (1992: 27–8); Guy (1994b: 302)
Notes
App – Approved by local planning authority or Urban Development Corporation (UDC)
All – Allowed by Secretary of State following a public inquiry
EZ – Deemed consent under Enterprise Zone legislation
* Allowed in 1993 after a second public inquiry, confirmed by House of Lords in 1995 following overturning of permission by Court of Appeal: for details see Evers (2004: 171–7).

level of impact upon existing town centres (URPI, 1990). Regarding the first of these reasons, the Department of the Environment took a strong stance in favour of the Green Belt, in one case ordering the developer (Town and City Properties) to pay the costs of the inquiry. Michael Howard, the Minister for Water and Planning, stated:

> The local planning authority and their ratepayers should not have to pay for resisting something which flies so flagrantly in the face of the Government's green belt policy. … We are certainly not opposed to new methods of retailing. But they do not belong in the Green Belt.
>
> (Planner, 1989: 3)

It should be recognised however that some regional centres gained the support of local planning authorities. The Sandwell Mall and Dumplington (later, Trafford) proposals have already been noted. Sheffield City Council approved the development of Meadowhall, despite opposition from its planning officials (BDP Planning, 1992: 137), and Essex County Council altered their draft Structure Plan at a late stage to incorporate the Lakeside proposal (ibid.: 138). Cambridgeshire County Council, aware of intense development pressure in the historic centre of Cambridge, included a policy allowing 'a large scale out of town shopping centre development' (ibid.: 140). Several proposals were then made by private sector interests to take advantage of this, but these were eventually dismissed by the Secretary of State following a joint planning inquiry in 1991.

The experiments in 'deregulation' of the planning system, noted earlier in this chapter, gave rise to some large schemes including regional shopping centres and retail parks. For each Enterprise Zone a protocol was drawn up by the Secretary of State, setting out the types of development which would still require planning consent from the local authority. In some cases, retail development was not included in this list,[7] allowing retail developers some freedom to build superstores, retail parks, and regional shopping centres including the Metro Centre and Merry Hill. However, in these latter two cases the wording of the protocol still required the developers to gain planning consent in respect of food retailing, which was granted by the local authorities concerned. In the Rotherham Enterprise Zone, developers were free to build any retail scheme. The result was one of the largest retail parks in the country (Retail World), and a planned regional shopping centre (Parkgate), which was however abandoned when consent was granted for Meadowhall, which was only six kilometres away and on a more accessible site (Davies and Howard, 1989: 13).

The other element of deregulation of the planning system had been the setting up of Urban Development Corporations. These encouraged retail developers in order to 'kick-start' projects for reclaiming derelict land (discussed further in Chapter 9). Not all the proposed schemes were built however, the most important example being the regional shopping centre at Royal Docks in east London.

Discussion and conclusions

One of the major reviews carried out during this period concluded:

> In general concept and detailed application, the framework of the retail planning system is found wanting and prompts the question of its precise aims and objectives in the current circumstances. Uncertainty and planning delay cannot be regarded as an efficient or satisfactory procedure for those seeking to invest or for planners trying to balance public and private benefit. Fundamentally, it does not resolve

the question of when public interest is sufficient to warrant intervention in the workings of a market founded on the presumption that the forces of demand and supply and investment will secure the most efficient retail sector and favourable benefits to the consumer and the use of land.

(DTEDC, 1988: 73)

The 1980s were a period of uncertainty and weakness in retail planning. The extent to which local authorities could control retail development according to what they saw as the wider interest was limited by central government's lack of concern over this question. The pace and style of retail development was driven more by developer pressure and wider political agendas.

This was exemplified in the summary provided by Davies and Howard (1989) of six main issues in retail planning:

1 The cancellation of the 1981 Census of Distribution.
2 The creation of Enterprise Zones and Urban Development Corporations.
3 The abolition of the Metropolitan Counties.
4 Pressures on the countryside.
5 The new inner-city initiatives.
6 The new planning guidelines on retail development.

Of these, 'new inner-city initiatives' are mentioned more as a lost opportunity than a retail planning initiative: the various measures announced in 1988 'add nothing concerning retail development or town centres to the old policies' (Davies and Howard, 1989: 11). We have seen how the other five issues affected types, rates and locations of retail development, and the ways in which local planning authorities struggled to implement what they felt to be retail planning policies which were desirable in the wider public interest. At the same time they could rightly be accused of failing to understand retail trends and the changing requirements of both retailers and consumers.

The 1980s marked a break from previous decades, in that there was clear evidence of political dogma affecting retail planning policy. The basic question was who was responsible for retail planning – the public or the private sector? It emerged that the private sector was expected by central government to take the initiative, within broad planning constraints of which the most important were the protection of the countryside, and avoidance of severe impact on traffic flows and town centre trading. This view of private sector priority was unacceptable to many public sector bodies and commentators, who continued to believe that retail facilities should be planned to the benefit of society as a whole rather than sectional interests.

Much of the policy emphasis of the 1970s was thus put aside in attempts to allow more retail-led development. This was officially justified by statements about the need for consumers to benefit from competition between retailers and methods of retailing, although Conservative antagonism towards local authority planning practice was also a factor.

One result of central government adopting a more 'liberal' posture was that decision-making on new store and centre development increasingly devolved to central government. This was because local planning authorities continued to refuse planning applications which appeared to be contrary to development plan policies, and developers appealed to Secretaries of State. However the procedure of 'calling-in' large-scale applications for determination in the first place by Secretaries of State was little used at this time.

The key element of central government policy was the statement that 'there is always a presumption in favour of allowing applications for development having regard to all material considerations, unless that development would cause demonstrable harm to interests of acknowledged importance' (DoE/WO, 1985: para 3).

This begs a few questions. What, in the retail planning context, were 'material considerations'? During most of the 1980s there was little consensus on this matter, although in England and Wales the issues set out in DCPN13 continued to be used. PPG6 however indicated that the trading impact of any scheme below a certain size was not a consideration which should be taken into account. This view was not accepted by most planners, as shown in a survey of local authority planners' and councillors' attitudes to retail planning (Sainsbury, 1989b: 5): impact studies continued to be required for most 'major' retail applications (see also Sainsbury, 1989a). Approved development plan policies, until 1991, were no more important in the decision calculus than 'other material considerations', and the experience of planning inquiries shows that they could be overruled by considerations which favoured retail development. These included the economic advantages of new development and the need for consumers to benefit from retail competition and innovation. Other material considerations included more local and site-specific questions of amenity and access (for a list see Guy, 1994a: 79–81).

When did 'harm' become 'demonstrable' and what 'interests' were of 'acknowledged importance'? 'Interests' did not appear to mean the same as 'material considerations': the need to uphold local planning policy was arguably not regarded by central government as an 'interest'. The focus was instead on private sector interests – both retail developers and traders in existing centres – but the latter could not, individually at least, be regarded as of 'acknowledged importance', since competition between retailers was not a matter of planning concern. 'Interests' also included the requirements of local residents and businesses for a pleasant, safe and efficient physical environment, and the potential effects of a retail proposal on 'amenity' continued to be an important consideration.

The criteria for and assessment of trading impact were gradually clarified as more and more experience became available. Following government advice that 'it should rarely be necessary to attempt detailed calculations or forecasts of retail growth or of changes in the geographical distribution of retailing' (DoE/WO, 1988a: para 11), complex methods of impact assessment such as spatial interaction models were put aside. The 1985 Parliamentary statement also attempted to downgrade the importance of impact assessment by stating that impact was only a planning issue when the vitality and viability of whole town centres would be threatened by a proposal. However, this did not stop trading impact continuing to be discussed at planning inquiries for routine superstore and retail warehouse proposals.

Basic to this and other issues was the lack of positive guidance to planning authorities on locating new forms of retailing. Planners assumed that these could/should go into town centres. However, developers required off-centre sites in order to accommodate large stores and car parks, and because they were cheaper and easier to purchase. In England and Wales, there was no advice to local authorities on catering for these requirements through explicit policies, which could be directed towards other planning goals, such as making land accessible for other purposes, or retaining expenditure within a town. Official advice simply stressed the advantages of large stores and off-centre development, but did not relate this directly to the plan preparation process. One analyst recommended that development plans should allocate suitable sites for retail warehouses: '... perhaps the best way of ensuring that development takes place in an acceptable location' (Gibbs, 1986: 27). But this advice was ignored by the DoE, although the Scottish Office in 1986 had made similar suggestions.

This lack of positive advice on acceptable locations for new development became another cause for concern amongst retail planners. As the decade progressed, local authorities began to accept that superstores and 'bulky goods' retail warehouses fulfilled useful purposes and should be developed in limited circumstances. The most suitable locations might usually be out-of-centre, but should be accessible to shoppers by all means of transport. Retail development could also help renovate derelict urban sites and provide employment (BDP Planning, 1992: 114). While few would argue against these propositions, they were not consistently supported by planning inspectors or government ministers, and less suitable proposals were often allowed to go ahead.

The other mainstay of 1970s retail planning – reconstruction of town centres with pedestrian precincts and improved car access – was less discussed in the planning press. Following the property slump of the mid-1970s and the economic recovery of the early 1980s, there was another boom in shopping mall development within town centres. However, a rising conservation movement put paid to some of the most ambitious schemes, and led to smaller-scale developments which fitted better into the traditional town centre streetscape. Government advice on this topic was lacking and local authorities took the initiative. However some commentators complained that town centres were not being supported by central or local government in the increasing competition they faced from off-centre developments, and the beginnings of the 1990s movement towards town centre management occurred.

Retail planning appeared to be uncertain and weak in the 1980s. However, some important new ideas came into being which fundamentally affected retail planning in subsequent years. Among these were the focus on vitality and viability of town centres, and the relationship between retail development and urban regeneration. More fundamentally, the experience of the decade demonstrated that a 'hands off' approach to retail development, and vagueness in government guidance, led to socially inequitable patterns of development and much wasted effort on the part of both developers and planners. We shall see that the 1990s were to see a revival of the ideological frameworks which had grown up in previous decades.

Chapter 4
Tightening up
Retail planning since 1990

Introduction

This chapter examines the history of retail planning policy in Britain, from the early 1990s to the time of writing (early 2006). During this period we see a gradual reversal of most elements of policy from the 1980s. The insistence that the private sector should determine the location, type and scale of retail development has been replaced by the doctrine that the public sector should take this responsibility. The idea of a 'balance' between town centre and out-of-centre development has been replaced by a 'town centres first' policy. In these ways, policy has to some extent reverted to that of the early 1970s. However, extra dimensions to policy have arisen, largely through the incorporation of concepts from other realms of land use and resource planning. These include the quest for 'sustainability', the ever-increasing focus on 'regeneration' in planning practice, and (under the auspices of the Labour Government first elected in 1997) the need to eradicate 'social exclusion'. These considerations, which were already to some extent embodied in retail planning policy, have become more explicit. In particular, the promotion of 'sustainable development' has come to subsume most other criteria in retail planning, as in land use planning generally.

These changes in policy have naturally been opposed by those interests which were most likely to be harmed. Disputes between out-of-centre developers and local authorities frequently have had to be settled through the intervention of central government, and decisions made at planning inquiries have remained an important indication of evolving government policy. Policy itself has become more and more detailed and complex, and open to varying interpretations.

Retail planning in this period has also been marked by an increasingly high political profile. Ministerial pronouncements and parliamentary inquiries on retail planning policy have become commonplace. Government departments beyond those responsible for land use planning have become involved in negotiations over policy. In contrast, local authorities have found less freedom to innovate in policy terms, or to deviate from central 'guidance'. There are signs however that the central government hegemony has been applied less rigorously in Scotland and Wales.

The chapter proceeds as follows. Changes in town planning philosophy, particularly the introduction of 'sustainable development' as a major theme, are discussed first. The next section describes broad trends and innovations in retail development. This is followed by a detailed examination of successive statements of government policy for retail planning, and the debates which preceded these statements. After a discussion of the ways in which policies have been implemented by local authorities and planning inspectors, we examine the ways in which retail planning policy has affected patterns of store and shopping centre development. The chapter ends with a discussion of some wider issues.

The growth of 'sustainability' in planning policy

The single most important change in land use planning generally since the early 1990s has been the growing emphasis on 'sustainability' and 'sustainable development'. The most recent government statement on overall land use planning policy in England is entitled *Delivering Sustainable Development* (ODPM, 2005b), and the ODPM logo now contains the phrase 'Creating sustainable communities'. In Wales, the National Assembly 'has a binding legal duty to pursue sustainable development in all it does'.[1] This emphasis has led to important changes in overall planning policy, particularly with respect to transport policy and new retail development.

At the beginning of the 1990s, the DoE was given *de facto* responsibility for developing broad goals which could assist sustainable development. Two of these goals were particularly relevant to land use planning, and came to dominate the government's advice to local authorities and developers in the 1990s. These can be summarised as:

1 Reduction of the need to travel: this arose from specific government commitments to reducing carbon dioxide emissions. This was to be achieved partly through land use planning policies where these involved controlling the location of new commercial and residential developments.
2 Conservation of resources: this led to stronger policies for preserving the natural environment and cultural heritage, and also to an emphasis on residential and commercial development within urban areas (in 'brownfield' rather than 'greenfield' locations).[2]

The origins of sustainability as a key element of planning policy can be traced back to the Brundtland Report (World Commission, 1987), and Resolution 44/228 of the UN General Assembly in 1989, which called for a UN Conference on Environment and Development.[3] This led to the first 'Earth Summit', held in Rio de Janeiro in 1992. As its contribution to the international discussion, the UK Government published in 1990 a White Paper entitled *This Common Inheritance*. This set out the ways in which policies across the whole of government should be developed in response to environmental concerns. A chapter entitled 'Land Use' summarised the role of the planning system in regulating development in the public interest, drawing attention to 'National Policy Guidance' in the form of Planning Policy Guidance Notes (DoE, 1990a: 86–7). It contained a commitment:

> to issue planning guidance on the location of new development in relation to traffic generation as part of the need to tackle global warming. One aim would be to guide new development to locations which reduce the need for car journeys and the distances driven, or which permit the choice of more energy efficient public transport …
>
> (ibid.: 87)

In a later section entitled 'Good Planning', it was stated that: 'The Government has asked local authorities to look to the reuse of existing sites before allowing new land to be taken for development' (ibid.: 115).

The revised PPG1 incorporated these ideas in its broad principles for planning policy:

> The planning system, and the preparation of development plans in particular, can contribute to the objectives of ensuring that development and growth are sustainable. The sum total of decisions in the planning field, as elsewhere, should not deny future generations the best of today's environment.
>
> (DoE/WO, 1992: para 3)

In 1993, John Gummer was appointed as Secretary of State for the Environment. He brought to this post a personal commitment to sustainable development, as well as an interest in the visual quality of the urban environment. Local authorities were now encouraged to insist on a high quality of design in new residential and commercial development (DoE/WO, 1992: Annex A). At the same time, central government began to take more interest in controlling the content of local authority planning policy. The Planning Policy Guidance (PPG) series was extended to cover new areas, and revised PPGs tended to be more detailed than previous versions. It became clear that local authorities were expected to follow the guidelines set out in the PPGs, in preparing their development plans and in appraising planning applications (Tewdwr-Jones, 1997: 150). Ministerial statements made in Parliament, or even speeches by government ministers, could comprise considerations, which in legal parlance were 'material' to development control and appeal decisions.

However, a Conservative government had to reconcile this new climate of greater regard for planning principles with its traditional belief in the private sector-led operation of land and property markets:

> There is no doubt that planners can provide an inspiration to economic development, but that inspiration must be realistic and not depend on investment that cannot be attracted. ... Above all, it is planning that is necessary, not organising; planning is about ensuring that the conditions in which competition prevails are conditions which do not destroy the overall environment, whereas organising is telling people what they should do because 'you know best'. There is a clear distinction between these – and when planners become organisers, they have ceased to retain the respect of the public: they have ceased to do the job they ought to do. When planners are seeking to create an environment in which others exploit opportunities and give people a chance to choose, in which others give variety and above all provide competition, then planners are doing their proper job.
>
> (Gummer, 1994: 79)

By 1997, just before a Labour government took office, a comprehensive package of land use planning policies had been assembled under the general title of 'sustainable development' in a revised PPG1:

> A sustainable planning framework should:
> - provide for the nation's needs for commercial and industrial development, food production, minerals extraction, new homes and other buildings, while respecting environmental objectives;
> - use already developed areas in the most efficient way, while making them more attractive places in which to live and work;
> - conserve both the cultural heritage and natural resources ...; and
> - shape new development patterns in a way which minimises the need to travel.
>
> (DoE, 1997: para 5)

Under the Labour government, the term 'sustainable development' came to have a stronger economic and social content. For example: '... development which ignores the essential needs of the poorest people, whether in this country or abroad, is not sustainable development at all' (DETR, 1999: para 4.2).

This signalled the arrival of social exclusion/inclusion as a major issue in land use planning policy: '[Planning authorities] should consider the extent to which they can address issues of social exclusion through land use planning policies' (ibid.: para 4.11).

Changes to the status of development plans

While these changes in planning philosophy were taking place, the role of development plans in the planning system was strengthened. During the 1980s, property developers had frequently been successful at planning inquiries when proposing schemes which were contrary to approved development plan policies (see Chapter 3). It was held that 'material considerations', which might include the supposed need for the development, could override development plan policies.

In 1991, however, the Planning and Compensation Act gave rise to an amendment (known as Section 54a) to the 1990 Town and Country Planning Act, which enhanced the status of approved development plans, such that 'Where, in making any determination under the planning Acts, regard is to be had to the development plan, the determination shall be made in accordance with the plan unless material considerations indicate otherwise'.

This was interpreted as indicating that planning policy and/or land allocation in the development plan (which could be an approved structure plan or local plan, or both) should become the main consideration in determining a planning application. This meant that local planning authorities could with more confidence refuse planning applications involving land designated for other purposes; and could also refuse applications on the basis that another proposed development which was supported by development plan policies should take precedence. Advice in Planning Policy Guidance Note 15 (DoE, 1990b: para 31) had already encouraged local authorities to take such a stance (see Lee Donaldson, 1991: 31–2 and BDP Planning, 1992: 104).

However, the DoE warned that this would only apply in limited circumstances:

> Where there are other material considerations, the development plan should be taken as a starting point, and the other material considerations should be weighed in reaching a decision. One such consideration will be whether the development plan policies are up-to-date and apply to current circumstances, or whether they have been overtaken by events ... for example, policies and proposals in the plan may have been superseded by more recent planning guidance issues by the Government.
>
> (DoE/WO, 1992: para 27)

Nevertheless, it was assumed that development plans would, because of their enhanced status, take a greater role in determining future patterns of development, in contrast to the 'planning by appeal' which typified the 1980s:

> One potential effect of the new Section 54a is to place greater emphasis, and hence increased pressure, on the plan-making process. Thus, instead of a sequence

of inquiries each concerning a particular proposal for a superstore on the edge of a town, there may now be a major inquiry into the local plan, deciding how many superstores are needed for that town over the next ten years, and where they should be.

(Mynors, 1991: 7)

It was also made clear that the location and characteristics of new development of all types was to be set out broadly in the development plan, and in this way 'ensure that new development is compatible with the objectives of sustainable development' (DoE, 1997: para 22). As a concession to the private sector, it was also stressed that 'the locational needs of businesses are taken into account in the preparation of development plans' (ibid.: para 21). However, the previous statement that: 'there is always a presumption in favour of allowing applications for development having regard to all material considerations, unless that development would cause demonstrable harm to interests of acknowledged importance' (DoE/WO, 1985: para 3), which had survived more or less intact in the 1992 version of PPG1 (DoE/WO, 1992: para 5), was now substantially watered down:

> applications which are not in accordance with relevant policies in the plan should not be allowed unless material considerations justify granting a planning permission. Those deciding such planning applications or appeals should always take into account whether the proposed development would cause demonstrable harm to interests of acknowledged importance.
>
> (DoE, 1997: para 40)

Finally, this statement was removed entirely from the revised PPG1 issued in 2005 (ODPM, 2005a). This suggests that the balance between adhering to the development plan and allowing some freedom from this constraint for commercial developers had been resolved in favour of the plan. However, it remains the case that relevant 'material considerations' can tilt the balance towards the developer, under circumstances which involve 'judgement' from all sides rather than under any specific circumstances. A House of Lords judgement in 1998 set out:

> the following approach to deciding an application:
> - identify any provisions of the development plan which are relevant to the decision;
> - interpret them carefully, looking at the aims and objectives of the plan as well as detailed wording of policies;
> - consider whether or not the proposal accords with the development plan;
> - identify and consider relevant material considerations, for and against the proposal; and

- assess whether these considerations warrant a departure from the development plan.

The weight to be attached to any relevant material consideration is for the judgement of the decision-maker.

(SEDD, 2002: para 47)

As the new series of structure plans, local plans and unitary development plans emerged in draft form from local authorities, commercial developers realised that planning applications which were clearly out of step with either local or national planning policy were unlikely to succeed on appeal. This led firstly to greater involvement of developers and landowners in local plan preparation, mainly through the process of submitting objections to draft plans (Booth, 2003: 158–9). Planning consultants were retained by leading private sector companies to carry out this process wherever a draft policy seemed to threaten the interests of the company concerned. Secondly, commercial developers became more involved in discussions with central government over the interpretation as well as the revision of planning policy. This was seen for example in 'evidence' submitted to Parliamentary inquiries, discussed later in this chapter.

By this time, the process of devolution had led to Wales formulating its own land use planning policies (WO, 1999), although these were generally similar to English equivalents.

The most recent years have seen major changes in the development plan system in England, with structure plans, local plans and unitary development plans replaced by 'local development documents'. Each local authority is expected to produce several of these, of which some will constitute the 'development plan' for statutory purposes. These changes have been paralleled by rather less drastic changes in Wales, where unitary development plans are being replaced by 'local development plans' (NAW, 2004). In Scotland, the structure plan and local plan system remains in force at the time of writing.

Retail development trends

It is a somewhat artificial exercise to describe and explain the main trends in retail development over this period without devoting at this stage much attention to the impacts of retail planning policy. This relationship however is examined in a later section. For now, we can identify some major influences on the pace and type of retail developments in Britain.

First, the general economic situation. Retail development should (theoretically) respond to changes in consumer demand for retail goods and services, but time lags and inflexibilities in the development process tend to obscure this relationship (Guy, 1994a). However, it is clear that the economic recession and property collapse experienced in Britain at the end of the 1980s had serious effects on retail developments in the next few years, particularly of retail parks and shopping malls, both inside and outside town centres. A combination of real declines in consumer expenditure on non-food goods, reduced demand by retailers for new premises, and high interest rates which made speculative property development extremely risky, were responsible for this sudden fall in retail completion rates.

The same influences created a slump in the demand for rented premises in shopping centres, especially from clothing and fashion retailers. In the early 1990s commentators became concerned over vacancy rates in high streets, and especially in recently completed shopping malls.

Food retailers

They were much less affected by these events, because consumer demand for food products remained more stable, and because the largest retailers were able to continue to buy land and build stores, using their own financial resources. They were however affected by a combination of other events, including the impact of newly arrived discount food retailers such as Aldi and Netto, and by a realisation amongst financial analysts that a failure to depreciate the value of land in company accounts was leading to over-valuation of assets (Wrigley, 1994). The largest companies began in response to develop a stronger non-food offer (including services). Initially this took the form of limited selections of low-value electrical and other household goods, but in the late 1990s, Asda and Tesco in particular began to develop highly competitive ranges of clothing. In-store services included pharmacies, photographic processing, dry cleaning, post offices and cafes, where sufficient space existed within the store, or where the retailer concerned was able to secure planning permission for a store extension.

At the same time, two of the major retailers (Tesco and J Sainsbury) began to diversify their development programme. Their main product in the 1980s had been the so-called 'conforming superstore', of between 2,500 and 5,000 sq.m. sales area and serving a catchment population of at least 30,000. Most of these stores were built in larger towns and cities. They now saw opportunities to serve smaller catchments, for example small market towns with an extensive rural hinterland, with smaller food-only stores of around 2,000–3,000 sq.m. Tesco also began to operate Metro stores in a few city centres, serving shoppers and employees in the centre itself, rather than the residential catchment. Towards the end of the decade, Tesco and Asda sought opportunities to develop very large stores equivalent to continental European hypermarkets, selling a wide range of non-food goods as well as a full range of foods. Finally, Tesco and Sainsbury began to operate convenience stores, either through new development or (increasingly) through purchase of established convenience store chains. Table 4.1 shows an example of differentiation of store formats in relation to location and catchment characteristics.

Table 4.1 Sainsbury's store formats

Format	Sales area sq. m. (approx)	Offer	Location
Local	300	Serving local communities: top up/grab and go	Towns, villages or railway stations
Central	800–1,200	Catering for city centre shoppers' differing needs throughout the day	Major cities throughout the UK
Country town	1,000–2,000	Small supermarket format – serving needs of weekly shoppers in small towns	Typically market towns throughout the UK
Supermarket	1,500–3,000	Offering a wide range of products expected in a modern supermarket	Where possible, in line with planning policy
Superstore	3,000–6,000	Full 'superstore' offer demanded by today's customers	Where possible, in line with planning policy
Savacentre	6,000 and above	Complete superstore offer, plus hypermarket offers catering for the demands of today's shopper	Where possible, in line with planning policy

Source: adapted from McNair (1999: 12)

Warehouse clubs

At the beginning of the 1990s, pressure emerged from North American operators to develop 'warehouse club' facilities in a few large towns. Similar in appearance externally to hypermarkets, and internally to cash-and-carry warehouses as used by independent shopkeepers, these facilities are intended to sell a wide range of goods, mainly non-foods and in 'bulk' quantities, to customers who become 'club members' for a small fee (Sampson and Tigert, 1994; Westlake and Smith, 1994). Two companies, the United States-based Costco, and Cargo Club, a subsidiary of the wholesalers Nurdin and Peacock, developed a small number of warehouses, but the latter company ceased trading in 1995 (Fernie, 1998). At the time of writing, only 17 Costco club warehouses had opened in Britain.

Retail warehouses and retail parks

As the economy recovered from recession, retail warehouse and retail park development quickly resumed, leading to a peak of completions in the late 1990s, almost at the level attained in the late 1980s (see Figure 4.1). Retail park developers made greater attempts to attract shoppers through better design, and many high street retailers selling clothing, footwear and other comparison goods sought outlets in retail parks (Guy, 1998c). Development and ownership of retail parks became dominated by property institutions such as insurance companies, as it became clear that growth prospects (in terms of rents and capital values) were probably the best in the whole field of commercial property (Guy, 2000). The growth of 'shopping' and 'fashion' parks, which arose partly from the effects of planning restrictions on new development of retail parks, is described later in this chapter.

Factory outlet centres

The major innovation during the early part of the 1990s was however the factory outlet centre. This type of development, already common in North America, made available to the public goods which suppliers were willing to sell at substantial discounts, in order to clear stocks. These included the previous year's fashions, unpopular lines or slightly damaged stock. The centres tended in America to be located several miles from the regional malls where the suppliers or retailers concerned would sell goods at full price, in order not to compete directly with the full-price offer. They became associated with family outings and hence tended to be developed along major interstate highways or in resort areas (Jones and Vignali, 1993; Fernie and Fernie, 1997).

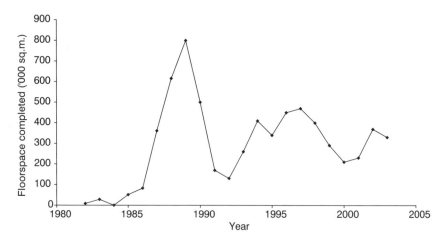

4.1 Annual completion of retail park floorspace in the UK (Sources: Hillier Parker, 1994; CBRE, 2004a)

Outlet centres entered Britain in 1993 with the conversion of some storage space and the addition of a simple 'shopping street' adjacent to the Clark's shoe factory in Street, Somerset, to create outlet stores for other retailers. Two companies – McArthur Glen, and Freeport – became specialist developers in Britain, and later on, in continental Europe. By 2002 there were over 40 such centres in Britain, mainly located outside town centres (Guy, 2002a). Formats varied, but the most common has been an 'open street' lined by relatively small outlet stores. Unlike conventional shopping malls, outlet centres (or 'villages' as they became known in Britain) have no anchor store, but they do have leisure facilities such as food courts and children's playgrounds.

Shopping malls

Development was badly affected by the economic recession of the early 1990s, but resumed again, with an emphasis on large-scale schemes in some of the largest town and city centres (Lowe, 2005). There were, in contrast to the 1980s, very few proposals for large out-of-centre malls (Hallsworth, 1994). There has also been substantial refurbishment, in some cases rebuilding, of town centre 'precincts' developed originally in the 1960s and early 1970s.

From the late 1990s onwards, 'mixed-use' developments which combined retail, leisure and residential space became commonplace within the larger town and city centres. Developers have thus to some extent overcome their traditional antipathy towards mixing residential and commercial uses.

Underlying trends

One major underlying trend was, as in earlier periods, increasing use of private cars for shopping trips (see Chapter 7). This clearly supported the rise in numbers of superstores and retail parks, but also supported the large and more attractive town and city centres for comparison shopping. It became clear that much of the investment in town centre retail schemes was being made in the largest 50 or so centres (CBRE, 2004b: 8–9). In such centres, development serving mixed uses became common.

The period saw an increasing disparity between, on the one hand, utilitarian 'big box' developments of superstores, hypermarkets and retail parks, emphasising choice, convenience and low prices; and on the other hand, city/town centre developments in which retail uses formed a part of more complex, varied and attractive schemes. Retailing increasingly became a focus for 'leisure' provision, including some explicitly tourist-oriented schemes, such as a few speciality centres and (perhaps surprisingly) the outlet centres.

One other trend should be mentioned here, although it lies largely outside the reach of physical planning policy. From about 2000 onwards, there was a rapid growth in 'remote' shopping, principally over the internet. On-line purchases amounted to 6.8 per cent of all purchases by the end of 2004 (IMRG, 2005). Tesco became the largest on-line grocer in the world, selling £577 million worth of goods in 2003–4 (Tesco, 2004). Other areas of rapid growth included computers, cameras and other electronic goods; books, CDs and DVDs; holidays and travel; and financial transactions and banking. Research by Dixon and Marston (2002) indicated however that impacts of internet shopping and personal finance upon conventional retail development were likely to be minor, in the short term at least.

Central government retail planning policy: 1990–8

Introduction

This and the following two sections describe the evolution of central government guidance on retail planning after 1990. The most important underlying trend during this whole period was an increasing emphasis on town centres as the appropriate place for retail development. Initially, while the enhancement of the vitality and viability of town centres was clearly an important part of overall policy, it was recognised that there could be a 'balance' between town centre[4] and out-of-centre development. The latter was recognised as more suited to large-format stores and retail parks. However, later guidance removed this concept of 'balance' and instituted a policy often known as 'town centres first'.

A second underlying trend was increasing reliance upon planning authorities (both regional and local) to specify the location and type and scale of new retail development. Policy moved away from the doctrine espoused in the 1980s, that the private sector should determine these matters, within a broad framework of planning policy.

A third trend was for increasing levels of detail in central government guidance to developers and local authorities, and increasing centralisation of decision-making on controversial development proposals. Government ministries, notably the Department of the Environment and its successors in England, initiated policy and, with important contributions from Parliamentary Select Committees, generally led the debates on the effectiveness of policy and the need for change. Local authorities continued to produce planning policies for retail development and town centres, but increasingly these did little more than replicate central government advice.

1990–93: introduction of sustainability principles into retail planning

Up to 1993, the relatively liberal policy outlined in the first versions of PPG6 (DoE/WO, 1988a) and NPPG8 (SDD, 1986) remained as official guidance to local authorities and developers (see Chapter 3). However, other publications including *This Common Inheritance* (DoE, 1990a) suggested that the 'sustainability' agenda was beginning to emerge as a key factor in retail planning. The following statement indicates a change of emphasis rather than any reversal of policy:

> Until a few years ago, people on shopping expeditions usually went into towns. Now many people go out of town, to the large supermarkets and shopping centres which have increasingly sprung up on the outskirts. This trend has its advantages: it has created new jobs, increased choice and given many people easier access to a wide range of goods. But there are disadvantages too: out-of-town shopping can be inaccessible to the least mobile people, including the old; it can lengthen car journeys; and it can sometimes threaten the town centre economy. The Government's guidance to planning authorities already emphasises the need to ensure that their planning decisions do not damage the vitality and viability of town centres as a whole. It will continue to stress this need.
>
> (DoE, 1990a: 115)

The change in planning legislation noted above, elevating the development plan above 'material considerations' in development control, gave rise to a new interpretation so far as retail planning was concerned, in this extract from the new PPG15:

> Where a planning authority have clearly stated that proposed development is inconsistent with an identified policy in an approved or adopted plan which is up-to-date and consistent with national and regional policies, and have substantiated this in their reasons for refusal of permission and in their written statement on an appeal, the applicant will run a serious risk of an award of the authority's costs against him if he pursues the appeal to inquiry but is unable to show that there are other material considerations which would justify an exception to the policies set out in the plan. This will particularly apply in respect of major developments, such as proposals for shopping centres ... where they are in conflict with policies in the structure plan.
>
> (DoE, 1990b: para 31)

Although this begged the question of precisely what the national policies for new retail development were, the statement would have been seen as helpful by local authorities, who had struggled during the 1980s to control new developments which were contrary to structure plan policies.

The publication of a new version of PPG6 (DoE/WO, 1993) marked the inclusion of the sustainability agenda in retail planning, although in a modest way compared with later revisions to policy. The main objectives were:

- to sustain or enhance the vitality and viability of town centres which serve the whole community and in particular provide a focus for retail development where the proximity of competing businesses facilitates competition from which consumers benefit; and
- to ensure the availability of a wide range of shopping opportunities to which people have easy access (from the largest superstore to the smallest village shop), and the maintenance of an efficient and innovative retail sector.

(DoE/WO, 1993: para 1)

These were claimed to be 'compatible with the aim of encouraging sustainable development' (ibid.: para 2), although this does not in retrospect seem obvious.

Although the new PPG6 showed no change in its encouragement of retail competition, it strengthened tests of impact upon town centres, and the role of development plans in allocating new retail sites. It also set out a more positive role for local authorities in town centre planning. Table 4.2 lists the main changes in policy compared with the previous version of PPG6.

Several broad principles underpinned this quite substantial series of changes. First, the sustainability agenda underlay the statement that stores should be located so as to be accessible by public transport and minimise vehicle emissions, although weaker versions of this policy existed in previous guidance. Similarly, the specification of 'vitality and viability' and the advice on measurement of impact should be seen as amplification of existing policy. However, the encouragement to specify the location of new developments when preparing development plans and regional strategies marks a significant change from the 1980s laissez-faire policies, although consistent with the advice in PPG15 (see above). The advice regarding 'diversity of uses' in town centres and the encouragement for town centre management was also new.

1994–98: the sequential approach and revised guidance

This advice was followed by a new version of PPG13 (Transport), prepared jointly by the Departments of the Environment and Transport (1994). This related retail planning to sustainability and transport policy in a clearer fashion, and took up recommendations from a previously commissioned report on Reducing Transport Emissions Through Planning (ECOTEC, 1993). The guidance reinforced policies

Table 4.2 New or amended policies in PPG6 (1993)

Policy	Typical quote	Where described
General	Town Centres and Retail Developments	Title
More detailed definition of 'vitality and viability'	'vitality and viability depend on more than retailing; they stem from the range and quality of activities in town centres, and their accessibility to people living and working in the area'	Paras 5–7 Figure 1
Diversity of uses within town centres	'local authorities should encourage diversification of uses in the town centre as a whole'	Paras 5–7 Para 16
Control over amusement centres		Para 9 Annex C
Access and traffic for town centres	'Development in town centres can therefore encourage the use of public transport, or enable one car journey to serve several purposes' 'In some town centres, there may be a need to control the total provision of car parking, to limit traffic congestion'	Paras 10–13
Town centres in decline	'The Secretaries of State … expect local authorities to be realistic in their expectations … diversification of uses may be the best way forward.'	Para 16
Development plans and town centres	'the development plan process can be a key catalyst and can help to guide development.'	Para 17 Annex B
Town centre management	'Local authorities should consider, with the private sector and the local community, the desirability of appointing a town centre manager to improve the links between public and private sector initiatives.'	Paras 18–19
Balance between town centre and out-of-centre retailing	'The Government believes that both town centre and out-of-centre locations have distinctive roles to play in providing for new retail development.'	Paras 21–25
Warehouse clubs	'should be treated for the purposes of this guidance as if they were retail businesses'	Para 26
Criteria for assessing new retail developments	'the key considerations are: • to enable the community at large to benefit from effective competition between retailers and types of retailer • to ensure that the likely effect of development on the vitality and viability of existing town centres and on the rural economy is properly weighed in plan preparation and development control decisions; and • to ensure that access is likely to enable a choice of transport mode, and that the location will not result in an unacceptable increase of CO_2 and other polluting emissions compared with the alternatives'	Para 31

continued …

Table 4.2 continued

Policy	Typical quote	Where described
Control over nature of retail parks	'it may be sensible to consider the use of planning conditions to ensure that … [changes in types of goods sold] do not subsequently change their character unacceptably'	Para 34
Location of food stores	'In many cases, the best solution will be the edge-of-centre foodstore that provides parking facilities that enable those shopping at the foodstore to walk to the centre for their other business in town.'	Para 35
Evaluation of impact on town centres	'In preparing plans, and in deciding applications for developments which seem likely to have a broad impact on a nearby town centre, authorities should weigh the benefits to the public against other economic, social and environmental impacts, such as: • the likely effect on future private sector investment needed to safeguard vitality and viability in that centre … • the extent to which the development would put at risk the strategy for the town centre set out in the local plan … • changes to the quality, attractiveness and character of the centre, and to its role in the economic and social life of the community • changes to the physical condition of the centre • changes to the range of services that the centre will continue to provide • likely increases in the number of vacant properties in the primary retail area.'	Paras 36, 37
Accessibility and transport	'retail development should be sited where it is likely to be accessible by a choice of means of transport, and to encourage economy in fuel consumption'	Para 38
Major retail developments	'The role and scope for major new retail developments may be addressed in regional guidance. It should be considered in structure plan preparation … these plans should suggest the role and scope of any such developments and the criteria to be applied in considering possible locations.'	Paras 40–6

Source: based upon DoE/WO (1993)

that new developments should be accessible by all modes of transport, and proposed (in effect) that new developments should not lead to an increase in private car travel: 'Local planning authorities should consider carefully the impacts on travel demand of all new development before planning permission is granted' (DoE/DoT, 1994: para 2.12). This was a stronger version of the advice in PPG6 that there was a need to 'encourage economy in fuel consumption'.

PPG13 also strengthened advice to local planning authorities on retail policies in development plans:

> Structure plan policies for retailing should seek to promote the vitality and viability of existing urban and suburban and rural centres. Shopping should be promoted in existing centres which are more likely to offer a choice of access, particularly for those without the use of a private car.
>
> (ibid.: para 3.9)

Local plans were advised to include policies which would:

- Maintain and revitalise existing central and suburban shopping centres ...;
- encourage local convenience shopping by ... ensuring such areas are attractive and readily accessible on foot or by bicycle;
- where suitable locations are not available for larger retail development, seek edge-of-centre sites, close enough to be readily accessible by foot from the centre and which can be served by a variety of means of transport;
- avoid sporadic siting of comparison goods shopping units out of centres or along road corridors; and
- provide for both local shopping and residential uses in large new developments, where feasible.

> (ibid.: para 3.10)

This was much more detailed advice concerning locating new development, and much more clearly related to principles of sustainable development. The fact that these quite significant changes in central government guidance occurred over a period of just eight months appears to be due to the timing of the Reducing Transport Emissions report (ECOTEC, 1993), which was too late to influence the wording of PPG6.

In the same year, the House of Commons Environment Select Committee carried out an inquiry into *Shopping Centres and their Future*. The report welcomed the government's 'new, more cautious stance on retail development' (House of Commons, 1994: para 4), but argued that a 'much more subtle and refined approach to retail development is required, especially if Planning Inspectors are to make informed and consistent planning decisions within the framework of Development Plans' (ibid.: para 5).

The Committee heard evidence from a wide variety of public and private sector interests. There was concern over increased vacancy rates and environmental deterioration in many town centres, due to a combination of general economic conditions and the impact of out-of-centre developments. The Committee, influenced by a visit to the Merry Hill regional shopping centre and the neighbouring town centre of Dudley, which had suffered severe trading impact (Tym, 1993; Guy, 1994b), seems to have decided that the problems affecting town centres were due mainly to retail impact. At the same time, research commissioned by the Department of the Environment into measures to improve the vitality and viability of town centres (URBED, 1994), pointed out the concern of local authorities about the actual and potential impacts of previously approved out-of-centre developments.

The Environment Committee's report noted confusion amongst planning practitioners and property interests over government policy on retail development:

> In PPG6 the relevant test of acceptability of a proposed development is whether it would, through its impact on retail trade, cause 'demonstrable harm' to the vitality and viability of a nearby town centre. Statements made by the Secretary of State, together with statements by other Ministers, suggest a further, 'sequential' test whereby there should be no out-of-town developments unless there is no suitable town centre site.
>
> (House of Commons, 1994: para 21)

This is one of the first published references to the 'sequential test' or 'sequential approach', which became one of the main features of retail planning policy. The sequential test/approach was not mentioned in the government's memorandum to the Inquiry, dated April 1994, but appears to have emerged in oral proceedings. One persistent rumour is that it was suggested informally during these events by a well-known academic, although it is clear that government policy was moving in this direction. A series of decisions on planning applications by Secretary of State John Gummer also indicated that policy was becoming less favourable to out-of-centre proposals (Smith, 1994).

The Committee's report (House of Commons, 1994) made a series of proposals for strengthening planning policy in favour of town centres. These included:

- Making it clear that both the sequential test and a retail impact test should be applied in considering retail development proposals.
- An 'automatic call-in procedure for large retail developments which are departures from the Development Plan and which the local authority has resolved to permit' (ibid.: xiv).
- Measures to improve the financial basis of town centre management and the ability of local authorities to 'facilitate approved town centre schemes' (ibid.: xv).
- Compulsory submission of a retail impact study to accompany planning

applications for 'superstores or other large retail developments in or around market towns' (ibid.: xv).

• Encouraging local authorities to place conditions on retail warehouses and large food stores in order to limit the range of goods sold.

• 'A more proactive approach to addressing the shrinkage of retail functions and areas in town centres' (ibid.: xvi).

The Committee also recommended that the forward planning process for retail development should continue to be modified to favour the public sector. Regional planning frameworks should be prepared, and 'Development Plans are crucial for setting a proactive rather than a reactive framework for retail development, ensuring that development takes place in appropriate locations' (ibid.: xvi).

Finally, the Committee recommended a substantial programme of research, into:

• The impacts of retail developments, particularly into the cumulative effects of out-of-town developments on the vitality and viability of existing centres.

• Consumer and resident attitudes towards and preferences for different forms of retail developments.

• Ways of quantifying 'sustainable development'.

• Improvements to the quality and coverage of retail statistics, particularly of employment, floorspace and turnover in town centres.

(ibid.: xvi–xvii, passim)

The Department of the Environment produced the government's response to the Committee's report, in February 1995. This confirmed that the sequential approach was now part of official policy:

This advice, to look at the town centre first and then edge-of-centre sites, before looking out-of-centre – a sequential approach to looking for suitable sites – is part of official policy. The Government believes that a sequential approach should be applied by both developers and local planning authorities in seeking to identify suitable sites, and that it is particularly important for identifying sites through the development plan. It should apply equally to food shopping and to comparison shopping.

(DoE, 1995a: para 10)

The Department agreed to support most of the Committee's recommendations. It was clear that PPG6, although less than two years old, required updating. A draft revision was issued the same year, and the final version published in June

1996 (DoE, 1996). For the first time, the Welsh Office was not a co-author; it produced its own rather more brief guidance (WO, 1996a), and a more detailed 'Technical Advice Note' (WO, 1996b), which was very similar in content to parts of the new PPG6.

The stated objectives of policy were now:

- To sustain and enhance the vitality and viability of town centres;
- To focus development, especially retail development, in locations where the proximity of businesses facilitates competition from which all consumers are able to benefit and maximises the opportunity to use means of transport other than the car;
- To maintain an efficient, competitive and innovative retail sector; and
- To ensure the availability of a wide range of shops, employment, services and facilities to which people have easy access by a choice of means of transport.

(DoE, 1996: para 1.1)

The new guidance was much longer than the 1993 version, and also longer than the draft guidance (DoE, 1995b). Most of the policies concerning shopping travel, access and parking were similar to those in PPG13, whilst policies concerning assessment of impact were almost identical to those in the 1993 version. The major changes were in two areas: detailed instructions on the preparation in development plans of retail policies and proposals for new development; and a much more restrictive approach to out-of-centre development, centred around the sequential approach, and a new requirement for proposers of off-centre developments of over 2,500 sq.m. gross floor area to submit impact assessments with the planning application.[5]

In detail, the main changes in the new PPG6 are shown in Table 4.3.

Almost immediately after publication of the revised PPG6, the House of Commons Environment Select Committee (1997) produced another report. This supported the policy in general terms, but felt that problems were likely to arise over the meaning of the terms 'suitable' and 'available' in the description of the sequential approach. The Committee found that the policies concerning acquisition of town centre sites were likely to be difficult to implement as there was little recent experience of compulsory purchase by local authorities. They also regretted that the research projects suggested in their 1994 report had not taken place. The government's response (DETR, 1997) was essentially 'wait and see'.

At around the same time, revised guidance for Scotland was produced (SODD, 1996). This was generally similar in content to PPG6, but was shorter and carried less detail on planning and management in town centres. The overall objectives were similar to the English ones, but rather more neatly expressed:

Table 4.3 New or amended policies in PPG6 (1996)

Policy	Typical quote	Where described
Town centres favoured over out-of-centre	'Town and district centres should be the preferred locations for developments that attract many trips'	Para 1.3
Regional planning for major retail	'Regional planning guidance should set out the development strategy for each region, indicating the role that the network of town centres should play and proposing a broad strategy for its development, including the scope, if any, for additional regional shopping centres'	Para 1.4
Role of structure plans	'Structure plans and UDP Part Is ... should set out the hierarchy of centres and the strategy for the location of ... shopping, leisure and entertainment ... In particular, the development plan should indicate a range and hierarchy of centres ... where investment in retail and other development will be promoted and existing provision enhanced.'	Para 1.5
Role of local plans	'Local plans and UDP Part IIs should ... consider existing provision and sites for development.'	Para 1.6 Annex B
Positive planning	'Development plans should plan positively for such uses, working with the private sector to assess need or market demand, and identify locations and sites for development.' '... local planning authorities should consider preparing development briefs for key town centre sites'	Paras 1.7, 1.9, 2.9, 2.10
Sequential approach	'Both local planning authorities and developers selecting sites for [retail] development should be able to demonstrate that all potential town centre options have been thoroughly assessed before less central sites are considered.' 'Adopting a sequential approach means that first preference should be for town centre sites, where suitable sites or buildings suitable for conversion are available, followed by edge-of-centre sites, district and local centres and only then out-of-centre sites in locations that are accessible by a choice of means of transport.'	Paras 1.10, 1.11
Assessment of need	'If ... there is no need or capacity for further development, there will be no need to identify additional sites in the town.'	Para 1.10
Flexibility in development	'Developers and retailers will need to be more flexible about the format, design and scale of the development, and the amount of car parking, tailoring these to fit local circumstances.'	Para 1.12

continued ...

Table 4.3 continued

Policy	Typical quote	Where described
Development in small and historic town centres	'In such centres, developments should be of a scale appropriate to the size of the centre.'	Para 1.13
Treatment of out-of-centre proposals	'The following key considerations should be applied: • the likely harm to the development plan strategy; • the likely impact of the development on the vitality and viability of existing town centres …; • their accessibility by a choice of means of transport; and • their likely effect on overall travel patterns and car use.'	Para 1.16
Town centre uses and design	'The Government … wishes to … • encourage mixed-use development in town centres; • encourage an increase of housing in town centres; • promote town centre management …; • improve access and traffic management; • make more effective use of town centre car parking; and • encourage high-quality design of both urban spaces and buildings.'	Paras 2.3, 2.11–2.24, 2.33–2.38 Annex C
Monitoring of change	'local authorities should regularly collect information on key indicators'	Para 2.7 Figure 1
Car access to town centres	'If town centres are to compete effectively with out-of-centre developments, they must remain attractive to people who arrive by car. Local authorities should draw up a traffic management strategy and provide good quality car parking.'	Paras 2.26–2.32 Annex E
Large stores	'Some types of retailing, such as large stores selling bulky goods, may not be able to find suitable sites either in or on the edge of town centres. In such cases, the local planning authority should still seek to ensure that such developments are located where they will be easily accessible by a choice of means of transport.'	Para 3.3
Regional shopping centres	'full account needs to be taken of all likely impacts. Circumstances [where they could fulfil an important retail need] will be … where: • there is a deficiency of higher-order shopping centres; • continued private sector investment in nearby town centres is unlikely to be seriously jeopardised;	Paras 3.4–3.5

continued …

Table 4.3 continued

Policy	Typical quote	Where described
	• there is no loss of Green Belt, or important open space, habitats or countryside; • public transport can adequately serve a wide population; and • the effect on the road network and on overall car use would be acceptable.'	
Outlet centres	'the issue for planning policy purposes is not whether goods are sold at a discount, but whether such retail developments would divert trade in comparison goods from existing town centres, whether they would be accessible by a choice of means of transport and, in particular, whether they would have a significant effect on overall car use.'	Paras 3.9–3.10
Edge-of-centre definition	'… will be determined by what is an easy walking distance for shoppers walking … away from the store carrying shopping … 200 to 300 metres'	Para 3.14
Facilities in district and local centres	'Local planning authorities should encourage appropriately-sized, local supermarkets and seek to retain post offices and pharmacies in existing district and local centres, and in village shops, and discourage their inclusion in out-of-centre retail developments by imposing appropriate conditions.'	Paras 3.18–3.19
Land allocated for other uses	'planning applications for retail development should not normally be allowed on land designated for other uses in an approved development plan'	Para 3.23
Regeneration and retail development	'Retail development should not be used simply as a mechanism to bring vacant or derelict sites into development'	Paras 3.24–3.25
Impact on travel and car use	'local planning authorities should assess the likely proportion of customers who would arrive by car and the catchment area which the development seeks to serve'	Paras 4.9–4.11
Assessing major shopping proposals	'All applicants for retail developments over 2,500 square metres gross floorspace should be supported by evidence on: • whether the applicant adopted a sequential approach to site selection and the availability of suitable alternative sites; • their likely economic impacts on town centres, local centres and villages, including … cumulative effects of recently completed developments and outstanding planning permissions; • their accessibility by a choice of means of transport …; • the likely changes in travel patterns over the catchment area; and • any significant environmental impacts.'	Paras 4.12–4.19

Source: based on DoE (1996)

The Government's main policy objectives are:

- to maintain an efficient, competitive and innovative retail sector offering consumer choice;
- to sustain and enhance the vitality, viability and design quality of town centres, as the most appropriate location for much of that activity; and
- to ensure that ways of meeting these objectives are compatible with Sustainable Development: The UK Strategy, and, in particular, that new retail development can be reached by a choice of means of transport.

(SODD, 1996: para 7)

The guidance differed from PPG6 in a few respects, outlined in Table 4.4.

A more detailed review, including comparisons of NPPG8 with its draft version published in 1995, can be found in Braithwaite (1997). NPPG8 was further revised and reissued under the title *Town Centres and Retailing* in 1998 (SODD, 1998), and additional advice was issued on improving town centres (SODD, 1999). This appears to have arisen from a wish to emphasise the more positive advice on town centre enhancement, in line with the English policy. The Welsh policy was similarly revised in 1999 (WO, 1999: Chapter 10).

Central government retail planning policy: 1998–2005[6]

Although PPG6 and NPPG8 were much more detailed than previous versions, areas of debate arose where the policies were different, not clearly expressed, or subject

Table 4.4 Policies in NPPG8 (1996) not found in PPG6

Policy	Source (paragraph no.)
The introductory paragraphs supported more strongly the role of the market in delivering efficient and innovative retailing, and of retail developments in providing 'a catalyst for economic, social and environmental benefits'	4, 5
More specific advice on dealing with centres in decline	30
Advice to planning authorities to consider the capacity of their area for new out-of-centre developments	49, 69, 70
Requirement for planning applicants to provide retail impact assessments for proposals of over 5,000 sq.m.	52
Encouragement for provision of new district shopping centres	55
Advice that new retail warehouses should normally be located within retail parks, in order to 'reduce the number of journeys'	57
A positive reminder of the social benefits of food discount stores	60

to various interpretations. This section describes these debates, and explains how they gave rise to modified versions of central government policy. The discussion is organised firstly around particular issues: the sequential approach, the treatment of 'need', and relationships with policies for social inclusion and urban regeneration. There follows a description of the revised English policies issued in draft form in 2003, and definitively in 2005.

The sequential approach

This approach, although simple in concept, embodied several areas of uncertainty. These are summarised in Table 4.5, along with the responses (where made) by government ministers.

The Parliamentary Answer by the then Planning Minister Nick Raynsford (1997) was the first in a series of such statements, which were announced as 'clarifications' of policy, but which in the eyes of most commentators amounted to modifications of policy. Particularly important was the DETR's (2000) statement that the 'class of goods' interpretation of the sequential test was to be applied. In a speech Raynsford stated that 'Most goods can be sold from town centres – wanting a large showroom or warehouse is not in itself a sufficient justification' (Raynsford, 2000).

Other problems in the application of the sequential test were not satisfactorily resolved over this period. The definition of 'suitable' and 'available' sites in town centres was raised as an issue by the House of Commons Environment Select Committee (1997), but the government's reply claimed that there was no need for clarification (DETR, 1997: paras 2–5).

The review of the sequential approach, commissioned by the National Retail Planning Forum and supported financially by DETR, pointed out that the 'suitability' and 'availability' issue, the 'format' issue and the question whether developers were obliged to demonstrate a 'need' for their proposal (see below, and in more depth, Chapter 5) were 'inextricably linked' in a 'triangle of inter-related decisions' (CBHP, 2000: 73). The policy issues involved are shown in Table 4.6, assuming a hypothetical proposal to develop a large-format store in an out- or edge-of-centre location.

This analysis made clear that the basic question was whether the sequential approach to be applied was the store format (or 'built form') proposed by the developer, or whether 'disaggregation' should take place so that the goods which were likely to be sold were at issue. If the latter, then the local authority could insist that the developer should seek town centre sites (perhaps several in number) in order to sell the goods required. This course of action was supported by the requirement in PPG6 (para 1.12) that developers should show 'flexibility' in tailoring their proposals to fit appropriate sites. As we have seen, the government

Table 4.5 Areas of uncertainty in sequential test, and government responses

Area of uncertainty	Typical comment in practitioner literature	Government response
Whether a particular site could be classified as 'edge-of-centre'. This would typically occur when the developer and local planning authority disagreed, the latter maintaining that the site was out-of-centre and therefore development would be contrary to policy. The definition of 'edge-of-centre' in PPG6 attempted to overcome this problem, but still gave room for uncertainty.	'The distance guideline of 200 metres to 300 metres from the primary shopping area set out in PPG6 is widely applied, but also widely criticised by developers and retailers. ... limited regard is paid to functional linkages between the proposed edge-of-centre development and existing town centre shopping and services ... There appears to be a lack of understanding by local authorities, Planning Inspectors and the Secretary of State [on this question].' (CBHP, 2000: 75)	None
The definition of 'suitable' and 'available' as applied to town centre sites. Typically the local authority would consider certain sites as suitable for the type of development concerned, and available for development within a given period, often five years. The developer would dispute either or both of these claims.	'There is inconsistency and confusion as to how sites should be assessed for suitability and availability. ... there is no consistency in decision taking over the criteria which are applied by local authorities, Planning Inspectors and the Secretary of State in assessing whether sites are suitable and available within a reasonable period of time.' (CBHP, 2000: 74)	None
The 'goods' versus 'format' distinction. The developer would claim that the proposed format was of a specified format (usually large, single-storey with adjacent free car parking provision), the local authority would insist that the developer should be 'flexible' regarding format, so that a more central site could be used. Each of these arguments seemed to find support in PPG6.	'Retail warehouses are specifically defined in PPG6 as large single-level stores, catering mainly for car-borne customers. ... Forcing developers to abandon their format through a goods-based approach to the sequential test potentially means that retail warehouses could never be justified. This could not possibly be described as a "flexible" approach.' (Rhodes, 2000)	'Class of goods' interpretation to apply (DETR, 2000)
Whether the sequential test applied to proposals to extend existing stores.		Sequential test did apply (Raynsford, 1997)
Whether the test applied when owners of off-centre stores applied for consent to alter conditions on the original planning permission (usually retail warehouses whose owners wished to sell a wider range of goods).	'In three recent appeals, ... planning inspectors have concluded that the two-fold test of "need" for the development and the sequential test should not apply for applications to change conditions on existing planning consents. ... the potential effect of that approach is far from insignificant ... all three operators concerned ... purvey goods or services which overlap with those which one might anticipate in a town centre.' (Tucker, 2000)	None

Table 4.6 Interlinked issues in the sequential approach

Issue	Developer's interpretation	Local authority's interpretation
Need for the development	Built form is needed	Goods to be sold are needed
Suitable and available sites in town centre	None, for the built form intended	There are sites suitable and available for selling the goods
Location of development	Edge- or out-of-centre	Town centre

Source: based upon CBHP (2000)

imposed the 'class of goods' interpretation, shortly after the publication of the Hillier Parker report.

The question of 'need'

One other modification of policy was made through a Ministerial statement in 1999. In PPG6, it was not made clear whether the developer was required to justify an out-of-centre or edge-of-centre proposal in terms of a 'need' for the scheme. A High Court judgement in 1998 held that there was no such requirement. The government was however unhappy with this decision, and Richard Caborn's statement reclaimed the situation:

> This statement is intended to add to and clarify the guidance in PPG6 in the light of a number of issues raised in recent litigation which concern the interpretation of PPG6 and Government policy. ... Proposals for new retail and leisure development which accord with an up-to-date plan strategy or are proposed on sites within an existing centre, should not be required to demonstrate that they satisfy the test of need because this should have been taken into account in the development plan.
>
> However, proposals which would be located at an edge-of-centre or out-of-centre location and which:
> - are not in accordance with an up-to-date development plan strategy; or
> - are in accordance with the development plan but that plan is out of date, is inconsistent with national planning policy guidance, or otherwise fails to establish adequately the need for new retail and leisure development and other development to which PPG6 applies, should be required to demonstrate both the need for additional facilities and that a sequential approach has been applied in selecting the location or the site.
>
> (Caborn, 1999a)

This statement made it clear that out-of-centre and edge-of-centre proposals would have to show that there was a need for additional retail floorspace, but further parts of the statement did not made clear what evidence should be used in support of such claims. The statement also explained that proposals within a town centre did not require such justification: this view also met with criticism, and appeared inconsistent with the view expressed in PPG6 and in subsequent Ministerial speeches that new development within town centres should be in keeping with the scale and function of the centre concerned. Further discussion of the background to Caborn's statement and of its implications may be found in Chapter 5.

Social inclusion and urban regeneration

One other set of issues became prominent during this period. The advent of a Labour government in 1997 brought a greater concern for social justice and equality of opportunity. The government was quick to identify 'social exclusion' as a specific concern, and a Social Exclusion Unit was set up to report directly to the Cabinet Office. The Unit, along with the Department of Health, showed concern for residents of areas in which access to fresh food and other retail goods and services was problematic. These areas, which became known as 'food deserts' (Wrigley, 2002), became a focus of attention in retail planning (see Chapter 8 for further discussion). A report by Policy Action Team 13 of the Unit (DoH, 1999a) suggested that 'local retail strategies' should be set up to investigate the situation regarding access to essential goods and services, and suggest improvements.

There was little reference in PPG6 to this issue. However, the revised NPPG8 indicated that social exclusion was considered relevant in retail planning:

> As part of its policies related to welfare to work and overcoming social exclusion, [the Government] ... wants as many as possible to take advantage of the changes in retailing and leisure, and to ensure that most people, including the disabled, have access to them.
>
> (SODD, 1998: para 4)

At the same time it became clear that retail development was viewed in many parts of Britain as an important potential source of employment, as well as a means of facilitating improvements to brownfield sites and infrastructure. More and more retail development proposals were being promoted as 'regeneration' projects. PPG6 had little advice on this matter, other than

> Retail development should not be used simply as a mechanism to bring vacant or derelict sites into development, unless it would help to support the vitality and

viability of existing centres. ... The local job creation benefits from retail proposals should be carefully assessed as there may be off-setting losses elsewhere in the area when trade is diverted ...

(DoE, 1996: paras 3.24, 3.25)

These issues are examined in more detail in Chapter 9.

After it became clear from Caborn's (1999a) statement that proposals for out-of-centre developments would have to show 'need', the question arose whether 'social exclusion' and 'regeneration' could be classed as elements of 'need'. In a Parliamentary statement of April 2003, the Minister for Planning Tony McNulty stated that:

Regeneration has also been argued to be a component of the need for additional retail floorspace. There is no Government guidance that supports this interpretation. The First Secretary of State considers that the contribution that a proposed development might make to the regeneration of a site or its area could be a material consideration to be taken into account in determining an application, but does not consider it to be an aspect of retail need.

Equally, the net additional employment created by a proposed development is not an indicator of retail need but may be a material consideration.

For the avoidance of doubt, the First Secretary of State does not regard regeneration or employment creation as aspects of retail need for the purposes of the tests set out in PPG6 and the Caborn statement.

(McNulty, 2003: 2)

This statement confirmed the position which planning inspectors had already taken on this issue. Nevertheless, the increasing level of concern over social exclusion and regeneration in retail planning debates indicated that a more positive policy stance might be helpful.

The 'effectiveness' reports

By 2001, it was becoming clear that interpretation of government policy was becoming increasingly disputed. Both the Office of the Deputy Prime Minister (the successor to the DETR) and the Scottish Parliament thus commissioned reports on the 'effectiveness' of policy (CBHP, 2004; CBRE, 2004c).

In England, the series of modifications to official policy had led to a complex and somewhat confused situation. The 'effectiveness' report concluded that the basic policies were widely understood and accepted in both local government and the private sector. However, details of the policy were often seen as unclear, ambiguous or conflicting:

There is a consensus that PPG6 works in theory, but not in practice, and that it has been interpreted in different ways, according to different local circumstances and decision-makers. Only regular users of the planning system find PPG6 satisfactorily clear, and there is a need for a single point of reference for town centre and retail planning policy, as opposed to the current guidance contained in PPGs and subsequent ministerial statements.

Even where the guidance is considered to be clear, there is an almost universally held view by Planning Inspectors, retailers and developers that the interpretation and application of policy and practice has been inconsistent on some occasions. Our consultation exercise has identified a number of areas that have given rise to confusion.

(CBHP, 2004: 8)

Despite the 'clarifications' of policy, and the continuing refinement of policy implied in analyses of Inspectors' decision letters, the report claimed that:

There is evidence of a perceived inconsistency in decision-making, largely due to a lack of clarity in the guidance. The sequential approach has given rise to debate about the rigour with which it should be applied, the extent to which operators in the retail and leisure sectors should be required to disaggregate their operations, and the uses to which it should be directed. Clarification is needed, either in a policy document or in good practice guidance, on how to apply the sequential approach and the class of goods approach.

(CBHP, 2004: 14)

Two other basic problems were diagnosed from questionnaire surveys and interviews with local authorities, planning inspectors and private sector developers and retailers:

the objectives of PPG6 contain elements of internal conflict – notably the third objective ('to maintain an efficient, competitive and innovative retail sector') in relation to the other three objectives which are conventionally taken to seek to concentrate development in town centres. Most regard the objectives in practice as falling within an overarching objective to sustain and enhance town centres.

... while the plan-led approach is a fundamental element of the guidance, requiring local authorities to plan positively for new development and identify sites, a combination of lengthy adoption process, and the failure of many local authorities to rise to the challenges set out in the guidance has meant that in practice, PPG6 is increasingly used by local authorities as a development control tool to prevent out-of-centre development, instead of as a basis for positive planning for town centres.

(ibid.: 9)

The report also confirmed the state of confusion over the interpretation of the sequential approach, especially the 'disaggregation' issue, and the related topic of 'need' and its definition.

At around the same time, a report on the effectiveness of NPPG8 was published in Scotland (CBRE, 2004c). Its main recommendations included the following:

- … the Scottish Executive should introduce a new approach to 'urban centres'. This should raise the profile of town and other centres in government policy, redefine town centres in the future to be sustainable, accessible and viable urban locations and new guidance should present a list of credentials which qualify a centre to be one of importance in future planning policy.
- the launch of a new profile to promote town centre initiatives. The new aspect involved in this recommendation is some form of annual round of bidding for central funds, in order to secure investment in appropriate development sites, town centre extensions, transport improvements, environmental enhancement and other initiatives.
- policy on sequential sites should be improved, with guidance on location and site development issues. This could be more specific in terms of appropriate linkages between new sites and existing centres, to promote a 'pre-test' of various sites, before developments come forward and to promote more detailed site development guidance.
- There is a need for best practice guidance on the preparation and promotion of town centre strategies, vitality/viability indicators and the identification/ assembly of town centre sites. In addition, some respondents have highlighted the need to promote design quality, improve the public realm and promote good practice on town centre management.
- that transport for shopping should be reappraised. Key trends should be identified through updated household shopping and leisure survey information. From this, different patterns of accessibility and transport facilities should be assessed, with a view to complementing future policy on shopping centres.

(CBRE, 2004c: Chapter 10, passim)

The report also recommended eventual revision of NPPG8 into a more concise form, supplemented by detailed advice notes on aspects of retail planning.

The two 'effectiveness' reports are thus rather different in tone. Neither research team was required to question basic policy or to rewrite official guidance.[7] However, while the English exercise focused mainly on the wording and implementation of policy, the Scottish exercise examined more broadly the purposes of policy, and the factual information which was needed in order to carry out policy more effectively.

Two other problems in retail planning implementation also affected the revision of government policy. First, it was clear from both 'effectiveness' reports that few local authorities were using powers of site assembly in order to facilitate town centre developments, despite advice to this effect in PPG6 and NPPG8. Second, research into consumer spending patterns showed that the largest 50 or so city and town centres were expanding their share of comparison goods expenditure, and as a result gaining much of the financial investment by both retailers and property developers. Smaller town centres were struggling to maintain their local market share and were not able to attract investment on the same scale (BCSC, 2004; CBRE, 2004b).

Policy revision

In Wales, amended guidance was issued in 2002, to reflect the content of Ministerial statements in England (NAW, 2002).

During 2003, a consultation draft of a revised policy statement for England was prepared by ODPM and circulated around Whitehall for comment. This clearly took note of the findings and recommendations from the 'effectiveness' report, although the latter was not officially published until February 2004. In particular the early versions of this draft confirmed the Ministerial 'clarifications' regarding 'need' and the 'class of goods' interpretation of the sequential approach, and appear to have taken a strongly promotional line regarding town centres. Interdepartmental negotiations, however, had the effect of weakening the sequential approach and emphasising the need to consider the benefits to consumers of large-format developments in retail planning (for further discussion see Chapter 6, and Guy, 2006a).

The consultation draft of the new Planning Policy Statement 6 (ODPM, 2003) was open to outside comment up to March 2004. Another long period of interdepartmental negotiation followed until the definitive version of PPS6 was released in March 2005 (ODPM, 2005a). This retained most of the policies in the consultation draft: some changes in wording are noted later in this section.

One of the most important changes in the guidance was the explicit incorporation of wider government policy aims into the retail planning framework, although within a hierarchy of objectives. Table 4.7 lists the main and subsidiary objectives of retail and town centre policy. These include references to social exclusion and regeneration, as well as those relating to sustainability and competition which were also in earlier guidance.

The policies were stated as referring to retail, leisure and entertainment uses; offices; arts, cultural and tourist facilities (para 1.8).

Much of PPS6 reaffirmed the 'town centres first' policies already stated in PPG6 and the subsequent Ministerial clarifications, particularly that relating to 'need' for development of additional floorspace. Some important modifications

Table 4.7 PPS6: summary of objectives and purposes

Principal objective: to promote vital and viable town centres (para 1.3)	• 'planning for the growth and development of existing centres' • 'promoting and enhancing existing centres, by focusing development in such centres and encouraging a wide range of services in a good environment, accessible to all'
Secondary objectives (para 1.4)	• to enhance consumer choice • to support an efficient, competitive and innovative retail and leisure sector • to improve accessibility
The government's wider policy aims: (para 1.5)	• promotion of social inclusion • regeneration of deprived areas • promotion of economic growth • delivering more sustainable patterns of development • promotion of good design

Source: ODPM (2005a)

to policy, as well as a few new policies, were however incorporated in PPS6. These included (see Table 4.8 for details):

- Strengthening of the role of regional spatial strategies in defining a hierarchy of centres and determining locations for major growth, including possible creation of new centres.[8]
- Mention of regeneration and social inclusion as 'other' and 'material' considerations in both development planning and development control.
- Inclusion (with definitions) of 'need' as an essential criterion in both locating new development within the development plan, and assessing planning applications (where outside town centres).
- Partial withdrawal of the 'class of goods' interpretation of the sequential approach, with a requirement instead that both applicants and local planning authorities should be 'flexible' in preparing proposals and assessing them, respectively.
- Confirmation that the sequential approach should apply to store extensions, but only where the proposed extension is over 200 sq.m. (the consultation draft PPS6 excluded extensions altogether from the sequential test).
- Advice to local authorities to assess the quality of local shopping facilities, especially in areas of social exclusion.

Table 4.8 New or Amended Policies in PPS6 (2005)

Policy	Typical quote	Where described
Retail hierarchy	... regional planning bodies and local planning authorities should ... develop a hierarchy and network of centres each performing their appropriate role to meet the needs of their catchments	Para 1.6 Para 2.1 Paras 2.9–2.11
Expansion of town centres	[Planning authorities should] focus development in, and plan for the expansion of, existing centres as appropriate	Para 1.6 Paras 2.5–2.6
Town centre uses subject to this guidance	Retail ... leisure ... offices ... arts, culture and tourism	Para 1.8
Managing the 'role' of centres	Local planning authorities should ... manag[e] the role and function of existing centres by, for example, promoting and developing a specialist or new role and encouraging specific types of uses in some centres	Para 2.3
Plan for new centres	Local planning authorities should ... plan for new centres of an appropriate scale in areas of significant growth or where there are deficiencies in the existing network of centres The identification of new centres which are of more than local importance should be addressed initially at the regional level through regional spatial strategies	Para 2.3 Para 2.7 Para 2.10 Para 2.13 Para 2.53
Facilitate large format store development in edge-of-centre	Larger stores may deliver benefits for consumers and local planning authorities should seek to make provision for them ... [they] should seek to identify, designate and assemble larger sites adjoining the primary shopping area (i.e. in edge-of-centre locations)	Para 2.6
Treatment of centres in decline	Where reversing decline is not possible, local planning authorities should recognise that these centres may need to be reclassified at a lower level within the hierarchy of centres ... this may include allowing retail uses to change to other uses	Para 2.8
Role of regional plans	Regional spatial strategies should set out a vision and a strategy for the region's growth, particularly for higher level centres in the region ... and provide a strategic framework for planning at the local level The need for major town centre development of regional or sub-regional importance should be addressed through the regional spatial strategy	Paras 2.12–2.14

continued ...

Table 4.8 continued

Policy	Typical quote	Where described
Avoidance of over-concentration of growth	The regional planning body should develop a strategic framework ... taking into account the need to avoid an over-concentration of growth in the higher level centres	Para 2.13
Role of plans at the local level	Local planning authorities should ... set out a spatial vision and strategy for the network and hierarchy of centres, including local centres, within their area ... identify the centres within their area where development will be focused, as well as the need for any new centres of local importance	Paras 2.15–2.18
Policies for deprived areas	[Local planning authorities should] develop spatial policies and proposals to promote and secure investment in deprived areas ... and to seek to improve access to local facilities	Para 2.16
Primary and secondary frontages	Local planning authorities may distinguish between primary and secondary frontages ... these ... should be realistically defined ... the appropriate local development documents should ... make clear which uses will be permitted in which locations	Para 2.17
Design policies	Policies for the design of development for main town centres uses, regardless of location, and for development in town centres, should promote high quality and inclusive design Local planning authorities should formulate planning policies which encourage well-designed, and where appropriate, higher-density, multi-storey development	Paras 2.19–2.22
Evening and night-time economy	Local planning authorities should prepare planning policies to help manage the evening and night-time economies in appropriate centres	Paras 2.23–2.26
Markets	Local authorities should seek to retain and enhance existing markets and, where appropriate, re-introduce or create new ones	Para 2.27
Site selection and land assembly	In selecting sites for development, local planning authorities should: a) Assess the need for development b) Identify the appropriate scale of development c) Apply the sequential approach to site selection d) Assess the impact of development on existing centres e) Ensure that locations are accessible and well served by a choice of means of transport	Paras 2.28–2.50

continued ...

Table 4.8 continued

Policy	Typical quote	Where described
Other considerations	In selecting sites for allocation in development plan documents, the local planning authority should .. consider … [whether] other considerations, including specific local circumstances, may be material to the choice of appropriate locations for development. … [including]: • Physical regeneration … • Employment … • Economic growth … • Social inclusion …	Para 2.51
Providing for local shopping	Local authorities should work [in deprived areas] with the local community and retailers to identify opportunities to remedy any deficiencies in local provision	Paras 2.55–2.59
Development control	[Until their plan is] reviewed to reflect this planning policy statement, local planning authorities should have regard to the policies in this statement as material considerations which may supersede the relevant policies in their development plan	Para 3.2
Development control criteria	Local planning authorities should require applicants to demonstrate: a) The need for development[1] b) That the development is of appropriate scale c) That there are no more central sites for the development[1] d) That there are no unacceptable impacts on existing centres e) That locations are accessible	Paras 3.3–3.27
Flexibility in the sequential approach	Developers and operators should be able to demonstrate that in seeking to find a site in or on the edge of existing centres they have been flexible about their proposed business model in terms of : • The scale of their development • The format of their development • Car parking provision • The scope for disaggregation Local planning authorities should take into account any genuine difficulties, which the applicant can demonstrate are likely to occur in operating the applicant's business model from the sequentially preferable site A single retailer or leisure operator should not be expected to split their proposed development into separate sites where flexibility … has been demonstrated	Paras 3.15–3.19

continued…

Table 4.8 continued

Policy	Typical quote	Where described
Assessing impact	Where a significant development in a centre, not in accordance with the development plan strategy, would substantially increase the attraction of the centre and could have an impact on other centres, the impact on other centres will also need to be assessed	Para 3.20
Other considerations	Material considerations to be taken into account in assessing planning applications may include: Physical regeneration Employment Economic growth Social inclusion	Para 3.28
Extensions	The sequential approach is only a relevant consideration where the gross floor space of the proposed extension exceeds 200 square metres	Para 3.29
Monitoring and review	Comprehensive, relevant and up-to-date monitoring is essential to the effective planning and management of town centres	Paras 4.1–4.4

Source: ODPM (2005a)
Note
1 Only if the development would be edge-of-centre or out-of-centre (para 3.9)

The Statement, although already longer than the consultation draft and previous guidance, was to be supplemented by detailed guidance on:

- Assessing need and impact of new retail and leisure development
- Applying the sequential approach
- Strategies for smaller centres, and
- Planning for town centres: guidance on design and implementation tools.

The first of these to be issued related to design and implementation tools (ODPM, 2005c). This explained how the design principles should be applied to retail and other town centre development proposals. Local authorities were advised to 'draw up master plans or development briefs for key sites or areas which are suitable for town centre uses. Such guidance should include a clear urban design framework', involving potential developers and investors (ibid.: para 3.5). Developments themselves should respect existing street patterns and the scale of the existing built environment (ibid.: para 2.4).

In examining PPS6, it is useful to review the extent to which the ODPM responded to the problems and criticisms identified in the 'effectiveness' reports and elsewhere, during the period in which PPG6 was being implemented. This is summarised in Table 4.9.

Table 4.9 Responses by ODPM to perceived problems in policy interpretation and implementation

Problem	Response in Draft PPS6	Response in PPS6
Interpretation of sequential approach	• 'Class of goods' interpretation dropped • Sequential approach not to apply to store extensions	• 'Class of goods' interpretation dropped • Sequential approach not to apply to store extensions below 200 m²
Definition of 'need'	Quantitative and qualitative need defined	Quantitative and qualitative need defined
Difficulties for large-format store developers	Planning authorities should make provision for edge-of-centre development of large-format stores	Planning authorities should make provision for edge-of-centre development of large-format stores
Uncertain status of regeneration and social inclusion as indicators of need	Material considerations rather than indicators of 'retail need'	Material considerations rather than indicators of 'retail need'
Lack of positive town centre planning by local authorities	Further encouragement	Detailed advice, referring to Planning and Compulsory Purchase Act 2004
Concentration of central area developments in largest centres	Regional spatial strategies should discourage concentration of development in largest centres	Regional spatial strategies should 'consider whether there is a need to' discourage concentration of development in largest centres

Although the wording of the draft and final versions of PPS6 are generally similar in these respects, there was some weakening of what commentators considered to be a pro-developer stance in the draft, notably the reinstatement of the policy that applications for store extensions were subject to the sequential test.

The publication of PPS6 was followed by revised guidance in Wales (NAW, 2005), which broadly followed the policies in PPS6. As with previous statements, the guidance is relatively brief, and is intended to be read in conjunction with the technical note TAN4 (WO, 1996b), although the latter was by this time rather out-of-date. Revised guidance in Scotland was also issued in draft form (SEDD, 2005).

This and the previous sections have examined the development of government guidance on retail planning from the early 1990s onwards. The most important concerns in previous guidance, including impact of out-of-centre schemes upon town centre vitality and viability, assessment of the need for new development, recognition of the difficulties faced by non-car users, and, on the other hand, recognition of the importance of competition and innovation in retailing, have remained in the guidance. Of the many new features of guidance, three stand out. The first is the *sustainability agenda*. Although in principle this covers a wide range of economic, social and environmental concerns, it has been manifested largely in support for existing town and district centres, and the requirement that new development does not add to private vehicle travel. The second has been the *sequential approach* to local authority planning and the consideration of private sector proposals. Thirdly, the *role of regional and local planning bodies* has been greatly enhanced. Starting from a position whereby the planning of new development was left largely to private sector initiative, it is now the case that these planning bodies are expected to take responsibility for locating new development, in response to the needs of the whole community.

Implementation of planning policy

The period examined in this chapter has thus shown an increasing insistence by policy makers that town centres should be considered as the most suitable locations for almost all retail development. The period has also been one of increasingly detailed policy determination at the centre (particularly in England), with decreasing scope for local government to work out its own policy guidelines, where these might conflict with central policy.

Policies in development plans

At the start of the 1990s, 'Key Structure Plan Topics' in England and Wales included 'Major industrial, business, retail and other employment-generating development' (DoE, 1990b: para 18). However, the counties were not expected to consider in detail the need for new retail development, or to specify locations. Thus, structure plan policies tended to give a descriptive summary of various centres where development was to be encouraged, followed by criteria for development control which attempted to regulate out-of-centre development. Up to this time, retail developers had every expectation that such proposals would, if refused by local authorities, be considered 'on their own merits' by planning inspectors at appeal (see Chapter 3). PPG15 however gave greater authority to councils to refuse applications which were clearly at odds with structure plan policies – as long as the policies themselves were consistent with national and regional policy. This created some confusion because the national policy for retail development emphasised the advantages of out-of-centre development.

These uncertainties were largely resolved in the 1993 revision of PPG6, which included an Annex which set out requirements for retail planning in regional strategies, structure and local plans. The 1996 revision then made it clear that, in line with the general 'plan-led approach' introduced in the 1991 Act, development plans should be the principal method of determining locations for new retail development.

Although no detailed analysis of structure plan, local plan and UDP policies in the 1990s for retail development has been published, the overwhelming impression is that these policies were generally very similar, and almost entirely based (in their general principles) on PPG6 and its Scottish and Welsh equivalents. There would seem to be three broad reasons for this:

- It was clear from other government guidance such as PPG1 (DoE, 1997) that development plan policies should be in accord with national policy, and that Secretaries of State will determine appeal and call-in decisions in line with national policy.
- The policies in PPG6 and its equivalents were specified in sufficient detail to serve as development plan policies, apart of course from particular geographical references.
- The policies were largely in sympathy with the pro-town centre views consistently held by most local authorities since the 1960s.

Thus, development plan policies have increasingly become closely similar to the national in their general wording and particularly in their development control criteria. This has reinforced central government policy and led to its 'success' as noted in the various Select Committee reports. However, the 'effectiveness' reports (CBHP, 2004; CBRE, 2004c) both suggested that local authorities have been less successful at implementing the more positive aspects of central government policy. There has been a reluctance to accommodate retail change (either growth or decline), through estimating the scale of development needed, and selecting locations for new development or redevelopment. In few cases have local authorities facilitated development through use of land purchase powers, as advised in the 1996 version of PPG6. For example, the Scottish report observed that:

> The current NPPG8 makes frequent reference to the fact that local authorities should promote town centre strategies and other promotional activities and this

is encouraged by way of reference to less desirable forms of retail development emerging, if town centre efforts are not progressed.

However, the study team believes that much more resource and vigour is required, to re-energise the retail based sector into higher levels of competitive activity to prove town centres as appropriate locations for future development.

(CBRE, 2004c: paras 9.19–9.20)

While many local plans or Parts 2 of UDPs have specified locations and even exact sites for new development, the local authorities concerned have generally not been willing to use their powers in acquiring the sites concerned. For example, a study of 19 local plans or UDPs prepared in England since 1999 showed that altogether 83 specific sites were listed as possibilities for retail development, but that only two of these proposals were explicitly backed up by the local authority using site assembly powers, including compulsory purchase where necessary (Guy, 2004a).

It should be added that the great majority of these sites were located in town or district centres: only five were edge-of-centre. Seventeen sites were out-of-centre, but 12 of these were in existing retail parks. This was despite there being no specific prohibition for local authorities to designate out-of-centre retailing in their development plans: such proposals would be consistent with government policy if all the tests in PPG6 were applied successfully.

This review of recent plans showed also that policies for development control tended to be worded similarly to those in government advice.[9] There was generally a strongly negative attitude to off-centre development, amounting to a virtual prohibition in several cases.[10] This was noted also in the 'effectiveness' reports:

While the plan-led approach is a fundamental element of the guidance, requiring local authorities to plan positively for new development and identify sites, a combination of lengthy adoption process, and the failure of many local authorities to rise to the challenges set out in the guidance has meant that in practice, PPG6 is increasingly used by local authorities as a development control tool to prevent out-of-centre development instead of as a basis for positive planning for town centres.

(CBHP, 2004: 53)

However, in areas where retail development was seen to have a vital role in bringing new employment or the opportunity for site remediation, these criteria were likely to enter the list relating to the control of retail development. This phenomenon has been much more common in the so-called 'north', a region not precisely delineated by commentators but which appears to include Wales and Scotland as well as much of England. This issue is examined in Chapter 9.

The passing of the Planning and Compulsory Purchase Act in 2004 marked a change in England and Wales to a system of 'spatial planning' and (in England) to a more flexible system under which the development plan may comprise several local development documents. According to an advice note prepared by the Planning Officers' Society (2004: 13), spatial planning:

> derives from the unique features or characteristics of an area. By considering the needs and problems of communities, it can help to identify the spatial 'drivers' of change within an area. This in turn allows plans to express a sense of place for their area from which spatial vision and objectives can be derived.

It will be interesting to observe to what extent this view can be supported in retail planning, given the precise nature of the current guidance and the centralist views in government circles, which limits scope for initiative at the local level.

This advice to planning officers also notes however that development plan policies must be consistent with national policy and regional spatial strategies. Specimen policies for retail and other development in town centres and out-of-centre locations are shown in Table 4.10. The wording of these policies is, in line with advice in the document, different from PPS6, but the policies themselves are clearly consistent with national guidance.

Decisions on appeals and call-ins

For many years analysts have examined the implementation of government policy through the decisions of planning inspectors. Most of these relate to appeals against refusals of planning consent: analyses of such decisions for food store proposals show that, whereas in the 1980s around 50 per cent of such appeals were allowed, the proportion fell to around 30 per cent after the revision of PPG6 in 1996, thence rising to around 45 per cent (Drivers Jonas, 2003). In the case of non-food proposals, success rates were higher, but fell from around 70 per cent in the early 1990s to around 50 per cent after 2000 (ibid.).

An analysis of decisions carried out for the 'effectiveness' review in England (CBHP, 2004) show that over the period 1990–2001, about 43 per cent of appeals against refusal of consent for major retail development[11] were allowed. However, of those referred to the Secretary of State for decision,[12] only 27 per cent were allowed. In several instances, inspectors' recommendations to allow the appeal have been overturned by the Secretary of State.

Despite a widespread view that local authorities have been at least as restrictive as central government in refusing out-of-centre developments, central government in England has called in many retail proposals for the Secretary of State's decision,

Table 4.10 Suggested retail policies for local development documents

Note: These policies provide locational guidance for planned development throughout the city without being site-specific allocations.

Development in the city centre and neighbourhood centres

Proposals for new retail, leisure, entertainment and cultural facilities in the city centre and suburban/district centres of XX, XX, XX and XX will be permitted if they:

a) enhance or maintain the range and quality of facilities provided and contribute to the vitality and viability of the centre;

b) are in keeping with the scale and character of the surrounding centre;

c) can be accessed conveniently by public transport, bicycle and on foot;

d) do not cause unacceptable levels of disturbance to the local community.

Retail and retail hierarchy

Development proposals for large retail uses (including superstores, hypermarkets and retail warehouses), garden centres, recreation, leisure and entertainment uses located at the edge or outside of town centres, district centres and local centres will be permitted if:

a) there is an identified need for the development;

b) it is within a defined settlement boundary;

c) it is easily accessible by car, goods vehicles, public transport, cycle and foot;

d) it is not located on land currently used or allocated for housing, industry, business, or open space; and

e) government guidance has been followed regarding a sequential approach to location and the proposals' effect upon the vitality and viability of nearby centres.

Non-retail uses in shopping areas

Planning permission will be refused for non-retail uses in the primary shopping frontages of XX, XX and XX if it would:

a) have a harmful effect on the interest and appearance of the shopping frontage;

b) undermine the vitality and viability of the shopping centre as a whole; and

c) result in a continuous street frontage of three or more non-retail uses; or

d) result in over 40 per cent of street frontage (measured 50 metres either side of the application site) being in non-retail use.

Source: Planning Officers' Society (2004: 82, 109–10)

under Section 77 of the Town and Country Planning Act 1990. The stated principle behind this procedure is that the Secretary of State's:

> policy is to be very selective about calling in planning applications. He will, in general, only take this step if planning issues of more than local importance are involved. Such cases may include, for example, those which, in his opinion:
> - may conflict with national policies on important matters;
> - could have significant effects beyond their immediate locality;
> - give rise to substantial regional or national controversy;
> - raise significant architectural and urban design issues; or
> - may involve the interests of national security or of foreign Governments.
>
> (Caborn, 1999b)

However, commentators have observed that routine retail applications, for example for a single food superstore, have sometimes been called in. A statement by the DETR explained as follows:

> Where large out-of-centre superstores are proposed, the Secretary of State for the Environment, Transport and the Regions will call in applications for his own decision where the local planning authority proposes to allow a development in which the sequential test has been inappropriately applied and the need for flexibility has not been demonstrated.
>
> (DETR, 2000: para 9)

This statement coincided with an increased rate of call-ins, for which most applications were refused by the Secretary of State (CBHP, 2004: 64–5). In the late 1990s, at least 10 food store applications were called in each year in England, as well as up to 20 non-food applications (Drivers Jonas, 2003). Anecdotal evidence suggests much lower rates of call-in in Wales and Scotland (published data are not available).

No comprehensive analysis of inspectors' or reporters' decisions on retail proposals since about 1990 appears to have been published, in contrast to the situation in the 1970s and 1980s.[13] A brief review of trends in the 1990s concluded that 'Planning policy for retailing continues to be made on the hoof during appeals and call-in inquiries', raising the concerns noted earlier in this chapter about the interpretation of 'need' and the sequential approach (DTZ Pieda, 2000). However, in contrast to the 1980s, when much of the discussion at inquiries appears to have concerned the wording of development plan policies, the issues raised by inspectors' reports and/or Secretary of State decisions usually concerned the wording of PPG6 and equivalent Scottish and Welsh policy documents. Inspectors took the view, in line with PPG1, that these documents took precedence over any other considerations, except for up-to-date approved development plan policies which were generally consistent with government guidance. Unfortunately, the wording of government policy was often found to be unclear or ambiguous (CBHP, 2004), such that much of the discussion at inquiries was over interpretation of the wording. Inspectors (collectively) have often been criticised by practitioners for inconsistency, such that apparently similar cases can result in contrasting decisions. However, Goddard (2000: 15) has suggested that 'many "inconsistencies" simply reflect inherent contradictions in the evidence presented, and the fast changing policy climate in which Inspectors operate'.

A final area of disagreement between central and local government has concerned the official status of major out-of-centre schemes completed before the 1990s. Their owners, supported in some cases by the local authority concerned, would like regional shopping centres to be designated as town centres in development plans. This would allow (in principle) the owners to extend the centre, through adding a new department store for example. The guidance in PPG6 indicated however that proposals for 'extensions to ... [or] redevelopment of existing regional-scale out-of-town shopping centres' should be subject to the same criteria as proposals for new centres (DoE, 1996: para 3.4).

The implementation of policy in this matter seems to have been problematic. The Merry Hill regional centre, which was opened in 1989 alongside a retail park, cinema complex and office park was not designated a town centre in the UDP following intervention from the DETR in 1997, against the wishes of the local authority which agreed that the centre should be expanded and wanted to develop town centre uses around it (Lowe, 1998). However, a draft report by a consortium of local authorities proposed in 2004 that the Brierley Hill area, which includes Merry Hill, should become a 'strategic centre', which would allow expansion of the retail area (Chesters, 2004).

In contrast, Leeds City Council ignored the advice of the panel of inspectors at the inquiry into its draft UDP, that the White Rose regional centre should be designated as a 'district centre' instead of 'out of town', in the plan (Planning, 2000). In Scotland, a new town centre has been designated at Ravenscraig, as part of a large regeneration scheme of land formerly used as steel works, and is likely to be developed in a form which property interests in neighbouring town centres claim is a *de facto* out-of-centre regional mall. In 2003, the Scottish Executive approved an alteration to the Glasgow and Clyde Valley Structure Plan, which gave 'town centre' status to the site concerned (Brown, 2003). The local authority subsequently gave the proposal planning consent. However, appeals made by neighbouring town centre landowners are still proceeding through the courts at the time of writing.

Effects on retail development trends

This section examines the effects of retail planning policy on the main areas of retail development. The 1996 PPG6 and similar policy statements in Scotland and Wales have been seen by the retail industry as particularly important turning points in policy, ushering in a much stricter control of out-of-centre development. The section examines to what extent this change in policy, as well as later adjustments, affected rates of development as well as typical sizes and locations of new retailing.

Policy changes affected programmes of store development, and thus retailers' strategies for growth, across all sectors of retailing. One immediate effect of the 1996 guidance was that for any proposal of over 2,500 sq.m. gross area which was not located in a town centre or district centre, an impact statement had to be submitted with the planning application. These were usually prepared by town planning consultants who were frequently retained by the retailer concerned for this purpose. These impact statements examined the potential effects of the new development upon the trading performance of existing stores of similar type, and went on to predict the impacts on the vitality and viability of town centres close to the proposed site (see Chapter 5). The guidance also allowed local planning authorities to require impact statements for proposals of below 2,500 sq.m., and this course of action appears to have been common, particularly for food stores.

Examining the effects of changing planning policy is a complex exercise, since other effects upon store and centre development need to be taken into account. These include the general economic climate, consumer tastes and preferences, retailers' growth strategies, and the cumulative effects of past development trajectories, particularly at local level.

The government view is that the 'town centres first' policies applied since 1996 have had a beneficial effect of concentrating retail development in town centres:

> For the first time since the mid-1980s there is strong evidence that the pendulum is swinging back strongly to town centres. The latest statistics on new shopping centres demonstrate that PPG6 is working. Last year, for the first time since the early 1980s, new shopping floorspace in major town centre schemes exceeded new floorspace in out-of-town shopping centres and retail warehouse parks.[14]
>
> (Raynsford, 2001)

The 'effectiveness' reports confirm this general picture. Since 1996, the proportion of planning approvals and completed developments located in town centres has increased, partly because progressively fewer applications for out-of-centre development have been made (CBHP, 2004: 62), and partly because their refusal rates are higher. This is shown in Table 4.11, which relates to Scotland only. The proportions of town centre, edge-of-centre and out-of-centre proposed retailing were very similar in 1998 and 2002, but the tightening of planning policy is evident from an increasing proportion of town centre schemes approved.

Food superstores

Development rates for large food stores reached a peak in the early 1990s. The three major food retailers at that time, Sainsbury, Tesco and Safeway, were opening between 60 and 80 new superstores each year (Guy, 1996a).[15] Planning consents for out-of-centre development were relatively easy to obtain, and the retailers rapidly extended their influence across most of the UK. Rates of growth began to slow after about 1993, however, partly because of new concerns about the financial viability of new stores on very expensive suburban sites (Wrigley, 1994). It was also the case that in some areas the local market was now more than adequately served with large food stores, such that further stores were unlikely to take sufficient trade to be viable (Guy, 1994c; 1996a).

The publication of PPG6 in 1993 led to stricter impact assessments of out-of-centre development of food superstores, although Wrigley (1998a; 1998b) makes it clear that this was only partly responsible for changes in the development strategy of the retailers concerned. The introduction of the sequential test in the 1996 version of PPG6 however led to clear changes in development strategy, as exemplified in this statement by a leading retailer:

> The revision of national planning policy – and specifically the introduction of the 'sequential approach' towards the appraisal of new retail development – has influenced Sainsbury's site search and development activities. The results of this

Table 4.11 Planning applications for retail development in Scotland

Location	Applications 1998 (%)	Approvals 1998 (%)	Applications 2002 (%)	Approvals 2002 (%)
Town centre	24	39	26	49
Edge of centre	17	18	15	20
Out of centre	50	38	47	28
Out of town	9	6	11	3
Total	100	100	100	100

Source: SEDD (2000: Table 13; 2004: Table 13)
Note: Percentages are of total floorspace.

policy are reflected in a clear shift in our store location strategy over this period. A far greater proportion of our new stores are being developed in town centre and edge of town centre locations.

(Sainsbury, 1999)

This change in strategy, adopted also by other food retailers, had three major effects:

First, the annual rate of new superstore development declined, as the supply of out-of-centre sites with planning permission began to dry up after about 1998. Compared with development rates of around 60–80 each year in the early 1990s, less than 40 new superstores were opened in the year 2000. The proportion developed in edge-of-centre or out-of-centre locations also declined during the 1990s (see Figure 4.2).

Second, the food retailers partly compensated for this lack of sites through extending existing stores. In terms of overall floor area, extensions came to be more important than new stores in some years. The food retailers used store extensions to improve their offer to shoppers. Thus, superstores began to accommodate services such as dispensing chemists, post offices, dry cleaning, photo developing and printing, cafes and so on. In the larger stores, non-food sales were now significant: in most cases the terms of the original planning consent did not restrict the range of goods that could be sold. While modifications to PPG6 appeared to limit the opportunities for store extensions, in practice local authorities have been less restrictive than when considering proposals for new stores (CBHP, 2004: 66).

Food retailers also began to use their internal space more effectively. Improvements in logistics enabled a reduction in the amount of storage space

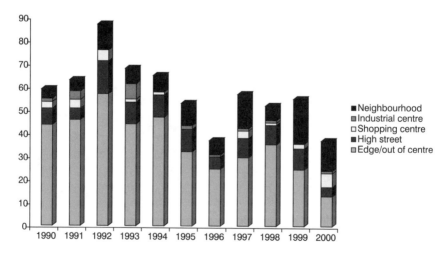

4.2 Superstore numbers and locations in the 1990s (Source: based upon data supplied by the IGD for the Review of the Effectiveness of PPG6, CBHP, 2004)

required, so that in many cases the sales area was enlarged through conversion of storage space. After about 2000, Asda and Tesco developed some mezzanine space in their largest stores, providing an upper floor which would be used for non-food sales. This became seen as a 'loophole' by commentators (e.g. FoE, 2004), and Section 49 of the 2004 Planning and Compulsory Purchase Act contained a provision to make such alterations subject to planning consent. This in itself required secondary legislation which was likely to be enacted in 2006.

Third, the retailers began to develop many more stores in or at the edge of town centres, in response to policy guidance. A town centre store would meet the sequential test and would not require an impact assessment. The most common response was the development of 'compact stores' (of around, or below, the lower size limit for superstores) into the centres of smaller towns, often as part of a larger mixed-use scheme involving other shops, and leisure, office or residential uses. In London, supermarket developments are now expected to incorporate residential apartments, above the store itself or its car park (Guy and Bennison, 2006).

As noted earlier in this chapter, Tesco started to develop 'Metro' stores within city centres, in the early 1990s: however, these are rather different from the company's 'conforming superstore', and this initiative (later copied by Sainsbury) was unrelated to planning policy changes.

In their public pronouncements, major food retailers claim support for the 'town centres first' policies. They also state that most of their large stores are within or at the edge of town centres: for example, Asda (1999) claimed that of their 229 food stores, 109 were in town or district centres, and 32 were edge-of-centre. This stance however has not prevented them from criticising details of policy, particularly the 'class of goods' interpretation of the sequential test, and the requirement to demonstrate 'need' for a new development (e.g. Lowe and Reeves, 2000).

Food discounters, particularly Aldi and Lidl, who expanded rapidly during this period, also found increasing difficulties in developing off-centre stores, although these were much smaller than superstores. In contrast to Tesco and Sainsbury, these companies have not generally been willing to compromise their standard model of store, in terms of location and design, to meet local authorities' requirements, and their relatively small size makes it difficult for the companies to argue that there are no 'suitable and available' sites within town or district centres.

Warehouse clubs

In the early 1990s, Costco, the leading developer of club warehouses, claimed that their product was not 'retail' in terms of land use, and that therefore PPG6 was not applicable. This view was challenged by J Sainsbury, Safeway and Tesco, and a High Court judgement in 1993 resolved that Costco's proposed warehouse in Thurrock, Essex should be considered as Use Class A1 (retail) (Westlake and

Smith, 1994). This position was reinforced in the revised PPG6 of 1996:

> Despite restrictions on those who may shop in warehouse clubs or the range of goods that can be sold, these outlets often share many of the characteristics of very large retail outlets, in which case they should be treated, for the purpose of this guidance, as if they were retail businesses.
>
> (DoE, 1996: para 3.8)

The company still claim however that their stores are 'cash & carry membership warehouses' (Costco, 2005), and it has been claimed by a planning consultant that 'Costco's had an easy ride because it's found a loophole in the U.K. planning system. It's amazing it calls itself a wholesaler rather than a retailer, because around 30 percent of its sales come from individual customers rather than businesses' (Bowhill, 2005).

Despite this claim, it appears that local authorities have regarded club warehouses as retail uses. The relatively low total developed in Britain by Costco (16 stores by mid-2005) reflects the difficulties experienced generally by developers of very large stores (Guy, 2002b). The other major company which began as a club warehouse operation, Matalan, now promote themselves as a conventional retailer, and had succeeded in opening over 170 stores by mid-2005. This greater degree of success can be ascribed to their smaller store size (typically 3,000 sq.m.), which enables them to trade from ordinary retail warehouse premises.

Retail warehouses

The early 1990s saw a gradual recovery in rates of development of retail warehouses and retail parks, following the economic recession. Until 1996 there was little resistance by local authorities to out-of-centre development of individual warehouses or retail parks, because the trading impact of such developments (where restricted to 'bulky goods') was unlikely to threaten the vitality and viability of nearby town centres. After 1996, these developments became subject to the sequential approach: applications took longer to process because of the need to justify the proposal, predict its impact and rule out sequentially preferable sites.

Retail park development therefore slowed down substantially after about 1998 (see Figure 4.1), reflecting (after a two-year time lag) the effects of the sequential approach and increased hostility amongst local authorities (CBHP, 2004: 72). In contrast with food stores, there was, however, little opportunity for development of retail parks in town centres, because of a lack of suitable sites. It was also obvious that the large-scale and utilitarian format of the typical retail park made it unsuitable for traditional town centre environments. In 2000 it became clear that, in line with the 'class of goods' interpretation of the sequential approach, developers were expected to consider 'disaggregating' a proposed retail park amongst more central sites. This guidance, which the development industry viewed as constituting an implicit ban on retail park development, further reduced the 'pipeline' of proposals, although there was a slight (and probably temporary) increase in openings in 2001–02. The longer-term outlook is that:

> Major planning obstacles in the way of out-of-town development remain and will continue to suppress pipeline rates and completion levels. Scheme attrition rates will also remain high (the planning-led focus on … [edge-of-centre] locations has inevitably led to a large number of poorer quality schemes being brought forward: many of which fall by the wayside). Finding sites that are viable for retailers, with a possibility of obtaining planning permission, will remain extremely difficult.
>
> (CBRE, 2004a)

Very large retail warehouses continued to be developed, partly through redevelopment of old hypermarkets or district centres (Guy, 2002b). After the 'class of goods' clarification in 2000, a small number of operators, notably B and Q, were able to develop a special case based on their unique 'format' proposition, and the difficulties incurred in splitting a proposed store into smaller separate town centre stores (B and Q, 2002; Guy and Bennison, 2006). Other instances of large store development took advantage of the 'regeneration' and 'social exclusion' agendas, which were gaining in importance in retail planning in less prosperous regions of Britain (see Chapters 8 and 9).

The increasingly restrictive stance of local authorities towards retail warehouse and retail park development had one further effect. In the light of continuing demand by retailers for large-format stores in easily accessible locations, the slowdown in development led to scarcity of opportunities for retailers attempting to expand, and hence inflation in rents. Retail warehousing has for many years shown the most rapid rate of growth in rents and capital values, of any property sector (Heaps, 2005). 'Open consent' retail parks which have had little or no planning restriction on the types of goods which could be sold, became especially valuable. A few well-designed schemes in good locations became known as 'shopping parks' or 'fashion parks', consisting almost entirely of retail outlets which would normally be found in the larger town centres (Guy, 1998c; 2000). Retail park owners have also subdivided large units into two or three smaller ones, creating more intensive use of space and a more varied offer for the shopper. This provides a good example of the unintended effects of restrictive planning policies, with scarcity of opportunity leading to increasing site value, asset management by landowners and hence an acceleration of the process of impact upon town centres.[16]

Regional centres

Some out-of-centre large-scale malls, notably Bluewater (Kent) and the Trafford Centre (Greater Manchester) were opened during the late 1990s, but all of them had received at least an outline planning consent before 1993. Their construction was delayed until the mid-1990s because of poor demand from fashion retailers and department stores, and the financial difficulties faced by developers in the aftermath of the economic recession.

Expansion of the existing regional centre at Merry Hill was refused, because the ODPM took the view that this was not a town or district centre (see above). It became obvious that further out-of-centre regional centres would not normally be permitted, so few proposals were made (for an early recognition of the importance of this change in policy, see Hallsworth, 1994). The only addition to the set of regional-scale centres in out-of-centre locations which was permitted during the 1990s was at White City in west London, on a site which although technically out-of-centre, is within the built-up area of inner London. This proposal, which includes around 135,000 sq.m. of retailing,[17] was surprisingly not called in by the Secretary of State for his determination. The scheme has suffered many delays, and at the time of writing is scheduled to open in 2008. Another such scheme in London, the Stratford City development, including up to 155,500 sq.m. of retailing, is currently planned to open in 2009, having received planning consent from its local council and the Greater London Authority. This scheme, which is linked with transport improvements and London's bid for the 2012 Olympic Games, provides a good example of the 'regeneration' agenda in retail planning, which is discussed in Chapter 9.

Factory outlet centres

These were the most important innovation in retail development in Britain during the 1990s. At first they appear to have been largely accepted by local authorities, particularly as their developers emphasised the attraction for tourists and the potential for regeneration of old vacant buildings or sites (Jones, 1995). The revision of PPG13 in 1994, with its emphasis on minimising the need to travel, became the determining factor in a key inquiry over a proposal at Tewkesbury, Gloucestershire (Fernie, 1998; England, 2000: 155). The 1996 version of PPG6, and similar guidance elsewhere, made clear that factory outlet centres should be considered in the same light as conventional retail developments: that is, subject to the sequential test as well as the 'need to travel' criterion and impact assessment.

The notion that outlet centres should be built within town centres did not appeal to developers, who argued that suppliers did not want to undercut their full-price offer in neighbouring high street stores. Out of around 45 outlet centres in the UK, only one is located clearly within a town centre. This forms part of the redevelopment of Livingston town centre, near Edinburgh, which was originally developed as the focus of a new town.

The rate of opening of outlet centres has declined substantially since the late 1990s, but this may be due to a lack of demand from suppliers and retailers as much as to the effects of retail policy (Guy, 2002a).

Town centre schemes

Very few schemes were built in town centres in the early 1990s, due to the economic recession and the lack of demand by retailers. Towards the end of the decade, pressure built up for renewal of shopping malls built in the 1960s and 1970s: many of these were now in poor physical condition, and lacked the climate control and spacious walkways which shoppers now expected. A series of 'regional' scale schemes (over 50,000 sq.m. gross retail area) in city or large town centres were completed from about 1999 onwards. Some of these, including the Oracle in Reading, and West Quay in Southampton, were new retail space, whilst others such as the Bullring in Birmingham, replaced obsolete shopping centres; for a list see Lowe (2005: 453). At the time of writing, further large replacement schemes are planned for Cardiff, Bristol, Nottingham and other cities.

These town and city centre developments were of course in line with overall planning policy, although their sheer size led to long negotiations with local authority planners over their design and access arrangements. They were encouraged by city councils as a means of moving up the 'league table' of largest centres in the UK, thus adding to the status of the city concerned (Lowe, 2005). However, concern has arisen that (re)development schemes are increasingly taking place in the 50 or so largest centres (CBRE, 2004b: 8–9; CBHP, 2004: 68). The advice in PPS6, that regional spatial strategies should seek a more equal distribution of growth across town centres in the region, will take several years to make a significant impact.

There has also been a movement towards mixed-use schemes in city centres, in line with government advice. An increasing number of schemes have been partially open to the elements and designed along 'streets' (existing or new), rather than entirely closed, as in the 1980s. This has partly reflected design trends (CABE, 2004; ODPM, 2005c), but also the consequences of incorporating residential and leisure uses which require access at any time of day or night.

This brief analysis has suggested, in line with government thinking (Raynsford, 2001), that the 'town centres first' policy has begun to take effect. Rates of development of off-centre food stores, retail warehouses and regional centres have substantially slowed down since the early 1990s, and after a long spell of little activity, town centre developments have almost reached the very high levels of previous decades. Equally important has been the increased variety of styles of development, with retailing frequently mixed with leisure, office and residential uses. However, some forms of off-centre development, particularly free-standing hypermarkets and 'bulky goods' stores, have continued to grow in importance.

Discussion and conclusions

Retail planning since 1990 has been characterised by an increasing emphasis on town centres as the favoured location for almost all types of development. At the beginning of the period, official policy was seen as vague and ambivalent. The 1993 Guidance responded to the new 'sustainability' agenda by emphasising the benefits of development in town centres, whilst still seeking 'balance' between in-centre and out-of-centre development. This was almost immediately superseded by the sequential approach, which has remained dominant ever since. The 'town centres first' policy received widespread support from politicians at all levels, and also from some sectors of the retail and property industries. A series of modifications to the guidance in the late 1990s presented more and more problems for some retailers and developers, but by 2004 there were signs that a more liberal approach had been accepted by the government, under pressure from economic interests in both public and private sectors.

One of the main themes in this chapter has been the changing relationship between the development plan process (including, most recently, formulation of regional spatial strategies) and the strategic planning process for major retailers and property developers. At the beginning of the period, private sector interests would select the store or centre formats and locations thought to be the most suitable for growth and increased profitability. Local planning authorities could accept or reject their proposals, but were given only limited discretion in this matter. At the time of writing, it is (in theory at least) the planning authorities who determine the broad pattern of future retail development and redevelopment. The private sector has to adjust its strategic planning to fit in with this pattern.

One other trend over time has been the increasing complexity and comprehensiveness of the official guidance. Taking PPG/PPS6 as an example, and excluding Annexes, the 1988 version contained a mere 24 paragraphs; the 1993 version contained 48; the 1996 version 103; and PPS6 contains 109.

In the light of this major intensification of retail planning, it is interesting to revisit the statement by John Gummer noted earlier in this chapter, remembering that Gummer was one of the key figures in this history: 'There is no doubt that planners can provide an inspiration to economic development, but that inspiration must be realistic and not depend on investment that cannot be attracted. ... Above all, it is *planning* that is necessary, not *organising*' (Gummer, 1994; my emphases).

This view implies that the private sector should take a lead in providing or modernising retailing, within clear boundaries set by the public sector. This appears to be what has in fact occurred since the mid-1990s, rather than the government's vision of a retail pattern largely determined through forward planning by local authorities. Local authorities have been reluctant to do much more than specify where development should *not* take place, rather than positively enabling new development or redevelopment. It remains to be seen whether the recent English guidance will alter this situation. The detailed planning of retail requirements and the facilitation of specific schemes appear to require expertise amongst planners at regional and (especially) local level, which at present does not exist in sufficient quantity.

The evolution of the guidance also reveals the tension between the view that competition and innovation in retailing should be encouraged in order to benefit the industry and its customers, and the view that development patterns should be guided by wider social goals, particularly in this case 'sustainable development'. Government statements claim that the guidance respects both of these views. However, the long-running arguments between on the one hand, some retail interests, supported by the Treasury and other government departments, and on the other hand, environmental pressure groups and local authority interests, supported largely by ODPM, are by no means over.

It has been argued therefore that recent and present guidance constrains the private sector, through restrictions on location, access and design, such that the viability of some companies' development trajectories will be in question (Guy and Bennison, 2002; Edwards and Martin, 2005). The developers either have to waste time and money over proposals which are unlikely to be acceptable under planning policy guidelines, or come up with compromise schemes which meet planners' requirements but are sub-optimal financially, because of increased development and operating costs and/or reduced sales (Guy and Bennison, 2006).

On the other hand, environmental pressure groups such as Friends of the Earth (2004; 2006a) argue that the balance of power lies with the private sector, especially food retailers. They claim that local authorities are powerless to prevent socially harmful developments (see also NEF, 2002; 2004). These arguments are explored in more detail in Chapter 6.

A further unresolved issue in retail planning is the extent to which 'material considerations' specific to any particular case should overrule the main elements of planning guidance. This dilemma occurs for example when a retail proposal is located unsatisfactorily from the general planning perspective but offers substantial gains in terms of physical regeneration and/or employment. It has often been suggested that local authorities have been more willing to favour such developments in areas of economic decline.

These issues are too complex to be resolved in a brief discussion such as this. Chapters 6 to 9 take a more detailed look at four major themes which have featured large in the retail planning agenda: competition and innovation in retailing; shopping travel and sustainable development; social exclusion; and urban regeneration. In these chapters, arguments used by protagonists and opponents are examined in detail against empirical evidence.

Finally in this chapter, some comments are made on the *process* of retail planning, as carried out in Britain. Policy delivery is led by central government, as in other areas of environmental planning, but the detailed way in which policies are formulated and refined at central level is not easy to diagnose. The orthodox view would be that the broad outlines of policy are set out by ministers, acting upon various representations from other politicians and from special interest groups. Civil servants are then given the responsibility of drawing up detailed guidance. The wording of guidance has to conform to established practice, be compatible with planning and other legislation, reflect the views (where appropriate) of consultees within and outside of government, and finally be clear and unambiguous. It is difficult (perhaps impossible) to meet all of these objectives simultaneously.

In influencing broad policy, the reports of Parliamentary Select Committees, which deliberately canvass views from a wide variety of interests (Pal *et al.*, 2001), are important in establishing which issues are of concern to whom, as well as identifying ambiguities and perceived weaknesses in the current policy guidance. The report of the 1994 Environment Select Committee appears to have been particularly important in exposing issues and setting up a revision of retail planning guidance. Government departments are however under no obligation to take up any recommendations from Select Committees, and subsequent Environment or ODPM committee reports have been less successful in influencing policy.

The period since 1990 has seen an increasing level of control over patterns of retail development by central government, especially in England. This is due partly to the increasing amount of detail in the guidance, which can be replicated by local authorities to form an almost complete statement of policy at local level. In addition, Ministerial decisions on appeals or (increasingly) call-ins have directly influenced the development trajectories of a few leading retailers. This in turn has raised criticism from private sector interests.

At certain times, it has been felt that central government policy has differed from official guidance, usually in imposing more restrictive control over out-of-centre development. For example, between 1993 and 1996, the sequential test was brought into play by the DoE without the usual consultation process, and applied in a few key decisions. Writing from experience of planning inquiries, one planning consultant stated:

> We are currently faced with the problem that recent appeal decisions from the Secretary of State seem to be applying a different agenda than indicated in current

policy guidance. If the pendulum has swung so far towards supporting town centre policies irrespective of facts and evidence on the ground, then the Secretary of State should say so.

(Smith, 1994: 96)

This apparent change in policy was thought by commentators to derive directly from the then Secretary of State for the Environment, John Gummer, who berated 'sheds on the by-pass' when launching the revised PPG13 in March 1994.

The increasing level of detail in the guidance has led to more uncertainty over policy content and its implementation, particularly at public inquiries. This in turn has led to a series of policy 'clarifications', which in turn have been questioned and debated. During the nine years between PPG6 and PPS6, Ministerial 'clarifications', or more realistically, modifications of policy, had the effect of altering or even cancelling out parts of the published guidance. Criticism was raised, mainly from industry sources, about the ways in which these modifications were announced by Ministers, without any process of consultation or apparent support from research findings. This is exemplified in the following comment by Tesco representatives:

My principle [*sic*] concern in general terms is that policy is now being defined 'on the hoof' seemingly in an attempt to prevent any form of major food development. Whilst the Secretary of State may be entitled to take this approach, I am greatly concerned that he does so with very little, if indeed any, technical backup or factual evidence. Indeed, a significant proportion of current planning philosophy appears to be based on anecdotal evidence or 'spin' placed upon the little factual evidence that does exist.

(Lowe and Reeves, 2000: 148)

There was also widespread criticism of the Caborn (1999a) statement on 'need', which is discussed in more detail in Chapter 5. This was based more upon its lack of clarity than on the change in policy itself.

One widespread criticism of the policy-making process, exemplified in the above quotes, is that it does not take enough heed of empirical research. Furthermore, the research which does take place tends to be supported financially either by sectional interests, in which case the findings can be claimed to be partial or unrepresentative; or by government itself, in which case the terms of reference may be set such that existing policy is not questioned. Government does not seem to be very good at listening to views which oppose elements of current policy, even if these views are based upon sound evidence. This observation will be recalled several times in the chapters which follow.

Chapter 5

Demand, need and impact

Introduction

This chapter examines critically two key concepts – 'need' and 'impact' – which have characterised retail planning policy in the UK since the early 1970s. These concepts are examined firstly in relation to the criteria used by retail firms for assessing the financial outcome of developing or leasing new stores. Secondly, the justification for using these concepts as criteria in retail planning is examined: to what extent are they consistent with broader justifications for planning intervention? Thirdly, we examine to what extent there is agreement about the measurement of 'need' and 'impact', and how these concepts should be used in informing the control of retail development. Finally, we ask whether it is necessary to employ both 'need' and 'impact' as tools when assessing applications for retail development.

The chapter begins with an explanation of how 'demand' forecasting enters into decisions by retailers and property developers to build new stores or modify existing ones. This question is related to consumer demand for a more modern, convenient or varied shopping experience. The concept of 'impact' and the ways in which it has been measured or predicted by planning practitioners are then examined, together with ways in which these processes have been steered by retail planning policy. 'Impact' is then related to the important issue of town centre 'vitality and viability'. The following sections examine the concept of 'need', as practised in retail planning, and consider problems faced in its definition and measurement. The final section attempts to bring together the concepts of demand, impact and need, explores their interrelationships and suggests ways in which retail planning policy could be simplified without losing its most important features.

Retailer and consumer demand

Any discussion of 'impact' and 'need' in retail planning should take place in awareness of the broader context of retail growth and change. Typically a retail company sees an opportunity to operate a new store profitably in a particular location. This may be supported by arguments relating to consumer demand: that the local population would gain benefit from the store's development. The resulting application for planning consent to build the store is, understandably, assessed by a local planning authority using its own social and economic criteria, which differ from that used by the retailer.

Retailers' assessment of demand may be carried out in a variety of ways, the details of which usually remain confidential to the company concerned (for reviews see Hernandez and Bennison, 2000; Birkin *et al.*, 2002: Chapters 7, 8). A straightforward (and very important) case is that of a food multiple or other 'big box' retailer wishing to develop new stores. Here, the company will possess up-to-date databases of population, driving times and comparable stores across the whole country. Outline proposals for new stores are assessed by means of computer models which forecast the likely level of sales at that location for a particular size of store. The company will then assess whether this level of sales is sufficient to generate a rate of return at or above the company norm, once the costs of land purchase and store construction are taken into account. In some cases, the land cost is unknown, and the company then calculates how much it is prepared to offer for the land while still generating a satisfactory rate of return (Guy, 1995). This process helps to explain why food retailers have been prepared to pay land prices far in excess of expectations, in cases where the proposed store is likely to trade exceptionally well.

Store development takes place in a competitive situation where the new store may take market share from other stores owned by the same company, as well as those owned by rivals. Profitable development is more likely to occur in cases where the ratio of the retailer's share of the local market to its share of local floorspace (in that type of retail) is above some critical limit (Mahajan *et al.*, 1988; O'Kelly, 2001). New store development lowers that ratio and thus makes subsequent development less likely to occur. This type of calculation can be extended to cases involving all retailers of one type, in which case the debate then focuses on 'saturation'. This concept has evoked much discussion (Treadgold and Reynolds, 1989; Guy, 1996a; Langston *et al.*, 1997; Lord, 2000), and there is no agreed definition of saturation or of ways of measuring and identifying it in practice. In its most extreme form the concept would suggest that all existing stores in an area are only just profitable, indicating that any new entrant would cause an unstable situation in which all retailers (not just the new entrant) would operate at a loss, leading to the eventual closure of at least one store. This simplistic analysis ignores the ability of retailers to seek economies in operation, or diversify their range of goods, in order to compete more effectively in the local market. However, the concept of saturation is useful in general terms, indicating a situation in which it appears unlikely that a new entrant could operate profitably, in the short term at least. It can be applied most successfully in areas of retailing such as supermarkets and retail warehousing, in which rival firms are selling broadly similar ranges of goods at similar prices and using similar methods of retailing.

The inverse of saturation is often termed 'spare capacity'. This means that retailers believe that the consumer demand for their mix of goods and services is not being fully met in the area concerned, because there are insufficient stores of the right size and quality. Two indicators of spare capacity are:

- A significant proportion of consumers obtain the goods concerned in other places: this is known in the academic literature as 'outshopping' (Guy, 1990), and in the practitioner literature as 'expenditure leakage'.
- Existing stores in the area have sales density (measured for example as annual sales in £ per sq.m.) well above the normal value for the company concerned: this is known as 'over-trading'.

Retailers often attempt to justify proposals by citing 'consumer demand' for a specific new development. This may simply reflect the apparent inadequacy of existing stores, as explained above. However, 'consumer demand' may (it is claimed) exist in situations where there is no obvious spare capacity. Here, the retailer claims to offer a novel or superior quality shopping experience which is not currently available in the area concerned. A good example of this occurred in the 1970s when food retailers were building a case for developing superstores in areas where none existed.

In the case of comparison goods retailers in areas such as clothing and personal goods, the assessment of 'demand' and the appraisal of possible new locations takes a rather different form. The main criterion is usually the strength of the shopping centre concerned – its size and retail characteristics:

> Retailers will use generic catchment data to give them an idea of the trading potential for a town and whether it is worth their while considering taking space. They will, however, either undertake their own catchment research or other investigations into trading potential to decide whether to pursue a store acquisition. They will be confident to invest if there are complementary traders either in a location already or who will commit with them, and conversely will steer clear of saturated markets or where the competition will get stronger.
>
> (A 'retail advisor', quoted in BCSC, 2004: 26)

This indicates that the assessment of opportunities for retail growth can be more complex than in the case of large-format stores. However, since growth through acquiring store units in existing shopping centres is not usually a matter of concern in town planning terms, retailers do not need to argue a case for 'demand'.

The arguments used by large-format retailers to defend their proposals for new stores tend to be rather less precise than one might expect. Their own decisions to develop new stores are usually made on the basis of a precise forecast of sales, and a derived estimate of the profitability of the new store. However, the case presented in public for a new development tends to rely on vaguely-defined concepts such as 'spare capacity' or 'consumer choice', partly because retailers are generally unwilling to divulge their sales forecast for the new store.

Retail impact: definitions and methods

Town planners have for many years taken the view that, as guardians of the public interest, they have the duty to prevent development which may produce harmful external effects. The effects of any type of proposed development on the long-established concerns of 'amenity' and 'convenience' are routinely assessed in the process of development control. Thus, a retail scheme will be assessed in terms of visual appearance, relationship with neighbouring buildings and land uses, effects upon traffic flow, and so on, just like any other commercial scheme.

'Retail impact' has, since the 1960s, when the first superstore and regional shopping centre proposals were made (see Chapter 2), taken on a further dimension. Here, 'impact' can be defined broadly as the competitive effect of new retail facilities upon existing retail facilities elsewhere, and any other effects upon local people and the built environment which arise from these competitive effects. Sometimes, 'impact' can be used in a positive sense, as for example an increase in employment.

A detailed justification for retail impact assessment and its status as a criterion for planning control was provided in the report commissioned by the DoE, on the effects of major out-of-town development:

> In beginning to consider the possible impacts upon town centres of new forms of retail development, we are faced first of all with a series of conceptual and definitional problems. Impact studies for retail development, we would suggest, seem from the literature to be quite different from assessments of the significance of other kinds of development proposals within the town planning system. Applications and appeals for office developments or business parks, for example, fail to generate the kind and scale of concern and research associated with that for major new retail development. Much of this has to do, of course, with retailing being much closer to the public's interest than other activities.
>
> Retail development begins by being of legitimate concern to the planning system in the same way as any other form of land use development. What is significant, and how it is assessed, is related to the purposes of planning in intervening in the market place.
>
> Impact is of legitimate concern, it can be argued, for five principal reasons.

- Understanding the effects of change: any change in an economy or a physical environment is of legitimate concern to constituent institutions, organisations or individuals;
- Control of public costs: unregulated private actions may give rise to undesirable public, or environmental costs (such as an effect upon transport infrastructure);
- The efficiency argument: the planning system is concerned with the efficient use and allocation of resources, particularly land;
- The equity argument: the degree of accessibility of different types of retail outlet and of shopping centres directly affects the standard of living of all consumers;
- The quality of life argument: the degree of accessibility of different types of retail outlet and of shopping centres indirectly affects the quality of life of individuals and groups in society (through changes in the quality of town centres and other places where people shop).

(BDP Planning, 1992: 33)

Impact is often categorised as economic (or trading) impact, social impact and environmental impact: these categories are explained in Table 5.1. For many years, analysis of 'retail impact' was restricted in practice to trading impact, usually

Table 5.1 Typical impacts of retail development

	Negative impacts	*Positive impacts*
Economic	• Loss of trade in existing centres • Diversion of retail investment from existing centres	• Improvement in scale, structure and diversity of centre (where retail development is in-centre) • Employment gains and income multiplier effects
Social	• Increasing disparity in access to retail between social groups	• Improvement of access to retail in areas of social exclusion
Environmental	• Increased vacancy levels and/or poor quality shops and services • Increased traffic • Other consequent environmental deterioration	• 'Planning gain' associated with proposal • Remediation of contaminated land • Visual improvements

Source: based upon BDP Planning (1992: 37–8)

expressed as a percentage loss in sales from existing town centres. 'Rules of thumb' were informally established, such that a trading impact of more than *x* per cent was serious enough to prejudice against the proposal.[1] It was also assumed by planning practitioners that losses at or above this level were likely to lead to social and environmental impacts, although before the 1990s these were rarely examined in any detail.

It should be noted that impact upon employment patterns – the balance between 'new jobs' provided by the new development, and jobs lost in existing shops affected by trading impact – is not usually considered in British planning practice. Official guidance makes no reference to this issue, nor to the possible loss of other jobs in local suppliers and services. These matters are however discussed in Chapters 6 and 9.

Predictive impact assessment

In assessing the scale and nature of trading impact, two types of analysis are relevant. The first is the prediction of potential trading impact before the new development takes place, the second an estimation of actual trading impact after development, through empirical research. The second type is sometimes termed *post hoc*. This and the following section examine these types of analysis in turn.

Predictive assessment tends to follow a standard pattern. The basic assumption is that new development will not generate new consumer spending: rather, it will attract spending which would otherwise go to existing stores. Therefore the analyst must make some estimate of the amount of consumer spending in the surrounding area, and then predict how this pattern of expenditure will be rearranged by the inclusion of the new store in the consumers' choice set. This in turn requires some knowledge of the sales levels of both the proposed store and existing stores or centres.

The first noteworthy exercise was concerned with the potential trading impact of the first regional shopping centre proposal at Haydock Park, Lancashire. Two studies were carried out by the Manchester University Department of Town Planning, the first employing a method of market area analysis similar to those already used in North America to predict the sales levels of new shopping centres, and the second a spatial interaction shopping model (Manchester University, 1964; 1966). These exercises both concluded that the proposed regional centre would have substantial impact upon nearby town centres, a conclusion which affected the decision to dismiss the appeal for this scheme (for a summary see Evers, 2004: 165–7).

Following the publication of advice from central government in 1972 that retail impact was a matter of concern in assessing planning applications, impact prediction became a routine procedure. As the volume of applications for superstores and retail warehouses rose in the 1970s, a relatively small group of planning consultants built up experience in methods of prediction, usually acting for retail developers but sometimes for the local authorities opposing planning applications. These consultants, sometimes termed ironically the 'travelling circus', got to know each other and their methods well through encounters at planning inquiries. In this way, a consensus over appropriate methods of impact analysis and interpretation became established.

The broad method used by consultants has been summarised, in a report on impact assessment commissioned by the Scottish Office, as follows:

  i.   Identify catchment or study area
  ii.   Estimate expenditure within catchment area
  iii. Estimate turnover of existing shopping centres
  iv.   Estimate turnover of new retail proposal
  v.   Estimate the amount of spending in each existing centre which will be diverted to make up the new store's turnover, and the locational source of that spending
  vi.   Express the amount of diverted trade from each shopping centre as a percentage of the estimated pre-impact turnover of that centre.

(Drivers Jonas, 1992: 60)

In introducing this summary, the report stated:

There is remarkably little dispute as to the stages to be undertaken in calculating percentage impact. This is despite the impression given by authors of articles on the subject during the past twenty years that there are a great many different approaches. …Very few methods do not involve all six stages, although variations in approach to some of the stages mean that the 'running order' may vary. Inevitably the disagreements as to how to calculate impact precisely generally arise towards the end of the process, usually from stage (iv) onwards.

(ibid: 59–60)

In the early stages of impact assessment, spatial interaction models were sometimes used to estimate loss of trade in existing centres. However, this was found to be problematic for technical reasons, and results were difficult to present clearly at inquiries. This was exemplified at the joint planning inquiry into retail proposals on the edge of Bristol, held in 1972. Here, several models were used by different consultants, all apparently similar in form but leading to substantially different conclusions (Couper and Barker, 1981: 634–6). The Department of the Environment and Scottish Office both eventually made it clear that such models were not generally acceptable for use in planning inquiries:

Mathematical models have been produced which aim to help those concerned with shopping development to assess the need for floorspace and the best locations to satisfy new demands. These models may be complicated and based on a number of arguable assumptions; they have not, so far, been of great help to Inspectors at inquiries.

(DoE/WO, 1977a: para 13)

England (2000: 65–9) presents a useful review of the problems faced by practitioners in attempting to use spatial interaction models in retail impact assessment, and emphasises that such models are still used in other contexts where good quality information on shopping trip patterns is available, such as sales forecasting by retail chains.

Consultants therefore generally adopted methods based upon market area analysis, derived loosely from central place theory and already used for many years in North America (Berry and Parr, 1988; Thrall and Del Valle, 1997). A report of a Unit for Retail Planning Information seminar on superstore impact assessment (Wade, 1983b) set these methods out in detail. However, it would be wrong to assume that this consensus over broad methodology led to consistently accurate predictions. Considerable differences arose between practitioners, particularly in the latter stages of the procedure, in which market penetration or trade draw rates had to be estimated. Here, practitioners tended to rely on 'experience', and were reluctant to explain their assumptions and methods in detail. Referring to the admittedly difficult topic of impact assessment for regional centres, Norris (1990: 104) claimed that

my review of over fifty Impact Studies has revealed the imperfect solutions which result from the imperfect arena in which such studies operate. No two studies look the same or reach the same conclusions. No two studies can agree on all, if any, of the data assumptions.

A general problem with market area methods was that within the common 'six-stage' framework set out above, each practitioner seemed to have their own version, which depended substantially upon 'informed opinion' or 'rules of thumb', or more frankly, guesswork, delivered with some obscuring of the more questionable stages in the procedure. The fact that impact assessments are always carried out by either proponents or opponents of a particular proposal, due to the adversarial nature of the planning inquiry process, means that they cannot be viewed as entirely neutral 'expert' judgements. The view has however been expressed that, provided there is agreement between all parties over the data used, impact assessments can be regarded as 'impartial' (Drivers Jonas, 1992: 109–10).

One major consideration in predicting impact lies in the forecasting of sales for the new store or centre concerned. This is a vital stage because the amount of trade drawn from other stores or centres is assumed equal to the new development's level of sales. Unfortunately, it is only rarely that the retail developers concerned will reveal their own forecast of sales; therefore the consultants preparing an impact assessment must make their own estimate. The most common method is to assume that the store or centre will perform in line with existing stores or centres of that type; for example, sales at a proposed Tesco superstore would be estimated as the store's sales area multiplied by the company's average sales per square foot. Norris (1990) uses the term 'step-by-step' for methods involving this type of assumption. This method is often criticised for ignoring any special features of the proposal's catchment area, or of existing stores in the area and their competitive effects (Drivers Jonas, 1992: 74). It should also be expected that a new store would, in order to justify development costs, perform at above the company average: this is because the average is weighed down by poorly performing older stores, which are still viable because their development costs have been recovered.

A more reputable method, supported by England (2000: 80) is to calculate sales levels from knowledge of the store's catchment population and competitors, using market area analysis. Norris (1990) terms such methods 'market penetration'. This approach also bears the advantage that the results can feed into capacity studies and estimates of 'quantitative need' (see below).

The advice issued by the Department of the Environment in 1985, that assessments should take into account the 'cumulative impact' of more than one proposed development, raised further problems. The notion that (for example) two new superstores would have less than twice the impact of one, because they would compete for custom, proved difficult to implement (Drivers Jonas, 1992: 85–6; England, 2000: 85).

Government advice, also given first in 1985, was that impact studies should focus on the effects upon town centre vitality and viability, rather than simply estimating percentage loss of trade. This added more complexity and elements of qualitative judgement to impact assessment.

The relationship between trading impact and any decline in town centre vitality and viability had never been researched thoroughly and was hence subject to judgements usually based upon anecdotes and prejudice.[2] The DTEDC report (1988: 75–80) attempted to clarify the issues here (see Table 5.2). This table shows that much would depend upon the commercial strength of retailing in the existing town centre, and upon the extent of unfulfilled demand for retail premises. These conclusions were commonly supported by observations in planning inspectors' reports:

Table 5.2 The link between retail impact and loss of vitality and viability

Arguments	Comment
The proposed development will have an impact on some existing retail businesses	Assumptions: 1. There is only one market for consumer spending 2. Additional floorspace will not only serve unsatisfied demand 3. Consumer expenditure remains constant in total, despite price reductions and/or new product ranges
Impact damages businesses	1. A fall in trade will reduce the retailer's net margin 2. In the short term, retailers may respond by reducing orders to suppliers, but this will reduce the appeal of the shop to consumers 3. In the long term, retailers may respond by reducing input costs, especially labour and occupation costs (including rents) 4. Another tactic is to change commodity mix
Damage will cause lasting harm	True if the new centre operates more efficiently than the existing
Harm will be on a sufficient scale to cause extensive closure of shops	Depends upon the extent to which the new and existing centres' shops coincide in character and function
Closure of shops will not lead to redevelopment	More likely in less prosperous areas or in centres already in decline
The absence of major redevelopment will lead to a loss of viability and vitality of a town centre as a whole	Abandoned shop premises may be reoccupied by other uses

Source: based on DTEDC (1988: 75–80)

With ... estimates of impact, Inspectors have rarely relied wholly upon such data, but looked more realistically at the evidence on the strength or weakness of nearby town centres. ... Inspectors have always acknowledged the sensitivity of such estimates to initial assumptions, and have relied as much on qualitative evidence and arguments of need as on quantified forecasts.

(Lee Donaldson, 1991: 30; cited in Drivers Jonas, 1992: 15)

Research carried out into Scottish planning inquiries similarly found that reporters[3] paid attention to issues such as the prospects for new investment, the ability of affected traders to respond to new competition, and the effect of possible closures and other changes on the physical environment of existing centres (Drivers Jonas, 1992: 48–9). This report concluded however that most of such studies did not sufficiently investigate possible effects of impact upon town centre vitality and viability. It suggested relevant questions which should be asked:

i.   What appear to be the broad implications of the residual levels of post-impact turnover for either the convenience or durable sector being examined (with reference to retailer company reports, surveys of other areas)?

ii. Are there particular retailers who perform a vital 'anchor' function in the centre and who might close *as a result of* the new development (bearing in mind that closures are more likely to be due to relocation than competition)?

iii. If closures and vacancies are likely to occur, what are the prospects for re-occupation by other retailers, and will these new retailers reclaim trade which has been lost to the new development?

iv. Are there desirable committed developments or other investment which would be unlikely to take place if the proposed development proceeds?

v.   How important is the affected retail sector (convenience or durable) in the context of the shopping centre *as a whole?* How large is the anticipated loss of turnover in terms of the centre's *total* (durable *and* convenience) turnover?

vi. Are there other activities and functions in the centre which would be likely to continue to maintain its vitality despite the estimated loss of trade?

vii. Is the location of the proposed new development sufficiently close to the existing centre to enable it to function as part of that centre or be supportive of it, and contribute to its total economic activity?

viii. Will the new development itself provide useful and accessible community facilities to replace those which may be lost from existing centres?

ix. Are there existing retailers in the centre with a strong trading base who can be expected to respond to trade diversion by implementing competitive measures and service improvements?

x.   Will the new development result in an *overall* improvement to the range and quality of shopping facilities in the area?

(Drivers Jonas, 1992: 127–8)

These and other such comments led eventually to the incorporation of town centre 'health checks' (see below) into retail impact assessment.

Further experience during the 1990s has given rise to comprehensive statements of good practice in impact assessment, the best known of which is in the report on impact of superstores in market towns (CBHP, 1998: Chapter 9). This framework, termed 'CREATE' (Combined Retail Economic and Transportation Evaluation), introduces a broader interpretation of 'impact', including transport and employment effects, and is summarised in Figure 5.1 and Table 5.3. England (2000: 194–7) proposes a similar framework, adding extra detail where relevant.

Post hoc impact studies

Studies which measured the actual impact that had taken place as a result of new store or centre development began to be published in the early 1970s. Rather than focusing simply on trading impact, several of these studies attempted to examine the environmental impact of new store or centre development. The most common technique was to measure changes in retail composition of existing centres through

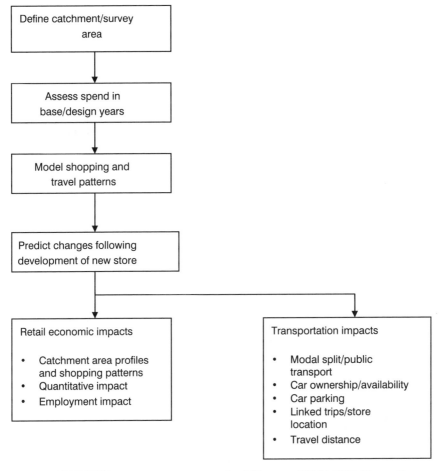

5.1 The 'CREATE' impact assessment method (Source: CBHP, 1998: Figure 2)

Table 5.3 The 'CREATE' Method: Assessment Criteria

Retail and economic impacts	
Catchment area profile	To what extent will the new store alter the catchment profile of the town. For example, has it increased clawback of expenditure?
Quantitative impact	Before and after market shares, and trade diversion from the town centre
Employment impact	Changes in the level and type of employment
Transportation impacts	
Modal split/public transport	Modal split to stores in the area and any likely changes due to the new store
Car ownership/availability	Level of car ownership within the primary catchment area. Whether a car is normally available for the main food shop. This will have an influence on the mode used for food shopping
Car parking	Provision, pricing and level of use of car parks in the town and whether there is likely to be any perceptible change as a result of the new store
Linked trips/store location	Are people likely to combine food shopping with other activities on the same trip, particularly within the town centre? Is the occurrence of linked trips likely to be affected by the move to the new store?
Travel distance	Is there likely to be any material change in vehicle mileage as a result of the new store?

Source: CBHP (1998: 99, 101)

'before and after' shop counts. Some also attempted to measure environmental impact through surveys of changes of use, vacancies etc. or through opinion surveys of town centre traders. Social impact was less commonly examined, but in some cases evidence was derived from surveys of users of new retail developments, or from interview surveys of randomly sampled households within the new store's catchment area. These generally showed that younger and more upmarket and mobile customers were the main users of new stores.

The concern at that time was mainly over hypermarkets and superstores. The first well publicised *post hoc* study was of the impact of the Carrefour hypermarket at Caerphilly, South Wales (Lee *et al.*, 1973). This, together with further studies of the Caerphilly area (Lee and Kent, 1975; 1979) concluded that the hypermarket had possibly led to closure of eight food shops in Caerphilly town centre, but these shop premises had quickly reopened under new operators. The overall effect was to replace food shops by comparison goods and retail-related services, a trend which was happening in town centres anyway. At about the same time, a study of the impact of a Sainsbury superstore in Peterborough, conducted (unusually for *post hoc* analysis) through 'before and after' shopper surveys, concluded that the new store was drawing custom principally from existing supermarkets rather than small grocery or general stores (Rogers, 1979). This conclusion was supported in other early studies, summarised in Thorpe *et al.* (1976).

Later studies of the trading impact of superstores and retail warehouses found little evidence of serious impact on town centres (for a summary see BDP, 1992: 45–53). However it should be noted that most of these studies concerned stores built in large towns, in which the comparison and specialist goods offer of the town centre remained far superior to the limited range available in superstores and retail warehouses. In the early 1990s, concern grew over the impact of large stores in small market towns and district centres. The House of Commons Environment Select Committee (1994: para 69) recommended that 'a proper study be urgently undertaken … to assess the effects of out-of-town developments on town centres'. Partly as a result, a report on the impact of such developments on market towns and district centres (CBHP, 1998) was commissioned by the DETR.

This study found a wide variety of effects. A survey of local authorities, carried out for that report, found that in 50 per cent of cases, out-of-centre food stores had 'led to an adverse impact on the range and quality of foodstores in nearby town centres' (CBHP, 1998: 39). It is not clear from the report whether edge-of-town centre, or indeed, town centre food stores had also had similar effects.

The study found that the development of out-of-centre large food stores had led to a loss of between 13 and 50 per cent of market share of existing multiple food stores. The report did not provide any estimates of impact upon independently-owned food stores, although it reported that in two of the smaller towns examined, Fakenham and Leominster,

> there has been a marked decline in the number of convenience retailers since the out-of-centre foodstore opened. In other case studies, we have identified small convenience retailers who intend to continue trading until the expiry of their lease, but will then vacate their units.
>
> (ibid.: 82)

However, the report also admitted that:

> the decline nationally of small grocery outlets is not a recent phenomenon, but pre-dates the dramatic increase in the number of large out-of-town superstores which occurred during the 1980s and the early 1990s. Although we have not undertaken any specific analysis, our discussions with Chambers of Commerce and

retailers suggest that the decline in the number of specialist convenience retailers has been caused as much by large town centre supermarkets, as it has been by the latter development of out-of-town foodstores.

(ibid.: 77–8)

Until the mid-1980s, town centres were the main focus of larger-scale retail developments. They were losing food and bulky goods shopping to off-centre superstores and retail warehouses, but gaining from shopping mall and precinct developments. However, the sudden boom in regional shopping centre proposals described in Chapter 3 seemed to threaten those town centres which were located close to these schemes, and especially those which were weak in other respects.

Studies of the impact of the Metro Centre, the first regional centre to be completed, were carried out at the Oxford Institute of Retail Management, relying mainly upon telephone interviews of households within the centre's catchment area (Howard and Davies, 1993). This research, together with that carried out on the effects of Meadowhall (Williams, 1991; Howard, 1993) showed that serious impacts tended to fall on medium-sized centres such as Durham, although Sheffield itself was also affected initially by a loss of around 15 per cent of its retail trade. An analysis of changes in property values in town centres affected by various regional centres showed losses of between 10 per cent and 20 per cent (England, 2000: 160).

The study of the impact of the Merry Hill regional centre, commissioned by the Department of the Environment, showed an unusually severe impact upon the nearby town centre of Dudley (Tym, 1993). The most significant conclusion was that Dudley had lost (temporarily at least) some 70 per cent of its comparison retail sales as a result of the impact of Merry Hill. It appeared that a 'spiral' of decline had been triggered by both the initial diversion of trade and the consequent decision of many of the town centre's retailers to close their branches in Dudley (see also Guy, 1994b). The process is summarised in Figure 5.2.

The Tym study, coupled with a site visit by the House of Commons Environment Select Committee (1994) proved to be an important motivation for the revision of government retail planning policy in the mid-1990s (see Chapter 4).

Town centre vitality and viability

The impacts (anticipated and realised) of off-centre developments upon town centres gave rise to concern over their vitality and viability. The regional shopping centres, with their climate-controlled environments, clean and safe pedestrian ways and free car parking made the problems of traditional town centres more evident.

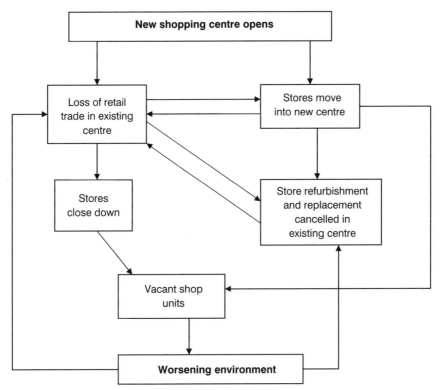

5.2 The spiral of decline following trading impact

An early indication was in an article praising the new Milton Keynes town centre: 'For anyone used to shopping in Milton Keynes a visit to a shopping centre in any historic town is an uncomfortable experience' (Thomas, 1983: 249).

Planning policies for town centres had up to the mid-1980s been concerned mainly with traffic, parking and the design of redevelopments (see Chapter 2). Little thought had been given to supporting the commercial function of the centre, or the quality of its environment. Town centres were often unpleasant places to work or go shopping. They were seen by some commentators and, no doubt, many shoppers, as dirty and unsafe (Oc and Tiesdell, 1997). They had very little 'life' after 5.30 pm. Business interests became increasingly critical of what they considered to be local authority hostility and inaction (Evans, 1997).

Development of shopping malls within town centres in the 1960s and 1970s had, while improving shopping convenience and comfort, often taken trade away from the rest of the town centre, leading to lack of investment in shops and services, and shop closures (Bennison and Davies, 1980). These fringe areas were rarely pedestrianised, and experienced serious problems of heavy traffic, decaying buildings and a poor physical environment.

In the 1980s, as the number of off-centre superstores and retail warehouses grew rapidly, it was noticed that some town centres were failing to attract new investment, thus entering a spiral of decline (Figure 5.2). This tended to be worse in lower-tier centres, such as small town and district centres within conurbations, or towns which were losing their economic rationale.

This decline was blamed, particularly in the early 1990s, on the impact of off-centre developments. But it was (and still is) the case also that smaller town centres were generally suffering from competition with larger ones. As consumers became more mobile, they tended to travel further to visit the larger centres for their comparison and personal shopping. In 1971, about 50 per cent of comparison goods sales were made in the largest 200 town and city centres, whereas in 1998, 50 per cent of sales were in the largest 75 centres (CBRE, 2004b: 8–9).

This issue – of the impact of in-town centre developments upon town centres themselves – has been almost entirely neglected in the retail planning literature. The Scottish Office study gave this issue some attention, but concluded that impact assessment 'should be necessary only if a new retail development in the centre of a town seems likely to (i) cause harm to the retail function of another town, or (ii) result in a severe shift in shopping focus within the town [itself]' (Drivers Jonas, 1992: 118). This advice was however ignored by policy-makers, with the result that retail development within town centres is still not formally subject to impact assessments on behalf of prospective developers.

The Parliamentary statement of 1985 introduced the notion of 'vitality and viability' as key characteristics of town centres, and also as criteria for impact studies. It was not made clear however what constituted vitality and viability, or how it should be measured, other than a vague indication: 'for example, … a significant increase in vacant properties, or a marked reduction in the range of services the town centre provides, such as could lead to its general physical deterioration' (DoE/WO, 1988a: para 7).

In a speech the following year, the Minister for Water and Planning, Michael Howard, added some refinement:

> towns are not merely centres of trade. It is important not to equate a town centre with a shopping centre. In terms of land use or commercial activity shopping may well be the major function of a town centre, but the town centre is (or should be) also the focal point for a whole range of other commercial and community activities. … I said earlier that the fate of individual town centre shops in the face of competition from out-of-town was not a relevant planning consideration. What is relevant is the overall effect of one or more out-of-town developments on the character and cohesion of the whole town centre. Shops depend for much of their custom on other needs and attractions that bring customers to a town centre in the first place and the reverse applies also. It is this complex interaction between

the different town centre functions that creates much of the 'vitality and viability' that may sometimes need protecting from too much out-of-town development.

(Howard, 1990; cited in Drivers Jonas, 1992: 14)

Eventually, firmer definitions of 'vitality and viability' were included in government guidance. The 1993 version of PPG6 indicated that

[although] most aspects of vitality and viability will be difficult to assess with confidence ... The following indicators can usually provide the main criteria for the purposes of a planning application or appeal:
- Commercial yield on non-domestic property: (i.e. the capital value in relation to the expected market rental) demonstrating the confidence of investors in the long term profitability of the centre; and
- Pedestrian flow: in other words the people on the streets, in different parts of the centre at different times of the day and evening, available for businesses to attract into shops, restaurants or other facilities.

(DoE/WO, 1993: Figure 1)

'Other factors which may be relevant' included:

- The proportion of vacant street level property in the primary retail area;
- The diversity of uses;
- Retailer representation and profile;
- Retailer demand or intentions to change representation;
- The physical structure of the centre.

(ibid.)

The report commissioned by the DoE to examine vitality and viability in town centres supplied, for the first time in official literature, definitions of the terms vitality and viability:

vitality is reflected in how busy a centre is at different times and in different parts whilst viability refers to the ability of the centre to attract continuing investment, not only to maintain the fabric, but also to allow for improvement and adaption [*sic*] to changing needs.

(URBED, 1994: 55)

The report also commented that PPG6's indicators for measuring vitality and viability (commercial yield and pedestrian flows) were useful, but required reliable comparative data across several places and at several times, which could be difficult to obtain. Further measures which were easier to obtain for a one-off appraisal of a town centre were suggested. These were included in the 1996 version of PPG6, and the Welsh equivalent TAN4 (WO, 1996b) (see Table 5.4).

These indicators have since been used routinely in planning practice, in two different situations. The first common situation is where a vitality and viability assessment is made as part of an impact study carried out for a prospective retail developer. Here, the trading impact of the proposal has to be translated into an impact on vitality and viability of the town centre most strongly affected by the proposal. A survey of planning consultants in England shows that they usually use most, if not all, of the PPG6 indicators in preference to other possible lists (Bray, 2003). The value of these indicators for this purpose was however criticised in the DETR-sponsored report on the impact of food stores:

> no guidance is provided as to the relevance of particular indicators for different sizes of towns. As practitioners, our experience is that the value of some of these health check indicators is limited in the context of small market towns and district centres. This is particularly apparent when attempting to analyse the change in the economic health of a centre over a period of time.
>
> (CBHP, 1998: 95)

The second context arises in the preparation of 'town centre strategies', as recommended in the 1996 version of PPG6. This process is usually known as a 'health check' and is likely to take a wider perspective than impact studies, to include for example shopper opinion surveys (for a comprehensive review see CASA, 2000). Town centre managers themselves are expected to carry out limited versions of health checks, as part of the process of monitoring their own achievements and effectiveness (Hogg *et al.*, 2000). This is partly due to pressure from major funders of town centre management schemes to show results (Williams and Baker, 1998).

'Need' in retail planning policy

A 'need' is commonly defined as 'a condition requiring relief' or 'anything that is necessary but lacking'.[4] This immediately recalls the discussion above of 'demand', a fairly clear concept which can easily be understood by consumers or retailers. In contrast however, 'need' has remained a woolly concept in retail planning over which there is little agreement, regarding either its definition or its utility.

In retail planning, arguments about 'need' have been used as justification for development and for refusals of consent. With regard to the latter, it is argued that retail planning involves attempts to ensure an efficient and effective pattern of retailing in a geographical area. This can create circumstances in which planners view existing patterns as close to the ideal situation: any major new development could

Table 5.4 Official indicators of vitality and viability

Diversity of uses	How much space is in use for different functions – such as offices; shopping; other commercial, leisure, cultural and entertainment activities; pubs, cafes and restaurants; hotels; educational uses; housing – and how has that balance been changing?
Retailer representation and intentions to change representation	It may be helpful to look at the existence and changes in representation, including street markets, over the past few years, and at the demand from retailers wanting to come into the town, or to change their representation in the town, or to contract or close their representation;
Shopping rents	Pattern of movement in zone of rents within primary shopping areas (i.e. the rental value for the first 6 metres depth of floorspace in retail units from the shop window);
Proportion of vacant street level property	Vacancies can arise even in the strongest town centres, and this indicator must be used with care. Vacancies in secondary frontages and changes to other uses will also be useful indicators;
Commercial yields on non-domestic property (i.e. the capital value in relation to the expected market rental)	This demonstrates the confidence of investors in the long-term profitability of the centre for retail, office and other commercial developments. This indicator should be used with care;
Pedestrian flows	The numbers and movement of people on the streets, in different parts of the centre at different times of the day and evening, who are available for businesses to attract into shops, restaurants or other facilities;
Accessibility	The ease and convenience of access by a choice of means of travel, including the quality, quantity and type of car parking, the frequency and quality of public transport services, the range of customer origins served and the quality of provision for pedestrians and cyclists;
Customer views and behaviour	Regular surveys of customer views. Will help authorities in monitoring and evaluating the effectiveness of town centre improvements and in setting further priorities. Interviews in the town centre and at home should be used to establish views of both users and non-users of the centre. This could establish the degree of linked trips;
Perception of safety and occurrence of crime	This should include views and information on safety and security;
State of the town centre environmental quality	This should include information on problems (such as air pollution, noise, clutter, litter and graffiti) and positive factors (such as trees, landscaping, open spaces).

Source: DoE (1996: Figure 1)

destroy the equilibrium and make some citizens worse off. The fact that retailers see some demand for a new facility does not create a 'need' for that facility.

However, retailers argue that new development allows innovative methods of retailing, increases consumer choice, and is therefore welcomed by most consumers. In an address to the RTPI 75th Anniversary Conference in 1989, Lord Sainsbury asked:

> How do planners or indeed anyone else know when exactly the 'right' amount has been provided to accommodate needs? It would seem to be a fairly simple point that much harm can flow from having too little of something. It is relatively rare for someone to complain about having too much choice. ... all too often negative decisions are made when there have been no significant environmental or heritage issues in the balance. It has just boiled down to the planning system arguing that there is no 'need'. This is not the same as no demand.
>
> (Sainsbury, 1989a: 18)

A requirement that local authorities should assess the need for new retail development first appeared in Government advice as long ago as 1977:

> Proposals for large new stores will involve an assessment of the need for the store – not only in terms of additional floorspace but also of alternative, modern or more convenient shopping facilities – in relation to the planning policies applying to the site and the contribution which the site makes to the policy objectives.
>
> (DoE/WO, 1977a: para 15)

This statement was motivated partly by the tendency at that time for local planning authorities to refuse applications for large new stores, because their approved development plan sought to restrict retail development to existing centres, and did not include any policies relating to large new stores. Whether the assessment of need was to be undertaken by the applicant or the local authority was not made clear in this guidance.

The case for including 'need' as a criterion in development control became implicitly more important in the 1980s as the government encouraged development and indicated that the 'market' should determine where and how retail development took place. Analyses of planning inquiry decisions during this period (e.g. Lee Donaldson, 1987; 1991) show that arguments put forward by developers to justify their proposal were often accepted by planning inspectors and in many cases outweighed (in their opinion) the negative arguments put forward by local planning authorities. Government guidance emphasised the advantages to consumers of retail innovation and the enhanced competition brought about by new retail development. For example, Scottish guidance advised that:

It is not sufficient, when considering the scope for new retailing development, to measure new proposals against the scale of current retailing provision for particular types of goods and local demand for such goods. Wherever possible consumers should have access to a variety of types of retail facility and to facilities of the standard they seek. They will also benefit from competition among retailers.

(SDD, 1986: para 7(g))

However, some Scottish structure plans argued that there was no need for speculative out-of-centre proposals, having surveyed their area to show that the population had adequate access to town centres, superstores and retail warehouses (Drivers Jonas, 1992: 24–6). Surprisingly, in view of the 1986 guideline quoted above, the Scottish Office approved such policies (ibid.: 27). In subsequent planning inquiries, developers attempted to produce a case for 'need', but the reporters tended to downplay the importance of this issue, making judgements instead on questions of impact (ibid.: 27–9).

In contrast, retail planning guidance in England and Wales at that time virtually ignored arguments relating to 'need':

There is a clear position adopted by the Department of the Environment in its PPG1 and PPG6 policy notes to the effect that retail impact analysis ought not to be necessary other than in exceptional circumstances. There is also a less clear but generally accepted view that the 'need' for a new retail development is not an issue requiring the attention of decision makers.

(Drivers Jonas, 1992: 113)

General planning guidance, in the form of the first version of PPG1, emphasised the role of the developer in identifying need for new development, and that this might override accepted planning principles:

it is not the function of the planning system to interfere with or to inhibit competition between users and investors in land, or to regulate the overall provision and character of space for particular uses for other than land-use planning reasons. Where development is acceptable in land-use terms, it is up to landowners, developers and tenants to decide whether to proceed with it. If, however, the applicant can demonstrate that there is a weighty national or local need for a particular type of development in that location, that consideration may be sufficient to outweigh important planning objections which might be a sufficient basis for refusal in the absence of the demonstrated need for development. The existence of alternative sites which might be suitable for a particular development is not normally a reason for refusing permission if the development is acceptable in planning terms.

(DoE/WO, 1988b: para 23; cited in Lee Donaldson, 1991: 9)

This advice appeared to favour developers who could ignore development plan policies and other 'important planning objections', so long as they could demonstrate a 'weighty' local need for their proposals. The term 'weighty' remained undefined, but its use suggests that the DoE were beginning to alter the balance in favour of local authorities.

This situation did not remain in effect for long. In the 1992 revised version of PPG1, all but the first two sentences of the above passage were withdrawn. In effect they were replaced by a weaker statement (from the developer's point of view) that 'An applicant who proposes a development which is clearly in conflict with the development plan would need to produce convincing reasons to demonstrate why the plan should not prevail' (DoE/WO, 1992: para 25), and:

> Local planning authorities or the Secretaries of State may find it appropriate, on occasion, to permit a development proposal which departs from the development plan because the particular contribution of that proposal to some local or national need or objective is so significant that it outweighs what the plan has to say about it. Such a consideration might be, for example, compelling argument by the applicant or appellant that a particular proposal should be allowed to proceed because of the contribution it will make to fulfilling an international commitment, or to some other particular objective which the plan did not foresee or address.
>
> (ibid.: para 30)

This change from 'weighty need' to 'compelling argument' seems to have tilted the balance away from the retail developer, in cases where the proposal was at odds with an approved development plan. It should be seen in the context of Section 70(2) of the 1990 Town and Country Planning Act, which 'requires the decision-maker to have regard to the development plan, so far as it is material to the application, and to any other material consideration' (ibid.: para 25). Having accepted that development plan policy should be the principal criterion in judging applications for development, the DoE could hardly maintain its previous stance that demonstration of 'weighty local need' should overrule such policy.

The change in emphasis in retail planning policy towards protection and enhancement of town centres also took the balance of the argument away from those developers who sought out-of-centre locations. The new version of PPG6 took a neutral stance on fulfilment of need:

> It is not the function of the planning system to preserve existing commercial interests or to inhibit competition between retailers or between methods of retailing. Nor is it the function of the local planning authority to regulate changes in the supply of retail services, unless interests of acknowledged importance would be adversely affected. Retailing must generally be able to respond to consumer

needs and demands; the public can then enjoy the benefits of improved choice and lower prices that may flow from the competition provided by new retail developments.

(DoE/WO, 1993: para 32)

The 1996 version of PPG6 took a more interventionist line. Selection of locations for new retail development was now to be the prerogative of local planning authorities rather than private developers, and the development plan would take a principal role in this process. In selecting locations for new development, local authorities should work 'with the private sector to assess need or market demand, and identify locations and sites for development' (DoE, 1996: para 1.7). After 'considering the need for new development', local authorities should adopt the sequential approach, so that the new development was wherever possible located in town centres. 'If, however, there is no need or capacity for further developments, there will be no need to identify additional sites in the town' (ibid.: para 1.10).

Thus, for the first time in England, local planning authorities were instructed to take the lead in assessing the need for new retail development, with the implication that development should occur only if a need was established. It was not made clear what methods local authorities should use to assess need.

In considering applications from the private sector for retail development, the new guidance made it clear that the development plan should take precedence over the developer's case, where these were at odds:

Development plans should specify preferred locations for retail development which sustain and enhance the vitality and viability of existing centres. Proposals for new retail developments in other locations should be assessed against the strategy in the development plan and be refused if it would undermine that strategy.

(DoE, 1996: para 4.2)

There was however no requirement in this guidance for any demonstration of 'need' for a proposed development. In November 1998 the food retailer Somerfield sought judicial review of a planning permission for a rival developer in Northallerton, Yorkshire, claiming that the developer had not demonstrated any need for the proposal, and that therefore a decision to grant planning permission was contrary to the advice in PPG6. The High Court judgement however stated that 'There is no indication in PPG6 that a developer must demonstrate need. ... If central government intended to require that need should be demonstrated as a precondition of the grant of planning permission, it was very odd that this was not spelt out clearly in the policy document' (JPEL, 1999a: Arnold, 1998).

In response the then Minister for Planning, Richard Caborn, took the opportunity to 'add to and clarify the guidance in PPG6' through a Parliamentary

Written Answer in February 1999 (JPEL, 1999b). He made it clear that 'need' was in fact a relevant consideration in the case of proposals for development outside existing centres which were not included in an up-to-date development plan, and that failure to demonstrate need would normally be justification for refusal of planning permission.

This was an important turning point in the treatment of 'need' in retail development. Previously, the need for a scheme was an argument which the developer could use in his favour, taking legally the status of a material consideration. Now, the developer was expected to demonstrate need, otherwise the application could be rejected on the basis that there was no need for it to be built. It is not clear whether the authors of PPG6 in 1996 had intended this to be the case: the speed with which the Caborn 'clarification' was introduced suggests that the intention had been there.

Caborn's statement attempted to explain how the developer should demonstrate need:

> In the context of PPG6 and this additional guidance, the requirement to demonstrate 'need' should not be regarded as being fulfilled simply by showing that there is capacity (in physical terms) or demand (in terms of available expenditure within the proposal's catchment area) for the proposed development. Whilst the existence of capacity or demand may form part of the demonstration of need, the significance in any particular case of the factors which may show need will be a matter for the decision maker.
>
> (JPEL, 1999b)

This rather negative explanation failed to make clear how 'need' should be defined or measured, leading to further uncertainty amongst developers (Lowe and Reeves, 2000). It was even suggested that Caborn's definition of 'need' was so broad that 'it allows any matter which is relevant to a decision to form part of the demonstration of need' (Adlard, 2001: 533).

However, planning inspectors quickly came to interpret 'need' in a more restricted way, as pertaining directly to retail matters, and any arguments based upon non-retail considerations, such as employment provision or physical regeneration, were classified as material considerations only (Bore, 2001; CBHP, 2004: 43–5).

As the 'need' issue grew in importance, a distinction began to be made between 'quantitative' and 'qualitative' need. This is now examined.

Quantitative and qualitative need

'Need' in retail planning is commonly classified as 'quantitative' or 'qualitative'. England (2000: 63) relates quantitative need to comparisons of supply of and demand for retail floorspace within a geographical area: 'An excess of expenditure, in the form of leakage of spending out of the area, is regarded as an opportunity for additional provision. Quantitative need can also be expressed as capacity for new development when ... [there is] population and expenditure growth up to the forecast year ...'. England also includes 'retailer requirements – demand by retailers for representation in a particular centre, and potential of competition and innovation' in a later section on quantitative need (ibid.: 103), although this definition does not concur with government statements discussed later in this section (see also Chapter 6).

According to England (2000: 103), quantitative need comprises:

- economic capacity in terms of demand arising from expenditure growth within the catchment area of a proposal
- leakage of trade from an area, which suggests a lack of provision to meet the needs of shoppers
- retailer requirements – demand by retailers for representation in a particular centre, and the potential for competition and innovation.

There are several commonly discussed technical issues concerning rates at which to project consumer expenditure (DTZ Pieda, 2004a), and less often discussed questions about the forecasting of price inflation and relationships between volume and value of goods (Thorpe, 1990).

England (2000: 63) defines qualitative need as 'a sectoral or geographical gap in the distribution of facilities. Less commonly ... a deficiency in the quality of provision'.

The Caborn statement in 1999 did not refer to 'quantitative' and 'qualitative' need as such, but this distinction was already commonly used in practice. There is clearly some overlap between quantitative and qualitative need: in some circumstances either category can be used to describe (or claim) the lack of any particular type of retail facility in an area. The main difference appears to be in the type of evidence used to support any such claims. Quantitative need is measured by comparisons of estimated supply and demand for floorspace, whereas evidence of qualitative need includes 'indications of over-trading' such as congestion within shops, or surveys of consumer views (ibid.: 119).

As part of the attempt to review the 'effectiveness' of PPG6, samples of local authority planners and retailers were asked to comment on aspects of existing policy (including Ministerial statements). It became clear that practitioners sought a more precise definition of 'need'. There was also 'some confusion as to how far in advance it was legitimate to look in order to attempt to predict a need' (CBHP, 2004: 43), given that in the medium term, retail expenditure was likely to increase. Thirdly, there was a general feeling amongst local authorities and retailers alike that the requirement to demonstrate need for development reinforced the control over out-of-centre development. One retailer commented that planning policy 'has moved from a presumption in favour of development; to the precautionary principle; to the requirement to demonstrate need for development' (ibid.: 44).

PPS6 responded to these criticisms by clarifying the concept of 'need', and explaining how it should be incorporated into retail planning policy. In considering applications for retail development, the guidance advises:

> A needs assessment prepared in support of a planning application should, wherever possible, be based on the assessment carried out for the development plan document, updated as required, and in the case of retail development should relate directly to the class of goods to be sold ... The need for additional floorspace should be assessed no more than five years ahead, as sites in the centre may become available within that period. Assessing need beyond this time period might pre-empt future options for investment in centres ... The catchment area that is used to assess future need should be realistic and well related to the size and function of the proposed development and take account of competing centres.
>
> (ODPM, 2005a: para 3.10)

Quantitative need is defined as:

> the likely future demand for additional retail and leisure floorspace, having regard to a realistic assessment of:
> - existing and forecast population levels;
> - forecast expenditure for specific classes of goods to be sold, within the broad categories of comparison and convenience goods ...; and
> - forecast improvements in productivity in the use of floorspace.
>
> (ibid.: para 2.34)

The guidance refers obliquely to qualitative need, stating that:

> a key consideration for a local planning authority will be to provide for consumer choice, by ensuring that:
> - an appropriate distribution of locations is achieved, subject to the key objective of promoting the vitality and viability of town centres and the application of the sequential approach, to improve accessibility for the whole community; and

- provision is made for a range of sites for shopping, leisure and local services, which allow genuine choice to meet the needs of the whole community, particularly the needs of those living in deprived areas.

(ibid.: para 2.35)

It is made clear in PPS6 that quantitative need should be seen as a more important criterion than qualitative. The relationship between the latter and the statement's emphasis elsewhere on a wider social and economic context for retail planning (including competition policy, social exclusion and urban regeneration and employment) is unclear. On the one hand 'qualitative need' can include any development which enhances 'consumer choice', but the guidance does not state whether the provision of better quality and/or novel styles of retailing can be justified in this way. It is clear however that assistance to regeneration or employment provision is not included in 'need'.

A further point of debate is whether retail developments within town centres should be assessed on the basis of 'need'. Some commentators have argued that large-scale developments within town centres – whether shopping malls or superstores – can produce impacts similar to those produced by off-centre development. PPS6 confirmed the existing position that town centre developments were excluded from the 'need' requirement. However, the guidance does state that development should be 'of an appropriate scale' for the town centre concerned. This refers to a debate over the propriety of developing large stores such as hypermarkets within small town centres or district centres, discussed further in Chapter 8 (see also Guy, 2002b; Wrigley et al., 2002a).

Relating demand, need and impact: the capacity study

So far, the key concepts of demand, impact and need have been treated separately. However, they are clearly interrelated. For example, consider an urban area in which all stores of a particular type are just profitable – a state of saturation, in the short term at least. In this situation there is no quantitative need for a new store, since none of the stores is over-trading. Were a new store to open, its trading impact would be severe, probably resulting in all stores operating at a loss, leading to eventual closure of one or more stores. This suggests that quantitative need and trading impact are inversely related.

This conclusion is reinforced if we consider a different situation, in which some stores are obviously over-trading. Here, a new store would 'mop up' some of this expenditure, closures would be unlikely and hence trading impact is not significant.[5]

The concepts of trading impact and quantitative need can be linked together through what have become known as 'capacity studies'. These attempt to estimate how much spare capacity exists within an urban area or local government area. According to England (2000):

> Capacity analysis uses the same base data as RIA [retail impact analysis] on retail expenditure. It takes expenditure growth from the base year over a long period, usually 10 years, over a wide area. The growth of retail expenditure represents turnover potential which can be converted to floorspace capacity by applying turnover/floorspace ratios. The net floorspace requirement needs to take account of any commitments and, particularly in the case of comparison shopping, the increase in floorspace efficiency of existing shops. The reuse of vacant floorspace should also be considered.
>
> (England, 2000: 101)

England considers that this analysis is suited more to comparison goods, where substantial increases in consumer expenditure might be expected over a ten-year period. In analyses of convenience shopping, a more limited version of capacity analysis is often used. Typically, the available expenditure on broadly defined categories of retail goods is compared with the sales potential of existing stores, if they were to trade at around company averages of turnover/floorspace. If expenditure appears substantially greater than sales potential, this means either that existing stores are over-trading, or that expenditure is leaking out to other urban areas, or a combination of the two. In any case, there appears to be a quantitative need for new development.[6]

Returning to the hypothetical example of a set of stores operating under conditions of saturation, we can also examine issues relating to qualitative need. Here, the conclusions could be different. If one or more existing stores is seen by many consumers as poor quality, because of high prices, poor layout and environment, limited range of goods, etc., then a prospective new retailer could claim that there was consumer demand for a new, better quality store. Hence, qualitative need might exist even where there is no spare capacity and where a new store might thus have considerable trading impact.

This recalls one of the most long-lasting and difficult issues in retail planning, exemplified in the regional centres debate of the 1980s. The proposed centres could be claimed to fulfil qualitative need, in the sense that they offered a new type of shopping environment which had proved popular in North America and elsewhere. However, they would clearly lead to significant trading impact upon nearby town centres. As we have seen in Chapter 3, the argument was eventually resolved in favour of town centres, although not always through considerations of need or impact.

Qualitative need has also been linked (at least, by prospective developers) with broader economic and social issues, including competition and innovation, sustainability (in the need to reduce aggregate travel), urban regeneration, and social exclusion. These issues are discussed further in the following chapters. However, PPS6 makes clear the government's view that these issues, while important and relevant to retail planning, do not constitute qualitative need.

Discussion and conclusions

This chapter has reviewed the history of retail planning policy in Britain, concerning impact and need. Although these two concepts are often considered in isolation, they are in fact closely related.

Impact is a long-standing criterion in retail planning which all interests are prepared to acknowledge in principle. Concern over the impact of new retail development is embedded in a broader town planning context of seeking to minimise the external effects of change in the built environment. The technical debate rests in methods of prediction, and in interpreting the likely outcomes of any particular level of trading impact. In researching impacts, problems arise in relating trading impact to other features of a fast-changing commercial environment. The policy debate rests in weighing the impacts of development proposals against other relevant matters.

Need is a more nebulous concept about which there is often little agreement between retail interests and public sector planners. We can detect a temporal cycle of opinion in official advice to local authorities. Originally, 'need' was seen as the prerogative of public sector planners: proposals for retail development were seen as necessary, or unnecessary, according to quantified perceptions of consumers' needs. Retailers and developers found that these arguments could be countered through their own interpretation of need, which was mainly qualitative in nature. New developments might not be justifiable in a strictly quantitative sense but were justifiable in terms of improving the quality of retail opportunities. In the 1980s, local authorities were instructed to stop trying to use quantitative need in their forward planning, and qualitative need became an important device to justify new development outside existing town and district centres. In the 1990s, qualitative need became downplayed in official guidance, and more recently, there has been a return to use of quantitative need as a major criterion in assessing retail proposals.

A comparison of methods used to identify need and predict impact show much similarity. The frequently used 'capacity study' can be regarded as an initial stage in both quantitative need assessment and impact assessment. It is also clear that quantitative need and trading impact are inversely related. The conclusion could be drawn that the concept of quantitative need, at least in appraisal of planning applications, is redundant: the demonstration of quantitative need by the retailer is unnecessary if trading impact is also used as a criterion for judging planning applications.

Qualitative need, however, is not necessarily related to trading impact, and deserves to remain an important criterion in judging planning applications. The comments of Lord Sainsbury (1989a) on the reluctance of planners to take heed of consumer views still seem as relevant today. This theme is explored further in Chapter 6.

Chapter 6
Innovation, productivity, competition and retail planning

Introduction

This chapter examines relationships between the economic performance of the retail sector and retail planning policy. The account is based around the key concepts of 'innovation', 'productivity', and 'competition'. We examine some of the untoward economic and social effects of imperfect competition in retailing, and ways in which the British government has attempted to regulate competition between retailers. Attention is also devoted to arguments used by retailers to justify new developments which may run contrary to planning policy. It will be seen that retail planning policy has not developed a consistent approach to these issues, and that the impacts of planning policies upon retail innovation and productivity are rarely fully understood by planners.

'Competition' turns out to be a particularly difficult concept. It is clear that retailers' attempts to become more 'competitive' can result in distortion or reduction of competition overall, as weaker contestants fall by the wayside. But almost all retailing possesses an element of monopoly power, simply through being an easily accessible choice for people living or working close by. This uncertainty about the meaning of 'competition' in retailing means that planners are accused of being both too lenient and too restrictive in their attitudes towards new retail development.

In this chapter, the key concepts of innovation, productivity and competition are initially treated separately. A summary of the arguments both for and against development of large-format stores by leading multiple retailers brings these concepts together and also illustrates the lack of consensus concerning their meaning and any need for government intervention. Ways in which retail planning policy approaches these issues are then discussed. It is concluded that planners generally lack understanding of economic concepts in retailing, and that planning policies may inhibit innovation and productivity, at the same time distorting competition between retailers.

Retail innovation and retailer strategy

In previous chapters, changes in methods of retailing and retail store and shopping centre development have been summarised briefly, and their implications for retail planning policy examined. At the retailer level, significant innovations which have affected the retail development process have been:

- Self-service in the 1950s and 1960s, which led to development of super-markets, and later, superstores and many kinds of non-food 'big box' store including retail warehouses.
- Widening of product ranges, particularly in large food stores in the 1980s and 1990s, which began to sell non-food items and consumer services, thus competing with an ever-widening range of non-food stores.
- Deep discount stores which aim to set low prices at the expense of in-store environment and customer service, both in food and non-food goods.
- Retail positioning (Davies and Brooks, 1989), so that retailers began to adjust their store profile (including product mix and standard of service) to the demographic characteristics of their catchment area. This has led to the growth of many retail innovations, including specialist fashion chains and city centre 'Metro' type food stores.
- Changes in distribution systems, such that multiple retailers started to deal directly with manufacturers and importers of goods, and develop their own warehousing instead of using locally based wholesalers. More recently, 'just in time' techniques have led to reductions in the space needed for storage of goods within the store. This has released space for extra sales, particularly in hypermarkets.
- Increasing integration of information and communications technologies (ICT) into the operation of supply chains, management information and retail transactions. The latter has allowed the collection of detailed information about customers, their household characteristics and buying behaviour (Birkin *et al.*, 2002).

At the level of shopping centres, innovations noted in earlier chapters have included:

- the retail warehouse park and its subsequent derivatives the shopping park and fashion park (Guy, 2000);
- the regional shopping centre (Guy, 1994a: 169–81; Guy, 1994b);
- the in-town centre shopping mall (Guy, 1994a: 181–8; Lowe, 2005);
- the factory outlet centre (Fernie and Fernie, 1997);
- specialist centres and 'festival' developments with a substantial non-retail 'leisure' component (Guy, 1994a: 188–91).

Innovation is often essential in maintaining a retailer's competitive advantage. More generally, competitive advantage arises through a suitable combination of those features which attract consumers to a store. Marketing texts refer to the 'four Ps': product, price, promotion and place (Bennison *et al.*, 1995: 8). Product, price and promotion tend to be similar across the whole range of stores operated by a typical multiple retailer, with some variation to accommodate local tastes and preferences, or to fit the size of store. The attraction to consumers offered by 'place', or store location, is of more concern to land-use planning.

Bennison *et al.* (1995) describe locational strategies through which multiple retailers develop new stores or rationalise their store network. These include:

- Contagion: a network of stores is developed outwards from the area in which the company initially operated. This typifies some grocery retailers, whose stores need to be within reach of the company's regional warehouses. Expansion into a new region may depend upon development of a new warehouse.

- Hierarchy: the retailer opens stores within a particular size of city, town or district centre appropriate to the products offered and the characteristics of the target population. For example, department stores require a large catchment population and therefore locate in larger town/city centres. On the other hand, a chemist or newsagent serves a local catchment and will seek a district or local centre.

- Defence/aggression: stores are developed in advance of possible competitors, in order to obtain the best site and to build up loyalty from the local population. This process has also been termed 'pre-emptive expansion' (Thorpe, 1990: 172). There may be capacity for only one store, for example a superstore in a small market town. Sometimes, sites may be purchased but not developed, as a spoiling tactic.

- Avoidance/collusion: stores are developed at a distance from existing competitors, in order to establish a loyal local market. In the UK it is noticeable that the major grocery operators hardly ever locate within easy walking distance of one another. This has led to allegations of collusion. On the other hand, many non-food retailers seek sites close to their main competitors, in the belief that shoppers will want to compare their offers.

- Acquisition: one way to establish a presence quickly in a country or region is to acquire existing outlets, often through takeover of or merger with another company. A notable recent example in the UK has been Wm Morrison's takeover of Safeway, resulting in store acquisitions for both Morrison and other grocery retailers. Tesco and Sainsbury have acquired several chains of convenience stores, in order to open a network of small food stores in local centres (Wood *et al.*, 2006).

- Outlet segmentation: partly as a result of past acquisitions, many multiple retailers own an assortment of stores of various sizes in several levels of centre. The network can operate more effectively if each store sells products and offers customer service appropriate to the local catchment area (Birkin *et al.*, 2002).

This summary of locational strategies suggests that competition between retailers does not correspond to 'perfect competition' as set out in economic theory, a conclusion reached by many commentators (for example in the essays in Moir and Dawson, 1990; see also Clarke, 2000). It is clear that the relationship between the retailer and the consumer is essentially skewed:

> Firstly, consumers are *small*, in terms of the average size of their purchases in relation to their overall spending power and retailers' overall turnover. Second, consumers are relatively *immobile*, in that they are either unable or unwilling to travel long distances to shop. Third, consumers are *uninformed*, in that they do not, necessarily, know which products are available where, and at what price, and in terms of specific quality.
>
> (Clarke, 2000: 985, original emphases)

It is clear also that retailers do not compete with one another in classical economic fashion. One obvious sign is that in some areas of retailing, a small number of companies take very large proportions of national market share. These proportions can be even higher in local markets, where one or two stores of a particular type serve the local population. Such 'local monopolies' have become a cause for concern, as discussed later in this chapter. They can restrict consumer choice, and (in theory at least) may lead to price increases and/or poor standards of customer service by the monopolist.

It should also be obvious that defensive or aggressive behaviour, and collusion between market leaders, violate the model of perfect competition: indeed, collusion is broadly speaking illegal in many countries. Aggressive behaviour can include the acquisition of development sites which are not immediately required, and payment of what appear to be inflated prices for such sites. Such behaviour carries the risk that 'sunk costs' will be incurred: disposal of these sites will in the long term fail to reclaim the initial investment (Wrigley, 1996; Guy, 1997; 1999). A market leader can however afford such risks in the interest of acquiring the best possible sites: 'best' in terms of the medium-term return on initial investment, expressed in the relationship between estimated sales and development costs (Guy, 1995). The reward may be a 'captive market', in which consumers are isolated from retail competition:

Allegations of price-fixing, collusion or other anti-competitive behaviour …
suggest that significant competition in the retail grocery trades, among the largest
businesses, is far from ubiquitous and does not affect all aspects of trading policy
and behaviour. Competition takes many forms and varies in intensity. It is greater
when retailers are seeking sites for new store development. It then falls away after
stores are built and trading. It is almost non-existent once a shopper is captured
in a store.[1]

(Moir, 1990: 116)

Clarke (2000: 985) adds that as grocery retailers sell more and more goods
through their own brands, comparison of items between stores by consumers using
criteria such as price and quality becomes more difficult. The stores themselves
also encourage 'loyalty' through point-of-sale coupons and other offers to regular
customers.

It also appears that entry into some areas of retailing can be very difficult.
Barriers to entry include the high cost of sites, advertising and marketing costs,
and difficulties in setting up supply contracts such that the firm can compete with
market leaders. Retailers in areas such as clothing will usually rent premises rather
than develop their own sites, but even here it can be difficult to gain access to
good quality town centre premises, in the absence of an established reputation.
The first-time independent retailer is less likely to seek an expensive town centre
site, or therefore to be affected by such considerations. However, (s)he must find
a way to compete with larger organisations, through unique location, or some
other advantage such as specialised range of goods or superior customer service
(Coca-Stefaniak *et al.*, 2005).

Retail productivity: international comparisons and the alleged role of the planning system

Another key issue in economic debates over retailing is that of productivity. Put
simply, a company is more productive if its practices enable higher levels of output,
in relation to the inputs needed to produce that output. In retailing, outputs are
commonly measured in terms of value of sales: measurement of inputs is more
problematic, as discussed below.

The simplest and most often used measure of productivity is labour
productivity: output per worker. This uses readily available information but has
the disadvantage of ignoring variations over space or time of hours worked by
both full-time and part-time employees. Therefore measures such as 'output per
hours worked' or 'value added per hour' are also used where suitable data exist
(Reynolds *et al.*, 2005; Griffith and Harmgart, 2005).

A more sophisticated measure is total factor productivity (TFP), which 'attempts to measure output per unit of inputs, where inputs are generally labour and capital' (HM Treasury, 2000: 4). This measure suffers however from problems in measuring capital inputs.

Academic authors have indicated that 'output' is a complex construct which should not be represented simply by retail sales or volume of goods sold. Output is often equated with those features of a retail operation which might appeal to consumers and influence their choice of retailer. For example, Nooteboom (1980), as summarised in Thorpe (1990: 164), suggested seven measures of output:

- Width of assortment: the number and kinds of different product groups offered;
- Depth of assortment: the number of kinds of different items per product group (i.e. brands, sizes, etc.);
- Prices;
- Service to customers within the store;
- Service generally offered by the retailer (guarantees, deliveries, etc.);
- Queuing time within the store;
- Attractiveness of the store environment.

Further discussion of retail productivity and its measurement can be found in a series of papers linked to the research carried out by Jonathan Reynolds and colleagues for the Department of Industry's Retail Strategy Group (Templeton, 2004; Sparks, 2005; Reynolds *et al.*, 2005). The latter conclude that:

> The most worthwhile estimates of both TFP and labour productivity are those that are able to overcome problems of definition and measurement of both outputs and inputs. However, these are particularly challenging in the context of cross-country comparisons of the retail trades. We conclude overall that these problems are such that any results obtained must be treated with considerable caution.
>
> Reynolds *et al.* (2005: 250)

This apparently esoteric issue became significant in retail planning in the late 1990s, when the UK government became concerned over apparently low levels of retail productivity, compared with other G7 countries. Retailing is one of the most important parts of the UK economy: in simple statistics it recorded £239 billion sales (35 per cent of total consumer spending) in 2002, and employed 3,077,000 people, amounting to about 11 per cent of the workforce (DTI, 2004: 9). Therefore the industry was expected to make an important contribution to achievement of the government's economic objectives.

One of the government's key economic objectives generally is improvement in productivity. The Treasury has for many years decried the UK's poor position with respect to the United States and most of Western Europe:

> UK productivity, however measured, lags that of other major industrialised countries. The labour productivity gap with the US was 45 per cent in 1999, that with France was 18 per cent and that with Germany 11 per cent. ... The challenge for the Government is to achieve its long-term economic ambition to have a faster rise in productivity than its main competitors as it closes that gap.
>
> (HM Treasury, 2000: 1)

Further analysis showed that

> although the country's most productive firms perform well, they are trailed by a long tail of far less productive firms ... The UK can therefore improve its overall productivity performance by the least productive firms lifting their performance towards the level of the best firms in their sector, and by strengthening the competitive pressures on them to do so.
>
> (ibid.: 39)

This led to five priorities for economic policy:

- Increasing investment in physical capital
- Developing human capital
- Promoting innovation and R&D
- Strengthening competition
- Encouraging enterprise and entrepreneurship

(ibid.: 40)

In coming to these conclusions, the Treasury were heavily influenced by an independent report on the UK's productivity (McKinsey, 1998). The McKinsey report chose 'food retailing' as one of its case studies, benchmarking the UK against the US and France. The report found output per hour worked to be about 25 per cent below France and 10 per cent below the US. However, the UK food industry achieved the best level of total factor productivity, through a much more intensive use of space. The relatively low level of labour productivity was seen to be due to two main factors:

- Use of 'low value-added workers' in areas such as bag packing and store cleaning, reflecting a lack of labour regulation compared with France.[2]

- Restrictions on store development through the land use planning system, which acted in two ways: through 'denying food retailers the full labour productivity benefits of scale', and through allowing the survival of 'relatively inefficient corner grocers and specialist shops'.

(McKinsey, 1998: 2)

It was acknowledged throughout the report that UK food retailing – particularly the largest companies – showed innovation in areas such as private label products and supply chain management. The use of low-paid labour also led to a better offer to consumers from stores which were seen as more attractive and with better customer service than typically was found in the US or France.

The report concluded that the government should

Further consider the economic costs of land use restrictions ... If PPG6 were removed, UK food retailing would be able to continue its evolutionary process. This would entail the further expansion of the 'modern format' – especially large-format retailers – and further contraction of the 'traditional sector'. ... another important effect of PPG6 is that it stops grocers developing tomorrow's ideal format ... a leading-edge format developed overseas but requiring a large amount of space may not come to the UK.

(ibid.: 14)

The significance of retailing in economic policy was reinforced in a more recent comparison of the US and the UK by Adair Turner, former director of the Confederation of British Industry. He claims that 'Lower productivity in retailing and wholesaling accounts for over a third of the total productivity gap between the UK and the US'. This was because 'it is simply far easier to run retailing and wholesale distribution at a high level of efficiency in a lightly populated, dispersed physical environment, such as in the US, than in more densely populated Europe' (Turner, 2003: 5).

Turner also states that 'Over the last 5–7 years, US productivity in retailing and wholesaling has been growing at a dramatic 6 per cent per annum, while typical European growth rates have been only 1 per cent or so'. This 'productivity spurt' appears to have been due entirely to 'the new entry of new, more efficient retailing establishments, new stores on new sites, and ... none is attributable to productivity improvements within existing stores' (ibid.: 6).

This view is supported in studies reported by Pilat (2005: 294), who states that:

The potential policy implications of such studies are considerable; if retail productivity is largely driven by entry and exit the policies that act as a barrier to entry and exit are likely to have highly detrimental effects on productivity growth in the retailing sector.

The argument is therefore that the UK's productivity gap in retailing is not just important in itself; it is also an important contributor to the overall productivity gap. Turner's reference to 'new stores' highlights the aggressive expansion of Wal-Mart Supercenters in the US, and the lack of any such store development programme in western Europe (it should be remembered that the average Supercenter is four to five times as large as the average British food superstore).

However, the research carried out for the DTI concludes that leading UK retailers are on the whole as efficient and innovative as their international rivals, and that measurement of productivity (particularly in international comparisons) is fraught with problems of definition and data quality (Reynolds *et al.*, 2005). The report did not recommend any changes to government regulation (of any kind) as this 'would be to enter upon broad social policy issues which would go well beyond our brief' (Templeton, 2004: para 1.16). Turner (2003) similarly concluded that the UK, in giving more weight to environmental arguments, is on a different societal path to that of the US, rather than being simply an inferior competitor.

Competition policy, consumer choice and planning policy

The nature of competition between leading retailers in the UK has also concerned government ministers for many years. After a series of earlier investigations, summarised in Clarke (2000), the Office of Fair Trading initiated a study of competition between major supermarket firms (Competition Commission, 2000a). This study was motivated by perceptions amongst many politicians and media circles that these firms were drawing excess profits, as indicated by higher food prices and net margins than occurred in other European countries. It was also alleged by some that the supermarket firms were colluding together in order to maintain high prices; and were behaving unfairly towards food suppliers in several ways later explored in Clarke (R.) *et al.* (2002).

Following comments made in McKinsey (1998), the Commission also investigated the role of the land use planning system in restricting supermarket development. Such restriction might reinforce local monopolies or duopolies by failing to allow new competitors into a local market.

The Commission distributed lengthy questionnaires to 24 multiple retailers involved in food retailing, carried out surveys of consumer behaviour and of local authority planning policies, and also received evidence from a variety of interest groups. The Commission found that these retailers all belonged to at least one of two 'complex monopoly' groups, as defined in the Fair Trading Act of 1973:

one monopoly being derived from pricing of retail goods, the other from the relationship between supermarkets and their suppliers. Furthermore, five companies (Asda, Morrison, Safeway, Sainsbury and Tesco) were sufficiently large to be able to exercise 'market power', and these companies were subject to more detailed investigation.

The Commission found evidence of local monopolies or duopolies in several local markets. Typically, a town would be served by one or two superstores or large supermarkets, most often Tesco and/or Sainsbury (Competition Commission, 2000a: paras 2.65–2.78; 2.598–2.603). There was also evidence that in such circumstances, prices were higher than in towns where there was a larger selection of supermarkets (ibid.: paras 2.394–2.405).

The Commission agreed with McKinsey (1998) in taking the view that land use planning in the UK had created high land values (and hence high development costs) compared with the US, and to some extent France. This view is also supported in the research carried out for the DTI (Templeton, 2004; Reynolds *et al.*, 2005). The Competition Commission found that planning control can inhibit competition: for example, both Asda and Wm Morrison had found difficulties in expanding into south-east England because their large store format is not acceptable to local planning authorities – hence the subsequent battle for control of the Safeway Group (Competition Commission, 2003).

Nevertheless, the Commission decided not to recommend any relaxing of the sequential approach to new store development. It appears to have been convinced that the overall policy of maintaining and enhancing town centre retailing drew support from many quarters and should not be jeopardised. It concluded that 'the latest planning guidance in our view balances broader social and environmental objectives relating to the vitality of town and city centres with the needs of consumers for stores' (Competition Commission, 2000a: para 1.4; see also Hallsworth and Clarke, 2001; Hallsworth and Evers, 2002).

Several other possible 'remedies' which had been presented for comment at an earlier stage in the investigation were not supported in the final report. These included:

- Restrictions on further development by the major players, and forced disposal of undeveloped sites or even existing stores in areas where one or two companies retained a very large market share.
- Changes to land use planning policy, including 'any mechanisms through which the extent of local competition or consumer choice could have some influence on which companies were permitted to acquire or develop a site' (Competition Commission, 2000b: 1).
- Various measures relating to pricing policy and relationships with suppliers.

The second proposal outlined above was altered in the final report to a recommendation that:

> in certain clearly defined circumstances, the Director General of Fair Trading's approval should be required for particular parties to be allowed to acquire or develop large new stores. These are that if Asda, Morrison, Safeway, Sainsbury or Tesco wish to acquire an existing store, or build a new store, having over 1,000 sq metres (about 11,000 sq feet) of grocery retail sales area within a 15-minute drive time of one of its existing stores, or significantly to extend the grocery retailing area of an existing store, it should be required to apply to the DGFT for consent.
>
> (Competition Commission, 2000a: para 1.15)

This recommendation, which would have required Parliamentary legislation, was not accepted by the government, although there were signs that it might be revived at some future date if warranted by anti-competitive trends in the food retail industry (Wrigley, 2001: 191).

The overall effect of this major investigation was thus to expose the issues rather than set in motion any significant tightening of rules concerning supermarket competition or relaxing of planning control (Hallsworth and Evers, 2002). This was broadly because in the Commission's view, any monopolies identified either at national or local scale were not serious enough to warrant new legislation.

This major review was followed by an investigation into the implications of the possible takeover of the Safeway chain by other food retailers (Competition Commission, 2003). The conclusion was that a takeover by Wm Morrison, or a non-food retailer, was in the public interest whereas a takeover by Tesco, J Sainsbury or Asda was not. The main reason for this conclusion was that the Morrison takeover would lead to a strong competitor to the 'big three', both nationally and (in many areas) locally. However, Morrison would have to dispose of stores (either Morrison or Safeway) in 48 areas, in order to avoid dominating the local market. Subsequently the OFT indicated which retailers were or were not allowed to acquire these stores, again on grounds of local market share. The OFT has also referred some one-off transactions of food stores to the Competition Commission, to investigate whether a local monopoly could arise.

Recent criticism has focused particularly on Tesco, who are not only increasing market share through continuing store development and mergers (see below), but are alleged to have held a 'land bank' of 185 undeveloped sites in early 2006. Both Asda and Sainsbury have issued statements urging the OFT to 'force' planners to take into account how many stores a food retailer already owns in an area when they consider new proposals (Finch, 2006).[3]

One of the most controversial aspects of the Commission's work has been the assumption that there are essentially two 'markets' in food retailing: firstly 'one-stop' food shopping trips, which are very largely served by large stores (of over 1,400 sq.m. sales area); and secondly, 'top-up' shopping trips, which are served by both large stores and smaller stores, the latter owned by both multiples and independents (Competition Commission, 2000a: paras 2.18–2.32). Thus, several takeovers of convenience store chains by Tesco and Sainsbury, beginning in 2002 with Tesco's acquisition of T and S Stores, have not been referred to the Commission by the OFT, on grounds that such takeovers do not create the possibility of monopoly conditions in the very fragmented convenience store sector. This policy has been vigorously opposed by organisations representing independent convenience retailers.

Evidence from a study of food shopping behaviour in Portsmouth tends to support the small retailers' view. Compared with a survey held in 1980 in the same area, households' food shopping patterns had become more complex. The distinction between main and secondary food shopping trips was now less clear. Secondary trips were made to large stores (including superstores) as much as to convenience or specialist stores (Clarke *et al.*, 2004).[4]

The Portsmouth study also found that the choices which households made were affected by accessibility and 'convenience' as much as by price, or customer service standards. Accessibility and convenience were not simply related to distance from the home. Many food purchases took place during trips made for another purpose, such as work journeys or children's leisure pursuits. It was made clear in interviews that most consumers want an extensive choice of food shopping opportunities, in terms of both location and retail characteristics. A limited choice within easy reach – even between very good retailers – is seen as inadequate (Jackson *et al.*, 2004).

Innovation, competitiveness and efficiency: the retailers' case

The focus now changes to individual retailers. In particular this section examines the search by large retail organisations for greater profitability, through a combination of expansion of operations, innovation and increased efficiency. This has led to pressure on government to simplify or modify various types of regulatory activity, including the operation of the land use planning system. While it can be argued that government should not intervene in order to increase private sector profitability, the retailers claim that their efforts in this regard also benefit the consumer, through such advantages as lower prices, improved product quality and range, and better in-store environments.

Some major retail innovations over the last 40 years have been listed earlier in this chapter. Many of these, such as replacement of counter service by self-service, have had important but indirect effects upon retail development and retail planning policy, through for example changes in the amount and nature of retail employment. Some aspects of innovation however are of particular concern to retail planners because they require the development of new types of store, often large single-level stores designed largely for car-borne customers. These stores, which include superstores, hypermarkets, and retail warehouses, have also been termed 'large-format stores' or 'big box stores'. They require sites of several hectares, to include car parking and servicing arrangements. Large floors and flexible internal layouts also allow innovation of product ranges and merchandising methods.

The arguments used by large store retailers in favour of further development usually involve economies of scale, such that larger stores are claimed to be less costly to develop and/or operate, relative to sales and other outputs. Cost advantages may relate to labour, in-store costs, goods delivery, etc.

The Competition Commission (2000a) found that, in the case of UK food retailing, labour productivity advantages seem to apply up to store sizes of about 3,000 sq.m. sales area, beyond which no further advantage generally occurred. This finding has parallels in other countries, with some variation in the critical store size (Guy *et al.*, 2005). Interviews with large store retailers suggest however that economies of scale exist more importantly in the ability to display and sell larger product ranges to the benefit of consumers, leading to higher expenditure per customer visit (ibid.). Larger formats also allow more innovation in merchandise, display methods and customer service.

As discussed in Chapter 4, large store retailers have become increasingly frustrated with retail planning policy, in particular the changes introduced by ministerial statements in England, and also with the negative way in which policy tends to be implemented by local authorities (noted in CBHP, 2004). This frustration led to an interest group, originally called the British Council for Out of Town Retail (BCOTR), to commission research on government policy and the views of a sample of retailers and developers. The report began by stating:

> The empirical research in this report reveals that government retail planning policies are restrictive to the point of being out of touch with consumers, out of touch with retailers and out of touch with the property industry.
>
> Current policy restricts the development of out-of-town superstores. Few town centre and edge-of-centre sites are large enough to accommodate the bigger formats. But research shows consumers like superstores, retailers gain economies of scale from them and developers get better returns on capital from them. But councils are interpreting the planning policies rigidly and unrealistically, leading to a de facto ban on out-of-town and consequently many new large stores.
>
> The embargo strengthens local monopolies and is anti-competitive in its effects. It has contributed to the consolidation of retailer sectors, entrenches the dominance of well-established retailers with a portfolio of large stores, blocks the

national expansion of regional operators and prevents new entrants coming into the UK market. The ultimate loser of the anti-competitive planning policy is the shopper who is deprived of consumer choice.

(BCOTR, 2002: 1)

These arguments, which echoed the views of the Treasury on retail productivity and the role of the planning system, were fed into the consultation process for the issue of PPS6 (for further detail see Guy, 2006a). In a comment on the draft PPS6 (ODPM, 2003), Accessible Retail (the successor to BCOTR) claimed that:

Experian estimates that expenditure on bulky goods has been responsible for about 35 per cent of the increase in retail spending and about 16 per cent of the increase in GDP in the last 5 years. It also indicates that retail warehousing has significantly contributed to the 2 per cent deflation per annum that retail goods have been experiencing over the past 3 years; out-of-centre retailers have seen volume growth exceed value growth over the last 10 years. Furthermore average out-of-centre sales densities are up 25 per cent higher than those in the high street, a difference that is especially apparent in bulky goods retailers. For example, DIY retailers trade almost three times as productively out-of-centre than they do in-town.

(Accessible Retail, 2004: 4)

This neatly summarises two arguments used by the large-format retailers: firstly, that large formats are more efficient, and add to the UK's productivity and combat price inflation; secondly, that they trade more successfully in out-of-centre locations.

The second argument is supported by research into large-format operators' reactions to the planning policy which requires them to be 'flexible' about their format and location: it is clear that operating from smaller stores and/or town centre locations reduces efficiency and imposes extra costs, both in development and operation (Guy and Bennison, 2006). A specific costed example has been provided by B and Q, who compared costs and potential prices of their products between, on the one hand a typical warehouse store in an off-centre location, and on the other hand, some 14 small premises or vacant sites within Reading town centre, which would provide the equivalent range of goods. Typical prices from the latter arrangement were estimated to be about 30 per cent higher, due to the costs of renting expensive town centre units and of staffing and servicing these stores (CBRE, 2003).

The local effects of retailer power: the environmentalists' case

Environmentalist pressure groups, including the Campaign to Protect Rural England (CPRE), Friends of the Earth (FoE), New Economics Foundation (NEF), and Sustain, have often raised arguments against the increasing power of major multiple retailers. Their case focuses partly on the multiples' impacts upon local communities and small-scale retailing and business: particularly, although not exclusively, concerning those food retailers who could potentially exert 'market power', as examined in the Competition Commission (2000a) report.

First, the multiples are accused of closing outlets in town centres and district or local centres, and replacing them with large suburban stores which are inaccessible to those who patronised the former stores (e.g. Sustain, 2000). A study of Cardiff by Guy *et al.* (2004) supported this view only to a limited extent, arguing that small supermarket closures and large store development had been carried out by different companies, and that some new supermarkets (mainly discount stores) had been opened in socially deprived areas.

Second, multiples are accused of distorting consumer choice by 'flooding' local markets with more and more stores under one fascia (FoE, 2005). The recent trend for Tesco and Sainsbury to grow through acquisition of convenience store chains has made this more likely to occur. Such complaints are supported by the conclusions of the Portsmouth research, that while many shoppers rely on a small number of stores for routine purchases, they may still welcome a variety of types of store in both town centre and off-centre locations (Kirkup *et al.*, 2004).

Third, the replacement of small independent stores by branches of multiple concerns is argued to affect the local economy, by reducing purchases of local goods and services (NEF, 2003; FoE, 2005). This may be particularly the case with food retailers, who use their own distribution systems instead of the local food producers and wholesalers which traditionally served small food shops. The evocative term 'food webs' has been used to describe these traditional linkages (CPRE, 1998). These arguments have to some extent proved effective in increasing awareness of local and regional food promotion and supply (DEFRA, 2003a; 2003b; AMT, n.d.). However, the spread of the major retailers, particularly supermarkets, into small towns continues to cause concern to supporters of traditional retail networks (e.g. NEF, 2003; CPRE, 2004). The most recent report by FoE (2006a) accuses major food retailers of 'trampling' on the planning system:

> Evidence, collected from some 200 planning disputes around the country, reveals that:
> - Supermarkets successfully lobby local authorities to alter local plans, allocating more sites for retail.

- Supermarkets ignore the planning system in pushing ahead with developments.
- Supermarkets bypass the planning system by entering into separate legal agreements with councils.
- Supermarkets use 'planning gain' to offer local authorities valuable facilities, including car parks, and affordable housing to help gain planning permission.
- Supermarkets buy up land which can be a barrier for local councils which want to develop housing or other facilities. Tesco, for example, owns around 185 sites around the country.

Some councillors also admit to being pressured into accepting supermarket planning applications because of concerns over costs of appeal, the report claims.

(FoE, 2006b)

Finally, the apparent replacement of traditional retailers and small businesses by standardised multiple fascias (including non-food retailers and service establishments) has led to accusations that town centres are losing their distinctiveness. The *Clone Town Britain* reports (NEF, 2004; 2005) set out these arguments:

In place of real local shops has come a near-identical package of chain stores replicating on the nation's high streets. As a result, the individual character of many of our town centres is evaporating. Retail spaces once filled with independent butchers, newsagents, tobacconists, pubs, book shops, greengrocers and family-owned general stores are becoming filled with supermarket retailers, fast-food chains, and global fashion outlets. Many town centres that have undergone substantial regeneration have even lost the distinctive façades of their high streets, as local building materials have been swapped in favour of identical glass, steel, and concrete storefronts that provide the ideal degree of sterility to house a string of big, clone town retailers. ... The assault on the character of town centres has been aided by planning and regeneration decisions that have drawn shoppers away from the high street and created a retail infrastructure hostile to small, independent businesses.

(NEF, 2004: 2)

The accusation that planning policies have helped create this situation has been ignored in the mainstream retail planning literature. Nevertheless, it deserves attention and will be discussed later in this chapter.

Planning policy responses to economic issues

The debates discussed so far in this chapter have taken place largely in economic fora. Land use planning has been seen as one of several types of government restriction, which may or may not have adverse effects upon economic progress. An alternative view has been that land use planning is not powerful enough to counteract the adverse effects of retail monopoly.

The focus now switches to the planning system itself, and its attitudes to retail innovation, competition and productivity. This has (in theory, at least) remained consistent throughout successive versions of planning guidance. The basic premise is that, in line with planning law generally, planning policies or decisions should not favour any one private interest over another. So, for example, consent for development should not be given to retailer A and at the same time denied to retailer B, unless there are good 'planning' reasons, such as an approved policy which prefers development to take place in the location chosen by retailer A.

This was made clear in the first retail planning guidance in 1972: 'It is not the function of land use planning to prevent competition between retailers or methods of retailing nor to preserve existing commercial interests as such' (DoE/WO, 1972b: para 6).

The revised Policy Note altered the wording to 'prevent or to stimulate', but also drew a more positive conclusion:

> Indeed, although it is not the function of the planning system to prevent or to stimulate competition among retailers or among methods of retailing, nor to preserve existing interests as such; it must take into account the benefits to the public which flow from new developments in the distributive and retailing fields.
>
> (DoE/WO, 1977a: para 7)

In the first version of PPG6 (DoE/WO, 1988a), the above wording was retained, except that 'prevent or stimulate' was replaced by 'inhibit'. However, advantages of superstores and retail warehouses for the consumer were emphasised, and it seems to have been assumed that such developments would naturally take place outside town centres. In this respect: 'it may be thought rather ironic that in the early 1980s, in order to attempt to increase competition, government action in land-use planning played into the oligopolists' hands by making it easier to create entry barriers through pre-emptive expansion' (Thorpe, 1990: 172).

This problem was exacerbated by the scale of modern store development, particularly in food and household goods retailing:

> Several of the new forms [of retail development], because of their scale, close off other options for change in retail provision. Thus retailers and developers may

get an effective spatial monopoly to trade and such a problem may arise relatively quickly because of the pace of change. Intervention in the market may be able to manage this process.

(Dawson and Broadbridge, 1988, quoted in Thorpe, 1990: 174)

The 1996 version of PPG6 showed little change, despite the new 'town centres first' emphasis (see Chapter 4). One of the four main government objectives was 'to maintain an efficient, competitive and innovative retail sector' (DoE, 1996: para 1.1), and it was emphasised that 'It is not the role of the planning system to restrict competition, preserve existing commercial interests or to prevent innovation' (ibid.). However, it became apparent to most commentators, especially after the Ministerial statements of 1998–2000 (see Chapter 4), that in practice this objective was frequently over-ridden by other objectives, particularly that of enhancing the vitality and viability of town centres. Restrictions on off-centre development, and instructions to retailers to be 'flexible' were, as noted above, limiting their ability to produce more efficient and innovative formats. This view was frequently expressed in surveys of multiple retailers and property developers (BCOTR, 2002), and planning consultants (Guy and David, 2002).

It is also clear from a survey of local planning authorities carried out by Moss (2004), that planners generally show little interest in the notion of using planning policy to enhance competition between retailers or to allow innovation in retailing. In so far as competition is an issue at all, there is widespread sympathy amongst planners for the view that out-of-centre large-format retailing has 'unfair' advantages such as free car parking, and that town centres should be supported through government policy in order to compete more effectively. An obvious way to do this is to prevent further growth of out-of-centre retailing, a view supported by many local authority planners (CBRE, 2004).

These views were, however, at variance with government policy on productivity and competition. Pressure from the retail sector, and (probably more significant) other government departments including the Treasury, gave rise to some concessions in PPS6. The requirement to be 'flexible' remained in the guidance, although local planning authorities were also required to take a flexible attitude and be aware of the possible advantages of the proposed format (ODPM, 2005a: para 3.16). However, the 'class of goods' qualification of the sequential test (see Chapter 4) was replaced by less restrictive, if unclear guidance (Guy and Bennison, 2006; Guy, 2006a).

More generally, PPS6 retained the overall objective to support 'efficient, competitive and innovative retail, leisure and tourist sectors, with improving productivity' (ODPM, 2005a: para 1.4), but made it clear that this objective was subordinate to the 'key' objectives which related to the growth and protection of existing centres. Furthermore, as with previous guidance, there was no indication to planning authorities on how to implement the advice on competition and innovation.

Discussion

Economic analyses of competition in retailing suggest that in some ways at least, competition is a long way from being 'perfect'; oligopolies operating at national level can manifest themselves in duopolies or monopolies at the local level. Lack of competition is in any case typical in small towns or residential suburbs, especially for those consumers who are not very mobile. This is because their choice tends to be restricted to a small number of retail outlets within easy reach of the home. This has of course always been the case, but relative disadvantage of those consumers restricted to a few local outlets can grow as the diversity of retailing in general increases.

Government policy claims to promote competition, innovation and efficiency in retailing. However, the evidence suggests that faster innovation and greater efficiency characterise the largest retailers, and that their continued growth can lead to reduced levels of competition, especially at local level. Retailers' pleas for greater freedom from planning control and other types of government regulation are often worded as promoting 'competition', whereas in fact they may be seeking a more 'competitive' (i.e. dominant) position for themselves. At the same time, smaller retailers seek greater regulation in order to protect themselves from what they see as 'unfair competition'. In several European countries, independent retailers are protected by government regulation from some aspects of multiple retail aggression. This includes restrictions on large store development, enacted in specific legislation rather than operated indirectly through the land use planning system (Guy, 1998a; 2001; Davies, 2004).

In contrast, current and previous retail planning guidance in the UK contains no explicit protection for small-scale retailing. In addition, policy initiatives by other government departments and agencies to support market towns and local food supply chains (DEFRA, 2003b; AMT, n.d.) seem to have had little influence. The only apparent reference to these initiatives to be found in PPS6 is a statement of support for street and covered markets 'which can make a valuable contribution to local choice and diversity in shopping as well as the vitality of town centres and to the rural economy' (ODPM, 2005a: para 2.27); and a mention of 'locally-based food and other products' (ibid.: para 2.60). However it can also be argued that the lack of sensitivity in the planning guidance, which seems to encourage almost any kind of retail development within town centres, can worsen the plight of existing small-scale retailing.

It could be argued that these debates are of little importance to consumers, in that the growing predominance of large multiples has brought generally lower prices, wider choice of goods, and a better shopping environment. This is certainly the view expressed by the multiples themselves (Guy *et al.*, 2005), and the Competition Commission (2000a) came to the view that 'complex monopolies' existed but their untoward effects were not serious enough to warrant substantial government intervention (Hallsworth and Evers, 2002). However, the Portsmouth research suggests that consumers want access to a wide choice of types and locations of retail outlet (Kirkup *et al.*, 2004). So, development of new, efficient and innovative store formats is both welcomed and deprecated: the latter because it may lead to closure of older, less efficient stores.

Retail planning policy in the UK is also inconsistent, in that it supports innovation and efficiency in retailing, but since 1996 has sought 'flexibility' from retailers, which adds to their costs and means that the most efficient format cannot easily be rolled out (Guy and Bennison, 2006). It now appears much more difficult for a large-format innovative retailer to expand rapidly than was the case in the early 1990s.

Retailers have also claimed that retail planning policies are anti-competitive, because existing stores are protected from the effects of new, more efficient stores by development control criteria, particularly the 'quantitative need' requirement and the sequential test. As an example, a small supermarket with a limited range of goods and an unsatisfactory internal layout may survive within a town centre, because more efficient stores are prohibited in out-of-centre locations. Of course, the planning policy would not prevent such a store being developed *within* the town centre.

Planners, as well as organisations of small-scale retailers, have countered this argument by claiming that allowing large-format stores constitutes 'unfair competition', because the buying power of the multiples and the scale of the store allow cost savings which the small retailer cannot match. A further complication is that on occasion leading retailers appear to support increasing levels of restriction on new development, perhaps because it hinders the growth of rivals, particularly new entrants.

The new guidance is somewhat confusing, in that local planning authorities are required to consider the possible advantages of large-format stores, whereas the large-format store operators are required to consider a more 'flexible' approach involving development of multi-level stores and/or smaller sales areas (ODPM, 2005a; Guy and Bennison, 2006). However, a more important requirement is that large-format stores should, if built at all, be located within or at the edge of town centres. There are several issues to consider here: the following account lists briefly the main arguments, familiar from the experience of past public inquiries (Bore, 2001).

First, does this meet the requirements of large store developers? Evidence presented to the BCOTR survey (Guy and Bennison, 2002) suggests that in many cases, edge-of-centre sites are satisfactory for both single store and retail park developments. The main problem which can occur relates to vehicle access, particularly for goods deliveries. Operators need 24-hour access for large trucks, which may be prohibited in town centres. In addition, food retailers do not like to share car parking for their customers with other town centre users (Guy and Bennison, 2006).

Second, can edge-of-centre sites easily be made available? PPS6 encourages local authorities to consider assembling edge-of-centre sites, through compulsory purchase if necessary. This could raise substantial problems of cost and delay to the private sector, because local authorities have little recent experience of compulsory purchase procedures, and recent experience has shown that edge-of-centre sites are often difficult to assemble (Adams and Hutchison, 2000; DTZ Pieda, 2004b).

Third, are large stores in edge-of-centre locations an effective planning solution in other respects? Here it becomes difficult to generalise across different towns with different physical make-up. On the positive side, edge-of-centre stores can generate extra trade for town centres through 'linked trips', although evidence suggests that this effect may be slight in some cases (see Chapter 7). Stores can also form the basis for mixed-use developments including residential accommodation (Greater London Authority, 2004). On the negative side, large stores and their car parks are unlikely to blend with small-scale historic environments, will bring extra car trips into town centres and can form a barrier between the town centre and its residential surroundings.

Fourth, large store development within town centres also meets opposition from the environmental lobby. Planners are not supposed to discriminate between retailers, so they cannot for example protect a long-established local company against proposed new multiple stores, if these are to be located within town centres. In a small town centre, a large supermarket can have severe impacts on established food retailers. However, planning committees with sympathy for this view are hampered by retail planning guidance, which does not protect small retailers as such, and encourages almost any form of town centre development as long as it is of a 'scale' consistent with existing development.

Conclusions

This chapter has shown that the terms 'productivity' and 'competition' are not only difficult to define and measure, but also carry different meanings depending on which business or political interest is involved. Policies which are intended to enhance innovation and productivity in retailing may at the same time restrict competition in ways which are detrimental not only to existing business interests but also, arguably in some cases, to consumer welfare.

The government's concern for improved competition and productivity in the retail sector has for many years influenced the wording, and at times the application, of retail planning policy. Local authorities have been less enthusiastic over these matters, partly because the small retailer tends to have political support amongst councillors, and there is sympathy for long-established businesses which use local labour and local sources of supply of goods and services.

A consistently applied rule in planning policy generally has been that planning authorities cannot discriminate between private companies. This has, since 1972, given rise to government statements that competition between retailers or methods of retailing should be encouraged, leading to a rule that the potential trading impact upon individual retailers should not enter into the consideration of proposals for new development. This tradition that land use planning is 'neutral' between business interests is now seen as problematic by both business and environmental interests. Large-scale businesses see it as supporting inefficient traditional concerns, whereas small businesses and environmentalists see planning at the local scale as 'powerless' to resist the growth of large retailers (e.g. FoE, 2006a). Unlike many other European countries, there is in the UK no explicit protection for small retail and service businesses, and no provision for such businesses to be consulted on retail planning issues. The 'neutral' stance taken traditionally by land use planning means that it is unable to influence the nature of retail competition in a consistent manner.

This lack of clear guidance also reflects deep disagreements between not only pressure groups but also government interests. In the case of the preparation of PPS6, it is clear that representations from the Treasury pressing for greater retail productivity had some effect upon the eventual wording of guidance, particularly at the draft stage (ODPM, 2003). However, the 'local food' agenda of DEFRA seems to have been ignored in the guidance, possibly reflecting a lack of influence at political level. In addition, the notion that small businesses might legitimately ask for some protection against aggressive behaviour by multiple retailers, an issue frequently raised in Parliament by backbench Members, seems to receive no sympathy at Ministerial level or from the administrators who produce detailed policy.

Statements in retail planning guidance concerning innovation, productivity and competition appear to have little effect in practice upon planning policies or the control of development. Their purpose may be simply to remind planners that their actions – negative or positive – affect the economic performance of the retail sector, as well as the nature and extent of consumer satisfaction. The Competition Commission was probably correct in taking the view that planning policies or methods of control could not be easily adapted in order to improve economic performance or consumer welfare.

Chapter 7
Sustainability, shopping travel and retail policy

Introduction

This chapter examines critically the assumptions behind the 'sustainable development' agenda in retail planning, and reviews the evidence of shopping travel behaviour in an attempt to ascertain whether this agenda is realistic and attainable. The following broad questions are addressed:

- What does 'sustainable development' mean in the retail context?
- Can shoppers be weaned away from their cars?
- Does the 'compact city' ideal imply a more sustainable pattern of travel?
- Is the 'town centres first' policy more sustainable than a 'balanced' alternative involving both central and non-central development?

The current orthodoxy regarding sustainable development can be traced back to the early 1990s and in particular the revision of PPG13 in 1994 (see Chapter 4). These policies have become widely accepted within the planning profession as part of the 'sustainable development' agenda, in Britain and in continental Europe. However, they appear to rest upon several assumptions about the relationship between retail store location and shopping travel.

This chapter examines empirical evidence, drawn largely from the UK, to investigate to what extent these assumptions appear to be true. The next section explains in greater depth the views of policy makers, interest groups and academics on how retail planning and development should (or could) be made more 'sustainable'. This is followed by a review of empirical evidence on shopping trip patterns, examining travel to out-of-centre and town centre locations. The 'compact city' ideal is then reviewed in relation to retail development and shopping travel. Finally, some conclusions are drawn. It is suggested that existing retail planning policy is to some extent contradictory, and has probably been ineffective in reducing the environmental impacts of shopping travel. However, some current trends, particularly the growing substitution of telecommunications for shopping trips, show promise in reducing these impacts. These trends lie largely outside the control of official policy.

The issues for planning policy

As noted in Chapter 4, the early 1990s saw the establishment of 'sustainable development' as a guiding principle in land use planning. As explained in government publications at that time, this meant that any new development should be judged on the extent to which it was likely to consume non-renewable resources. In the context of retail development, two immediate implications could be drawn. First, new development should not involve irreparable loss of natural resources, implying that development on truly out-of-town sites used for agriculture or important for reasons of nature conservation should be prohibited. This policy was in line with existing Ministerial views on the undesirability of encroaching on 'green belts' (see Chapter 4). Second, new development should not add to the impact that transport (of all kinds) was already making on consumption of non-renewable resources, on air pollution, and (particularly) production of carbon dioxide, which was thought to be adding to the Earth's 'greenhouse effect' and climate change.[1] This second implication has become the major focus of debates on sustainable development in land use planning. The 'need to reduce travel' became a focus of debate. It was stated for example that:

> Sustainable development emphasises needs, not wants or desires. Transport policy should therefore have it roots in this needs-led approach: in short, we need to look at why and how we travel. ... land use changes ... have removed goods and service provision further away from where people live to locations primarily accessible by car. Only by reducing the overall length of trips, by encouraging public transport use when travel is necessary and by adopting a policy framework that gives walking and cycling precedence (within their limits) over other forms of travel can we possibly hope to shape a transport policy which minimises impacts.
>
> (Rawcliffe and Roberts, 1991: 310)

Underlying these ideas was a more general support for the 'compact city' as an ideal form of development (Commission of European Communities, 1990). This involved restriction of new urban development to existing urban 'brownfield' sites, high densities for new residential development, and mixing of land uses rather than strict zoning. These policies were expected to reduce transport energy consumption and thus intended to put the ideal of sustainable development into practice (Jenks *et al.*, 1996; for a sceptical view see Breheny, 1995).

The publication of PPG13 (DoE/DoT, 1994) was an important stage in the process of setting up land use planning policies which might reduce the need to travel. As part of this agenda, PPG13 proposed that the location of traffic-generating developments should be largely confined to existing centres, so as (a) to minimise the proportion of visitors using private cars, and (b) to avoid any increase in private car travel in the locality. It was also proposed that car parking provision should be controlled, in the interests of deterring 'unnecessary' car trips. It was hoped that these measures could form an important part of the government's commitment to reduce carbon dioxide emissions.

The land use planning policies proposed in PPG13 would, it was intended, help to reduce the need to travel in four ways (DoE/DoT, 1994; Banister, 1994):

- New development should be located where it is readily accessible by a choice of travel modes.
- New developments which have the potential to attract multi-purpose trips should be clustered together.
- New housing developments should include local facilities, in order to encourage walking and cycling trips.
- Traffic demand should be managed by planning authorities through control over car parking.

The first two of these policies led to an emphasis on town and district centres as the preferred location for retail development, as explained in Chapter 4. These centres are normally the focus of established public transport routes and hence are accessible to people who do not have the use of a car. Large stores (mainly food stores) which would not easily fit into traditional town centre environments should be located at the edge of the centre, accessible by foot from the main retail area (DoE/DoT, 1995: 74–5).

At that time it was assumed that these measures would be effective in reducing the amount of travel, especially by private car. An exercise in forecasting the 'possible economic effects' of PPG13 claimed that there would be 'a significant reduction in the distance travelled by car ... by consumers for most kinds of shopping and other service trips' (Land Use Consultants, 1995: 2). This was likely to occur in non-food retailing rather than food retailing (ibid.: 3).

The policies in PPG13 were welcomed by commentators, but thought by some to be insufficient to prevent the increasing use of private cars for shopping purposes. Banister (1997: 446) suggested that, as new developments were often accompanied by the closure of existing facilities, there should be a 'social audit' made for any proposed development. The costs to the community of both closures of existing facilities and the additional distance (if any) required to travel to the new facility should be weighted against the benefits of the new facility. In addition, local authorities could require the developer to guarantee that a certain proportion (Banister suggested 20 per cent) of all trips were to be made by transport modes other than the car. Failure to meet this target would result in a fine.

Along with many other writers, Banister (1997) also suggested that new residential developments should be at densities high enough to create viability for local services, and that facilities for walking and cycling within neighbourhoods should be improved. Both of these methods would divert some of the demand for shopping from more distant destinations for which the car was normally used, into local stores accessible through walking or cycling trips.

Two issues directly affecting retail development in town centres were raised in the report of the House of Commons Environment Select Committee (1994). It was claimed that there was '... a tension between PPG6 and PPG13 on the issue of car parking provision in town centres. PPG6 seeks to promote town centre vitality and development and yet PPG13 aims to restrict cars entering town and city centres' (House of Commons, 1994: para 28).

Despite the government's reply that these policies were not inconsistent (DoE, 1995a: para 45), this question has continued to be debated in the planning and town centres literature. Detailed guidance stated that:

> The importance of the provision of adequate car parking to support the vitality and viability of town centres is well recognised. The presumption should be that such car parking is allocated to, or favours in its pricing policy, short stay visits rather than long stay.
>
> (DoE/DoT, 1995: 75)

Secondly, the Committee raised the issue of food superstore location and the potential for 'linked trips' where such stores were located within or on the edge of town centres. The report quoted conflicting evidence on this question but recommended that:

> planning policy guidance be amended, to include a presumption that superstores are best located in or on the edge of town centres ... We believe that implementation of such a policy should help to reduce car journeys, as well as giving shoppers the opportunity to combine food and non-food shopping trips.
>
> (House of Commons, 1994: para 123)

Subsequent official guidance has accepted this view. Indeed, the provisions of PPG13 have changed little since 1994. It may be useful therefore to attempt to draw out the assumptions which appear to lie behind these policies. The final assumption is not usually stated in the planning literature, but seems to underlie much of the discussion:

- Out-of-centre retailing generates proportionally more car travel than similar retail provision in town centres.
- Therefore, building more out-of-centre stores will increase total car travel.
- Placing new retailing in town centres will reduce dependence on car trips.

- Building supermarkets in or close to town centres will encourage linked trips, therefore reducing total car travel.
- High density residential and mixed-use development will encourage local shopping and reduce car travel.
- Car parking should be restricted in order to discourage shopping trips by car.
- Public transport/bicycle/walking modes are seen by shoppers as appropriate for shopping trips:
  - essential for non-car owners
  - adequate for car owners.

The next four sections of this chapter summarise empirical findings on shopping behaviour in Britain, leading to an assessment of the assumptions listed above, in the final section.

Shopping travel in Britain

Large-scale surveys such as the National Travel Survey suggest that the average person carries out just under 200 shopping trips in a year, averaging over 4 miles and 17 minutes per trip. Since the late 1980s the number of trips has decreased, but the average length increased (see Table 7.1). However, after 2000, a more rapid decrease in the number of trips per person has led to a decrease in total distance travelled.

The majority of shopping trips are carried out by car, for both food and non-food shopping (Table 7.2). National Travel Survey data indicate that the average walking trip to shops is 0.6 miles return trip, whereas car trips average 5.2 miles (car drivers) and 6.8 miles (car passengers). For main food shopping, 76 per cent of people in 2002–3 preferred to use the car as their 'usual means of travel' (DfT, 2005a: Table 3.9). This was followed by walking (12 per cent), bus (8 per cent) and taxi (3 per cent).

Table 7.1 Shopping trips per person in Britain

	1989–91	*1992–4*	*1995–7*	*1998–2000*	*2002–3*
Number of trips	227	225	222	216	197
Number of miles	747	779	836	897	843
Average trip length (miles)	3.3	3.5	3.8	4.2	4.3
Average trip time (minutes)	16	17	17	17	17

Source: DfT (2005a: Tables 3.1, 3.2)

Table 7.2 Number of shopping trips per person by main travel mode, 2002–3

	Food shopping	*Non-food shopping*	*All shopping*
Walk	23	27	51
Car	58	65	124
Bus	7	10	17
Other	2	3	6
Average trip length (in miles, all modes)	2.3	5.6	3.7

Source: DfT (2005a: Table 3.8)

Most shopping trips are of over one mile and under ten miles (Table 7.3). Non-food trips tend to be longer than food trips. Comparison with previous surveys is difficult because of changes in definition. However, it is generally accepted that shopping trips have tended to increase in length. For example, average shopping trip length (based on trips of over one mile) rose by 14 per cent between 1985–86 and 1994–96 (Banister, 1999: 314).

A comparison with 1998–2000 data shows an increase in the use of cars for food shopping, and a decrease in walking trips (Table 7.4). There was little change however in the modal split for non-food shopping.

Research to be discussed below suggests that where stores or centres are provided with good facilities for car access and parking, then the car is overwhelmingly the favourite travel mode. Conversely, congested town centres with limited and expensive parking facilities may induce a substantial number of shoppers to use other means of transport, usually buses. It is also the case that those who cannot use cars tend to be an important source of custom for town centres. Unfortunately, little research has been carried out in the UK which would establish the circumstances under which the various transport modes are viewed as acceptable to the shopper, or how choice of mode influences shopping destinations.

Table 7.3 Shopping trips by purpose and length, 1998–2000

Distance (miles)	*Food shopping (%)*	*Non-food shopping (%)*
Under 1	32	26
1–2	22	14
2–5	29	26
5–10	12	17
10 +	6	17

Source: DTLR (2001: Chart 4.7)

Table 7.4 Percentages of shopping trips by main travel mode, 1998–2000 and 2002–3

	Food shopping		Non-food shopping		All shopping	
	1998–2000	2002–3	1998–2000	2002–3	1998–2000	2002–3
Walk	32	25	26	25	29	26
Car	58	64	63	61	60	63
Bus	8	8	8	9	8	9
Other	3	2	3	3	3	3

Source: DfT (2005a: Table 3.8); DTLR (2001: Table 4.11)

Qualitative research carried out in Sheffield reinforces the obvious conclusions that the car possesses powerful advantages over public transport, such as relative speed, comfort and flexibility in time and space (Ibrahim and McGoldrick, 2003). The disadvantages of car use – delays through traffic congestion and difficulties in parking – seem to be sufficient to deter car use only in traditional town centre environments.

Walking is clearly still an important means of access to shopping, valued for its low cost, flexibility and healthy image; cycling, however, hardly features at all in most British travel surveys, in contrast to some continental European countries.

Shopping travel and out-of-centre retailing

Much of the literature on sustainable development links the growth in 'out-of-town' shopping, particularly between about 1980 and 1995, with increases in shopping trip distances and use of the car, as noted above. This argument assumes that the new shopping opportunities have generally been more distant from people's homes than previously used destinations, and that (in some cases at least) people have switched travel mode from walking or public transport to car, in order to reach the new destinations more conveniently. It is also claimed that these trends have been inequitable, as shoppers who do not have the use of a car are unable to reach the 'out-of-town' stores, and are left with a degraded choice of local shops following the trading impact of the new developments.[2]

It is clear from many travel surveys that use of out-of-centre superstores and retail warehouses is dominated by car travel – typically over 90 per cent of shoppers arrive by car, with a small percentage arriving on foot and very few arriving by public transport or bicycle.[3] Research discussed in Chapter 8 indicates that some food shoppers who arrive on foot go home by taxi.

The proportion of car-borne shoppers is somewhat lower at regional shopping centres, reflecting their better quality of public transport provision. Usage of cars by shoppers at Merry Hill was measured in the early 1990s at 84 per cent, at the Metro Centre 79 per cent, and at Meadowhall 71 per cent, despite (in the latter two cases) good public transport service. This compared with Birmingham town centre (35 per cent) and Newcastle centre (38 per cent) (Tym, 1993: 30; Ibrahim and McGoldrick, 2003: 34).

The argument that new out-of-centre stores increase shopping travel is however rather simplistic. In the case of food shopping, since over three-quarters of households already use cars for main shopping trips, development of new stores is likely to result in redirection of such trips rather than the generation of new ones. Since many shoppers choose to shop at their nearest store, irrespective of its ownership, trips may on average be shorter where there is a higher density of food stores (Hay, 2005). A survey which compared food shopping destinations of car users living in areas of 'poor superstore provision' with those in areas with 'a good choice of stores' found that the former travelled 42 per cent further on average (Sainsbury, 1993: 13). Further evidence that increasing the provision of food stores, even where these are out of centre, tends to reduce total shopping travel is presented in Cairns (1995: 412–13); CBHP (1998: 30–3); and Banister (1999: 327–9). The latter source shows also that decreases in average trip length are compensated to some extent by increased trip frequencies, but the overall effect is still to reduce overall travel.

It has also been claimed that the largest stores – food or non-food – generate less frequent trips. There is evidence to support this view for food shopping (Cairns, 1995: 413–14). A comparison of very large (c.10,000 sq.m.) and smaller (c.4,000 sq.m.) stores operated by B and Q has shown that the large stores generate fewer trips, because of their superior range of items and lower likelihood of out-of-stocks (CBHP, 2002).

One issue which has received little attention in the transport literature concerns the structure of shopping trips which include visits to out-of-centre retailing. McIver (1999a; 1999b) has shown that conventional trip distribution models, used in transportation impact forecasting, tend to assume that such visits are made during single-purpose home-based trips. In reality, however, many visits take place as part of multi-stop trips, of which an important category is the journey home from work. Research on food shopping in Portsmouth shows that much food shopping takes place in this way, such that the location of the store visited is related to other trip destinations (shopping, work, social or leisure) rather than distance from the home (Clarke et al., 2004). Surveys carried out for B and Q (2002: 19) show that over 40 per cent of trips to these stores involved links with other activities – mainly non-food shopping.

In the case of both regional shopping centres and outlet centres, there seems more justification for the claim that new development leads to increased car travel. Surveys carried out in regional centres indicate very large catchment areas, with for example some 14 per cent of visitors travelling over one hour to visit the Cribbs Causeway centre near Bristol (The Mall, 2003). Such catchment areas are probably more dispersed than those found typically for city centres, although comparative data are difficult to find. Outlet centres probably also generate quite long journeys, although again, there seem to be no relevant published research findings.

Shopping travel and town centre retailing

The orthodox view is that retail development in town centres or district centres is more 'sustainable' than development elsewhere. This is because it is held to be less likely to attract car travel; and because it can generate a more efficient pattern of household activity, giving potential for multi-purpose visits at a single destination. Town centres are also becoming a focus for mixed-use developments which include substantial residential accommodation as well as retail and leisure uses.

Arguments supporting retailing in town centres as 'sustainable development' also tend to emphasise the contribution which new development can make to the vitality and viability of a town centre, as for example in guidance on the implementation of PPG13 (DoE/DoT, 1995: 74–9). This implies a wider definition of 'sustainable development' than that used in this chapter, although it is often claimed that reduced traffic volumes lead to a more pleasant town centre environment.

Two key questions need to be assessed against empirical evidence. The first is whether retail development within (or on the edge of) town centres creates less private car mileage, and environmental impact, than similar development elsewhere. The second is whether development of food stores or other large-format stores adds to town centre vitality and viability by creating 'linked trips'.

Travel characteristics of town centres

It is clearly true, in most cases, that public transport access is better in town centres than in suburban or edge-of-town locations. It is also likely that the town centre is the most accessible location by car over the town as a whole. However, this does not guarantee that use of cars or total distance travelled will be reduced.

In the case of food shopping, both Land Use Consultants (1995) and Cairns (1995) suggested that locating stores in or close to town centres would do little to reduce overall car travel. Data from surveys carried out at Safeway stores show that their town centre supermarkets tend to attract at least 80 per cent car trips (Hass-Klau *et al.* 1998: Table 26). Since households who cannot use cars for food shopping are most likely to use town centre stores, this percentage seems remarkably high and suggests that there is virtually no diversion of shopping trips into non-car modes amongst car users. In contrast, surveys of town centre supermarkets in inner London, such as that carried out in Camden Town (Warren and Taylor, 1991), have shown very low levels of car use (Hass-Klau *et al.*, 1998: Table 27). Such areas have special qualities which both deter car use (traffic congestion) and encourage public transport (high volume of services) or walking (high residential density). In more typical urban settings, supermarket customers would expect to be able to use the car. Indeed, research by Sainsbury (1993: 6) showed that 97 per cent of car-owning households 'used the car regularly for their main food and grocery shopping'.

Cairns (1995: 414) also suggests that any reduced use of the car for town centre food shopping is compensated by more frequent trips, so that overall mileage is unlikely to be reduced at all.

More generally, government publications (e.g. DoE/DoT 1995: 77) have stated that around 50 per cent of shoppers in town centres arrive by car, a figure apparently based upon a survey of eight town centres, reported in Donaldsons (1994: 10). Common sense and experience suggests that while main food shopping trips are least suited to walking or public transport modes, the proportions of these modes in other types of trip will be higher. This is partly because comparison goods such as clothing are more capable of being carried in a non-car journey.

Surveys suggest that those who travel to town centres for shopping purposes by car value the convenience and relative speed of the journey (e.g. BCSC, 1997: 10). In this survey of car-borne shoppers in five town centres, 77 per cent of those questioned agreed that public transport was an alternative mode for their journey, and 70 per cent 'considered that improvements to public transport would persuade them to use it' (ibid.: 11). Along with other studies, this research concluded that such improvements, along with improved access on foot and by bicycle, could reduce car use in town centre shopping.

A neglected question relates to the environmental impacts of car journeys to town centres. Common observation suggests that atmospheric pollution is higher than normal in town centres, and that town centre traffic is more subject to stop–start behaviour, and hence higher fuel consumption, than is the case in suburban areas. This indicates that a given length of car journey is likely to impose higher environmental costs when it takes place within a town centre.

Car parking provision in town centres

One of the major determinants of choice of travel mode is the availability and cost of car parking at the destination. The key question is whether restricting car parking space leads to fewer car trips, and whether the use of other modes is increased as a result. Government policy has been stated as follows:

The supply or pricing of car parking is a potential tool for influencing travel choices. By limiting parking provision, people may be encouraged to use other means of travel. By providing the right supply of parking for shopping and other town centre trips, the vitality and viability of town centres can be supported.

(DETR, 1998: Chapter 5)

However, it is not clear what is meant here by 'the right supply of parking'. Government statements have been criticised for inconsistency in this respect. The advice on implementation of PPG13 included the following:

The importance of the provision of adequate car parking to support the vitality and viability of town centres is well recognised. The presumption should be that such car parking is allocated to, or favours in its pricing policy, short stay visits rather than long stay. This represents a more efficient use of the available space.

(DoE/DoT 1995: 75)

On the other hand, the subsequently revised PPG13 stated:

The availability of car parking has a major influence on the means of transport people choose for their journeys. Some studies suggest that levels of parking can be more significant than levels of public transport provision in determining means of travel ... even for locations very well served by public transport. ... Reducing the amount of parking in new development ... is essential, as part of a package of planning and transport measures, to promote sustainable travel choices.

(DETR, 2001: para 49)

A feature of the practice literature on town centres has been a lack of consensus over car parking provision. The view of private sector interests, supported by most town centre managers, is that car parking which is adequate in scale not to deter shopping trips by car is necessary to maintain the competitive position of town centres in the face of competition from out-of-centre retailing:

Despite PPG13 which actively discriminates against the car, local authorities are still required by PPG6 to plan positively for car-borne shopping. Many shoppers will always shop by car and will continue to visit out-of-town facilities if they cannot gain easy access to town centres. Thus, city centres need to be more accessible by car, whilst encouraging those who travel by public transport and other modes of travel.

(BCSC, 1996: 10)

On the other hand, environmental interests wish to see car parking limited in order that shoppers will be persuaded to use other modes. In response to such views, the British Council of Shopping Centres commissioned research into 'the best way of reducing the number of town centre shoppers using their cars, without causing detriment to the vitality and viability of the town' (BCSC, 1997: 5). A literature review concluded that 'to date very little research has been carried out … previous research has proved largely inconclusive' (ibid.).

Linked trips in town centres

The third issue concerns the importance and nature of 'linked trips' in town centres. In the present context:

> The term is often discussed in relation to new retail developments and their potential to generate linkages with the near-by town centre. Once shoppers arrive at their major destination (e.g. a food store) a linked trip involves a trip on foot or by other mode of transport to an existing facility in the town centre. Such linkage could be measured either in terms of number of trips undertaken or by the amount of spend on the same trip.
>
> (OXIRM, 2004: 7)

Since the statement in the House of Commons (1994) report referred to above, government policy has consistently emphasised that generation of linked trips is an important argument in favour of the sequential approach:

> In the case of many smaller centres, particularly historic towns, the best solution may be an edge-of-centre foodstore with parking facilities, which enables car-borne shoppers to walk into the centre for their other business in town, and shoppers who arrive in the centre by other means of transport to walk to the store. One trip can thus serve several purposes, and the new shop is likely to help the economic strength of the existing town centre, be accessible to people without cars, and overall generate less car use.
>
> (DoE, 1996: para 3.13)

This statement was largely hypothetical, in that there was little empirical evidence available in its support. The Sainsbury survey suggested that 'only 11 per cent of car shoppers frequently buy durable goods on their main shopping trip' (Sainsbury, 1993: 14), but this figure included those who shopped at out-of-centre stores. Much higher proportions were reported in several surveys summarised in Hass-Klau et al. (1998: 36–41), although these were not measured on a consistent basis. A particular problem here is that town centre food stores (even where owned by the leading multiples) tend to be smaller and older than out-of-centre stores, and less likely to be able to fulfil main food shopping requirements. In addition, 'non-car customers usually make a higher number of shopping trips but buy a smaller quantity of goods at each visit, and clearly this type of shopping results in a higher number of linked trips' (Hass-Klau *et al.*, 1998: 38).

An example of empirical findings supporting the government's case may be found in the research on food store impacts in market towns, carried out for the DETR (CBHP, 1998: Table 20). Here, 'linked trips' ('particularly within the town centre', otherwise undefined in the report) were recorded as varying from 25 per cent to 65 per cent for out-of-centre stores across nine survey areas, whereas town centre stores recorded between 64 per cent and 79 per cent.

Policy statements enthusing over linked trips tend to assume that established patterns of shopping would be replicated when newer forms of development are brought into town centres. It is important therefore to compare linked trip generation between similar types of store in town centre and out-of-centre locations, and amongst car users.

Findings from another survey of Sainsbury shoppers suggest that proportions of linked trips for town centre stores are higher than those for edge-of-centre or district centre stores, although again it is not clear whether all the stores in this sample were of similar size (see Table 7.5). The low proportion for edge-of-centre stores does not give much support for government advice.

The most extensive analysis of linked trips lies in an unpublished report carried out for Tesco by Bennison *et al.* (2000).[4] This research, based on telephone surveys of 33 areas surrounding proposed Tesco stores, showed that, as in other surveys, linked trips were more likely to occur in the case of town centre stores, smaller stores, and for non-car users. When other shopping carried out in the same store[5] was ignored, it appears that no more than 8 per cent of visits to out-

Table 7.5 Linked trips in use of Sainsbury stores

Location	Number of stores in sample	Shoppers taking goods home by car (%)	Visiting a non-food shop on foot in same centre (%)	
			Car shoppers	Non-car shoppers
Major town/ city centre	6	34–68	25–48	22–50
District centre	5	40–94	1–19	10–28
Edge of centre	6	68–84	5–14	15–28

Source: Hass-Klau *et al.* (1998: Table 31). Based on exit surveys of c.1,000 shoppers at each store, carried out in 1994–96 (presumably includes both main and secondary food shopping trips).

of-centre stores involved a linked trip, compared with a maximum of 12 per cent for edge-of-centre stores, 9 per cent for stores in district centres and 22 per cent for stores in town centres (see Table 7.6). The authors note however that town centre stores tend to be smaller than those in other locations, hence a 'store size' effect partially explains the differences in rates of linked trips.[6]

This exercise concluded that:

> The project has also shown ... that in absolute terms, the volume of linked activities represented in particular by non-food purchases was relatively small given the overall number of trips recorded in the database: for example, only a quarter of all users of stores in or near town centres undertook a linked trip where a non-food purchase was recorded. Even for smaller stores located in or near town centres, the spin-off benefits to other traders may not be very substantial, especially if most of these purchases are for smaller items such as newspapers.
>
> (Bennison *et al.*, 2000: 46)

There is thus considerable difference between the high proportions of linked trips noted in the DETR supported research (CBHP, 1998), and in other studies supported by major food retailers. Variation in the survey method used and in the wording of questions may account for much of this difference.

The surveys also indicate considerable differences in the propensity of linked trips, between one store or town centre and another. The DETR report concluded that:

Table 7.6 Linked trips by location of food store and type of other destination visited

Type of destination	Town centre store	Edge of town centre store	District centre store	Out of centre store
Bank, post office, etc.	22	12	7	7
Other food store	15	6	6	6
Non-food store	21	12	9	8
Window shopping	10	6	4	3
Other services	3	2	2	2
Sports/entertainment	5	4	3	3

Source: based on Bennison *et al.* (2000: Tables 3.4, 3.7 and 3.8–3.13)
Note: All numbers are per cent of all main trips to that type of food store. Petrol purchases excluded from data, as are transactions made at the store already visited for main food shopping. Based upon main food shopping trips only.

The propensity to undertake linked trips depends on four interrelated factors:

- the extent to which the store complements the town centre/district centre;
- the distance and physical linkages between the two;
- the relative size of the centre as compared with the store;
- accessibility, parking and orientation of the store.

(CBHP, 1998: 10)

One way in which to study the effects of new food store development in town centres is through repeat surveys of shopping behaviour and attitudes, similar to those used in research on trading impact. Surveys carried out in Llanelli, south Wales, show that the development of an Asda superstore as part of a covered town centre shopping mall increased pedestrian flows within the town centre and improved shoppers' opinions of the centre as a whole (Bromley and Thomas, 2002). However, the surveys revealed no evidence of increased town centre sales of clothing or of DIY goods, indicating that linked trips based around the Asda store were doing little to improve the town centre's economic viability.

Summarising this diverse range of material, it appears that the extent of linked trips from town centre food stores will depend upon several factors, including the size of the store (the smaller the better), its distance from the main retail area, and the quality of the retail area itself. The most common form of linked trip appears to be a visit to a cash point or other source of personal finance. Whether town centre food stores attract shoppers who would not otherwise have gone to the town centre at all is an unanswered question. We also have little knowledge of the propensity for non-food stores (for example, in retail parks) to generate linked trips.

Shopping travel in the compact city

One of the key concepts in urban planning in recent years has been the 'compact city'. This concept idealises the 'traditional' European city, characterised by a relatively dense residential environment interspersed with mixed-use commercial developments, and promotes this as a model for sustainable development. Reviews of the concept and its applications can be found in Jenks *et al.* (1996) and Williams *et al.* (2000), while Gordon and Richardson (1997) and Neuman (2005) provide a sceptical view. Despite these doubts over the validity and relevance of this concept in an age of increasing personal mobility, the 'compact city' is embedded as an ideal in European Union policy for spatial planning.

It is often stated that the compact city will generate fewer car-based trips than a more typical twentieth-century suburban environment:

there are a number of concepts of planning and design aimed at reducing car-travel kilometres. Car-travel reduction can be achieved through three strategies:

(1) by mode shifting from car to walking, cycling, and public transport; (2) by reducing trip distance; and (3) by reducing the total number of trips. What the land-use concepts outlined above have in common is that they seek to reduce travel distances and to increase the share of public transport by increasing the population base for public transport. Situating residential, employment, and service locations closer to each other is generally assumed to reduce the distances which need to be covered. It is expected that the shorter travel distances will result in a reduction in the total number of kilometres travelled, an increase in the possibility of linking more destinations in one trip ('trip chaining'), and an increase in the attractiveness of walking and cycling in place of using the car. Higher densities are assumed to improve public transport use because distances to public transport stops are shorter.

It is assumed that, when nearby destinations are added to the choice set, average travel distances tend to get shorter because these destinations will be chosen rather than more distant ones. Moreover, as travel distances are shorter, individuals are assumed to be more likely to choose to travel by foot or by bicycle.

(Maat *et al.*, 2005: 37)

Maat *et al.* (2005) show however that these notions appear rather simplistic when examined in the light of theories of household travel behaviour. Nearby destinations may be ignored, in favour of more distant but more satisfactory alternatives: this is particularly the case with shopping trips in which 'individuals may maximise their utility by opting for a more distant destination in order to get higher quality, greater choice, or cheaper products' (ibid.: 37). In addition, time saved by visiting nearby destinations or carrying out multi-purpose trips will then be spent on other activities, which may themselves involve further travel. They conclude that the case for reducing car travel simply through 'compact city' measures is uncertain, although there is a case for improving the attractiveness of walking and cycling through 'slow mode friendly designs' which reduce speeds for motorists. It follows that road congestion, which is more likely to occur in high-density cities, will also discourage car travel.

Other writers distinguish between the 'need to travel' and the 'desire to travel':

Discussion about compact cities or alternatives to them often focuses on reducing the 'need to travel', by arranging land uses so that residents can live closer to jobs, shops, schools and other destinations. The effect of such changes depends on the degree to which residents actually travel to the nearest job, shop and so on. The preference for going to the nearest destination was very weak in 1990 [in the authors' research in the Bristol area] and will be further weakened by increasing car ownership. ... where travel costs are fairly low relative to incomes, and where there is a wide diversity of jobs, housing and so on, ... the value of ... going to a particular shop ... far outweighs the additional costs of the extra travel.

(Simmonds and Coombe, 2000: 124–5)

International comparisons of large cities have shown that more densely populated cities tend to show lower rates of car use and shorter trips (e.g. Newman and Kenworthy, 1989). The same applies within Britain, in that conurbations such as Liverpool, Glasgow and inner London show shorter aggregate distance travelled per person compared with other urban areas, and especially with small towns and rural areas (Barrett, 1996). Generally, denser residential areas tend to generate shorter travel distances in total (Barrett, 1996; Banister, 1999). However, much (although not all) of this variation reflects differences in socio-economic characteristics. Land-use characteristics in themselves appear to have only minor effects upon aggregate distance travelled, and some, including 'proximity to high street shops, bus stop or railway station ... do not have a clear, consistent or significant link with travel distance per person' (Stead, 2001: 506). There is evidence from the National Travel Survey that people living within three minutes' walk of local facilities (defined as post office, chemist and grocer) travel less distance than the average (ibid.: 512). Similarly, research comparing two areas of similar socio-economic profile and residential density in Cardiff found that in the older area where there were more shops, secondary food shopping tended to be more frequent and involved less use of the car. However, there was little difference in frequency or travel mode for main food shopping (Van and Senior, 2000).

It should be remembered that older high-density areas such as inner London benefit from a dense pattern of commercial uses, reflecting the availability in the past of cheap commercial premises, and until recently at least, relatively low personal mobility. This means that some trips, for example to a chemist or post office, are usually shorter than in less dense or more modern residential areas. It does not necessarily follow that new residential areas populated by busy car-owning families will generate less car travel if they are more densely developed.

There appears to have been no empirical research to compare shopping travel behaviour between newly developed areas at different residential densities. Research carried out in new privately built residential areas around Bristol shows that, not surprisingly, distance travelled to supermarkets, post offices, newsagents and food shops tend to be shorter in areas where these facilities have been provided (Farthing *et al.*, 1996; Winter and Farthing, 1997). However, the incidence of cycle trips in this survey was negligible, and walking trips to shops 'were much less likely' amongst car-owning households than non-car owning (ibid.: 186). The conclusion drawn was that 'The evidence from the research described here does not support the assumption in recent policy advice that increasing the local availability of facilities (and therefore their accessibility) per se will have a significant impact in encouraging walking to those facilities' (Farthing *et al.*, 1996: 188).

Evidence from North America, reviewed by Crane (1996), suggests that providing easier access from residential neighbourhoods to local facilities tends to raise the frequencies of trips, for both car and walking modes. Hence, total car mileage may even increase.

The research discussed in this section generally supports the view that land use planning, including 'compact city' measures, are unlikely in themselves to affect patterns of shopping trips, except possibly to encourage walking for minor food and convenience shopping. This prognosis assumes that the balance between costs of transport, and the perceived benefits of larger and more distant shopping opportunities, remains roughly as at present, and also that there is no major improvement in public transport facilities.

Discussion and conclusions

In a report to the Royal Commission on Environmental Pollution, it was shown that, contrary to the expectations of the early 1990s, land use planning had had only limited success in achieving sustainable development. Trends such as the growth of population in small towns and rural areas, and centralisation of services and facilities, were leading to resource depletion and increasing use of private car travel (Bartlett School, 2004). Closure of small shops, increasing use of edge-of-town supermarkets, and poor provision of facilities in new residential areas, were all stated to contribute to these trends (ibid.: 3). This recalls the arguments of Breheny (1995) and other earlier writers who warned that powerful forces of decentralisation of population and commercial activity were well established and likely to continue in the foreseeable future.

Evidence from National Travel Surveys and other sources confirms that the use of cars in shopping trips, and average distances travelled, have increased during the 1990s and early 2000s. The causal link between this trend and the increasing use of out-of-centre shopping destinations is however difficult to discern. Orthodox wisdom tends to hold retail trends to blame for increasing car use. However it can be argued that the reverse applies. Increasing car use – itself a result largely of increasing car ownership – favours shopping destinations which are easily accessible and possess good quality car parking, preferably free to the user. This has triggered the steady growth of such facilities. Research shows that for some types of shopping trip, for example main 'trolley shopping' trips to food stores, it is very unlikely that car users can be persuaded to change to walking or public transport. For other types of trip, for example 'basket' shopping for convenience goods such as newspapers and chemists' items, short-distance walking trips remain predominant.[7]

It can be argued that government policy since 1994 has actually encouraged an increase in shopping travel by car. First, by restricting the development of out-of-centre superstores and retail warehouses, trips to these destinations – which are overwhelmingly made by car – have tended to be longer than would be the case had development continued at previous rates. This is because these stores tend to offer standardised bundles of goods and services, such that many shoppers visit the nearest store irrespective of its ownership. This hypothesis was supported in surveys summarised by Cairns (1995), and can be demonstrated in simulation exercises such as in Hay (2005). However, there appears to have been no empirical research examining specifically the travel impacts of new store openings, since the early 1990s.

Second, policies which favour town centre retailing have helped developers to modernise and expand the retail areas of several of the largest town and city centres, thus attracting more and more shoppers, as discussed in Chapter 4. This is likely to have increased car travel, through shoppers abandoning small nearby town centres in favour of much longer trips to larger town and city centres. Despite problems of city centre congestion and parking, many shoppers – especially where travelling in groups – will prefer the car to the less flexible and (perceived) more expensive alternative of public transport. These extra trips also generate relatively more pollution than do trips to out-of-centre stores, through the effects of stop–start travel in congested streets, and queuing for parking spaces. Other measures to improve the attractiveness to shoppers of town centres, including short-stay car parking and park-and-ride schemes, may generate more car journeys (Marshall, 1999).

Thus, retail planning policy does not seem to have been effective in achieving one of its main goals, despite its significant effects on patterns of retail development. One of the weaknesses in policy formulation appears to be the assumption that observed patterns of behaviour, based around historic development trends, can be expected to continue as a consequence of appropriately designed new residential and/or commercial development. For example, observation suggests that many older high-density residential areas have an attractive mix of local shops and services, and generate many walking trips. However, commercial realities make this level of provision very hard to achieve in new residential areas, no matter how high the density. And typical residents of new residential areas may be more inclined to use cars than do residents of older inner city areas.

Given that reduction of 'greenhouse gases' and other pollutants should remain a key element of planning policy, the question arises whether means can be found to achieve these goals through land use planning. Some methods often suggested by commentators can be appraised briefly.

Imposition of car parking charges

One measure often suggested by pressure groups, and supported by the House of Commons Environment Select Committee (1997: para 38), has been to impose car parking charges for out-of-centre shopping. It is claimed that this would allow a 'level playing field' between out-of-centre and in-centre destinations, the motive being to enhance the competitive position of town centres rather than to reduce car travel. The government response was that:

> Research commissioned by the then Department of Transport and by others does not support the Committee's conclusion that the price of parking is the pivotal factor in determining whether people choose to shop in town centres or out of town.
>
> (DETR, 1997: para 35)

As a result, measures allowing local authorities to impose charges for parking at out-of-centre locations have not been introduced. In practice, it seems likely that out-of-centre retailers would refund car parking fees to the customer, provided that a minimum level of expenditure were made. However, the overall effect might be to reduce the frequency of car-borne trips.

Improvement of public transport

The evidence reviewed in this chapter indicates that improving public transport links with large food stores and most retail parks is likely to have little effect upon modal split. This is because these destinations serve 'trolley shopping' purposes for which the car is ideal. Casual observation suggests that the free bus services provided by some food store operators are largely used by elderly customers: it is not known whether these shoppers could have visited the store by car. On the other hand, there is evidence that improved public transport can generate greater use for town centre shopping, and probably this applies also for the largest off-centre developments in which there is a substantial fashion and leisure offer.

Alteration of shopping habits

Another possible way to reduce the increase in car use would be to persuade shoppers to carry out less trolley shopping and more basket shopping (suggested as a 'fourth solution' by Cairns, 1995). There is some evidence from the Portsmouth research (Clarke *et al.*, 2004) that this is happening, in the case of busy households who have to fit shopping trips into a complex pattern of daily activity. And an increasing proportion of new homes are being provided within or close to town centres, allowing good access on foot to a wide variety of shopping and leisure opportunities.

However, simply providing local shops (or trying to prevent small local shops from closing) does not in itself stimulate a more 'sustainable' pattern of shopping activity. In the case of convenience goods, small shops do not offer the variety and price savings found in larger stores, and the superstore will usually attract car trips no matter how close it is to the home. It is also unlikely that, except where residential densities are very high, small shops can be economically viable on the basis of walk-in trade generated locally, as shown in a North American context by Bartlett (2003). The evidence from research in areas of social exclusion, discussed

Table 7.7 Assumptions and evidence in transport policy relating to retail development

Assumption	Evidence-based conclusion
Out-of-centre retailing generates proportionally more car travel than similar retail provision in town centres.	Generally true
Therefore, building more out-of-centre stores will increase total car travel.	Not true in areas where other out-of-centre stores of similar type already exist
Placing new retailing in town centres will reduce dependence on car trips.	Not true for superstores or retail warehouses; not true for larger developments if they attract long distance trips
Building supermarkets in or close to town centres will encourage linked trips, therefore reducing total car travel.	Will encourage linked trips, but unlikely to reduce total car travel
High density residential and mixed-use development will encourage local shopping and reduce car travel.	Unproven
Car parking should be restricted in order to discourage shopping trips by car.	Unproven
Public transport/bicycle/walking modes are seen by shoppers as appropriate for shopping trips: • essential for non-car owners • adequate for car owners	Generally untrue in present circumstances

in Chapter 8, indicates that small local convenience shops often struggle even in areas of very low car ownership.

The second part of the 'fourth solution' suggested by Cairns (1995) was the development of on-line shopping, which would reduce the need for car trips, especially for food. More recent evidence suggests that a pattern of goods delivery of remotely ordered goods by dedicated vans is more efficient in terms of total travel than the normal pattern of store visits by private car (Cairns, 2005). However, not all on-line purchases substitute for store visits; and the use of time released through on-line shopping may generate more travel.

Shopping travel to the larger town and city centres also offers the potential to reduce car use, since the disincentives afforded by congestion and parking fees are at their strongest here. The development of more flexible, pleasant and fast public transport would appear necessary to achieve the modal splits typical of many continental European cities.

Finally, the evidence discussed in this chapter can be related back to the implied assumptions behind government policy, discussed earlier. The limited selection of research findings applicable to the UK are fairly consistent. As summarised in Table 7.7, only weak support (if any) can be made for most of these assumptions. There is however clearly a need for further research in many areas.

Chapter 8

Social exclusion, access to shopping and retail policy

Introduction

This chapter concerns the plight of those who, for various reasons, find access to routine shopping opportunities difficult. For many years one of the main justifications for retail planning has been that the free operation of the market is likely to leave some geographical areas, and parts of the population, inadequately served (Davies, 1984). Retail planners should therefore attempt to identify inequalities in access, and consider ways in which planning intervention could overcome such problems.

Retail planning guidance has since the 1970s recognised that a substantial part of the population is likely to have a restricted choice of retail outlets, because of their restricted 'mobility'. This term may signify some physical disability or weakness which prevents the person from walking more than a short distance or using public transport. More commonly, it signifies lack of access to a private car for shopping purposes. In some areas lack of mobility is made worse by a lack of good quality shopping opportunities within easy reach of the home. The resulting 'disadvantaged consumer' became in the 1980s an important topic in retail planning discussions, and the orthodox view was that such people could not easily benefit from the growing number of large stores and centres which were designed for car users. Since the arrival of a Labour government in 1997, the issue of poor access to shopping has been revived as part of a wider discussion of 'social exclusion' and the development of policies for 'social inclusion'. These terms have now entered the vocabulary of official retail planning guidance.

This chapter first examines what is meant by the terms 'social exclusion' and 'disadvantaged consumer', and their relationship with the longer-established research and policy focus on 'social deprivation' and 'areas of multiple deprivation'. The related but separate question of physical access to shopping opportunities is then examined. The recent 'food deserts' debate and policy initiatives are assessed. Finally, elements of retail planning policy which attempt to address these problems are evaluated.

Social exclusion and social deprivation

The government has defined social exclusion as 'a shorthand term for what can happen when people or areas suffer from a combination of linked problems such as unemployment, poor skills, low incomes, unfair discrimination, poor housing, high crime, bad health and family breakdown' (ODPM, 2004: 4); and:

> Social exclusion happens when people or places suffer from a series of problems such as unemployment, discrimination, poor skills, low incomes, poor housing, high crime, ill health and family breakdown. When such problems combine they can create a vicious cycle.
>
> (ODPM, n.d.)

Social exclusion became a key issue for the Labour government after its election in 1997. It was felt that the social policies of previous governments had exacerbated the relative poverty of the most deprived sections of the population, and the encouragement of sales of local authority-owned housing had marginalised those who could not take advantage of this policy. They were increasingly confined to areas characterised by poverty, unemployment, poor living conditions and health, and crime. People living in such areas were often stigmatised and found it difficult to obtain financial credit or employment. Although this phenomenon had already been recognised and described in terms such as 'multiple deprivation', the new term 'social exclusion' emphasised the view that people were being excluded from opportunities to improve their social and economic position, partly through living in a particular area.

The remedy therefore lay in policies of 'social inclusion', in which areas of social deprivation would be targeted in various ways. A Social Exclusion Unit was formed within the Cabinet Office, and during 1999, 18 Policy Action Teams produced reports on various aspects of social exclusion and ways in which social inclusion could be fostered. These reports led to the production of an Action Plan for Neighbourhood Renewal. This promised a 'vision that, within 10 to 20 years, no-one should be seriously disadvantaged by where they live' (Cabinet Office, 2001: 8).[1]

This exercise led to policies aimed at helping various disadvantaged groups. Some of these policies were related to specific 'disadvantaged areas', in which Local Strategic Partnerships were set up. These emphasised 'community-based approaches' rather than simply top-down distribution of extra funding. In England, the 88 most deprived local authority areas have received such initiatives.

The government's justification for this 'area-based' approach is that access to employment opportunities, services etc. varies geographically, and people can be disadvantaged simply through living in the 'wrong' area:

The causes and consequences of social exclusion cluster in particular areas, with the same areas tending to have the highest levels of disadvantage across a number of policy areas – for example in employment, education, housing, or health. Clear inequalities exist between different areas of the country and between different neighbourhoods within these areas. Difficulties are compounded where there are poor services such as fewer shops, poorly performing schools and fewer doctors' surgeries. ... A large proportion of those where the head of household is either unemployed (33 per cent) or economically inactive (29 per cent) live in the 10 per cent most deprived wards. This means that targeted area-based policies can help reach those at risk of social exclusion, though it is important to recognise that many disadvantaged people lived outside deprived areas.

(ODPM, 2004: 5)

As indicated in this statement, not all people living in areas of social exclusion are 'deprived', or have poor access to urban facilities. Equally, not all people with poor access are 'socially excluded' in a more general sense, nor do they all live in areas of social deprivation.

'Disadvantaged consumers' and 'food deserts'

It has been recognised for many years that considerable variations exist in accessibility to shopping. In part this is inevitable, because shopping tends to cluster geographically, and many people live in areas of low residential density in which it is not economically viable to have a dense network of convenience stores or local services. However, problems occur when a poor level of accessibility to shops is compounded with some form of personal disadvantage, such that travelling to shops becomes difficult.

The term 'disadvantaged consumer' appears to have arisen first in the late 1970s. A study of the Newcastle-upon-Tyne area commissioned by Tesco identified disadvantaged consumers as those in one or more of the social groups shown in Table 8.1; and also a much smaller group of 'neglected consumers' who found access to any form of shopping very difficult (Davies and Champion, 1980). This study found that about 25 per cent of the population of the Tyneside area could be classed as disadvantaged consumers, and about 3 per cent as neglected consumers. The latter included those suffering from severe physical handicaps, mothers of large numbers of young children, and families with bedridden relatives.

The RTPI Working Party (RTPI, 1988) categorised the 'disadvantaged shopper', in ways which are shown in Table 8.1 (see also Westlake, 1993 and Piachaud and Webb, 1996). Clearly these categories are very broad, and not all members of any such group in any typical urban setting would regard themselves as disadvantaged. Inclusion in two or more categories (for example, mother of

Table 8.1 Definitions of the 'disadvantaged consumer'

Davies and Champion (1980)	*RTPI (1988: 32)*
Head of household in unskilled manual employment	Low income earner
Head of household unemployed	
Large young family	Those with caring responsibilities, including young children or elderly relatives
Absence of a car	Those without access to a car for routine shopping trips
	Residents of locations poorly served by public transport
Elderly	Elderly
Physically disabled or infirm	Disabled and others with mobility problems
	The young
	Ethnic groups

young children in a low income household without a car) is much more likely to create disadvantage.

In the 1970s and 1980s, many female shoppers did not have driving licences, and it was less common for married couples to undergo joint shopping trips (Bowlby, 1984). As a result it was frequently asserted (for example, by Hillman, 1973) that new developments such as hypermarkets, which appeared to cater solely for those who could drive to the shops, were socially regressive. The sizeable minority of shoppers excluded from this new form of shopping by lack of mobility had to rely on a dwindling selection of small supermarkets or convenience stores which were close to home or accessible by public transport.

Further research showed that households who did not regularly use a car for shopping tended to rely upon local shops or district shopping centres for convenience purchases (Guy, 1985; Bromley and Thomas, 1993; 1995). These studies all demonstrated that lack of a car was the most important determinant of use of local shops, although other aspects of 'disadvantage' such as old age or low income were of some importance. Research in Swansea indicated that many such households wished to visit hypermarkets or large DIY stores, but were unable to do so because of the stores' inaccessible locations at the edge of the city (Bromley and Thomas, 1993).

More recent surveys confirm that a majority of disadvantaged consumers use local and district centres rather than free-standing superstores for main food shopping. In a survey carried out in 1999 of 503 adults, all in Social Classes D and E, some 43 per cent owned a car: these respondents were twice as likely to use an 'out-of-town supermarket' for their main shopping, and had more positive views about the advantages of such stores. However, the majority of the entire sample preferred to use 'local supermarkets' (58 per cent) and 'local corner shops/convenience stores' (41 per cent) (Robinson *et al.*, 2000). Families with children were particularly prone to using local shops (ibid.: 125). Asked what factors prevented use of food stores offering lowest prices and widest range of goods, 31 per cent of the sample stated they were 'too far away', 17 per cent mentioned lack of a car, and 15 per cent mentioned inability to 'carry home all the shopping' (ibid.: 129). Similar results were obtained in a survey of households living in deprived areas of Coventry: those households with one or more 'disadvantages' (approximately as indicated in Table 8.1) tended to use district centres the most often for main grocery shopping (Williams and Hubbard, 2001: 276).

As car ownership and licence holding amongst women has grown, and the cost of owning and running a car has decreased in real terms, the proportion of households who cannot easily use cars for shopping has steadily dwindled. In 2004, 74 per cent of households in Great Britain had access to a car, and 61 per cent of women aged 17 and over possessed a full driving licence (DfT, 2005b: Section 2). Extended opening hours in superstores and retail parks allow access by car in the evenings and at weekends, when the family car is unlikely to be used for work purposes. A survey of 1,900 adults representative of the population of Great Britain, carried out by the market research company MORI, showed that 90 per cent of people interviewed would be able to get to out-of-centre shopping if they needed to, and only 1.6 per cent of those interviewed needed to shop out-of-centre and could not get there by car (MORI, 2000). These findings indicate that many households without cars are in fact able to use cars for shopping. An earlier study of the isolated community of Ystalyfera (South Wales) also showed that some households without cars still ignored local shops for grocery purchases, and travelled some 15–20 km further in order to use superstores (Bromley and Thomas, 1995).

Qualitative studies, discussed below, throw some light on the apparent paradox that shoppers without cars can still gain access to somewhat remote superstores. Informal arrangements involving relatives or friends with cars are commonplace. Where the superstore is within a reasonable walking distance, shoppers can walk there and return home by taxi.

In the late 1990s the new policy focus on 'social exclusion' led to attention being focused particularly on housing estates built on the edges of towns and cities by local authorities since the 1940s. Here, the local centres originally built by local authorities had declined in quality, leaving in many cases a poor shopping environment with little or no food available within easy walking distance of the home (Speak and Graham, 2000).

The term 'food deserts' was coined by a working group for the Department of Health's Nutrition Task Force (Beaumont *et al.*, 1995) to describe such areas, and was soon being used somewhat uncritically in government pronouncements (Cummins and McIntyre, 1999; 2002a; 2002b; Wrigley, 2002). The research discussed below indicated however that poor access to food shopping was not confined to local authority housing estates. Remote rural areas generally have the poorest perceived levels of choice between outlets (Fitch, 2004), and probably the poorest quality and variety of food (see for example Skerratt, 1999), although they have been researched less in this regard than have urban areas.

The convention grew that a 'food desert' is an urban area which lacks adequate food shopping facilities within a certain distance – usually said to be 500 m – from people's homes. Definition of 'adequacy' may vary, but a single small shop selling little or no fruit and vegetables is not usually seen as an adequate outlet. In more detail:

> There appear to be five primary features that characterize a 'food desert' and the population that live in them:
> 1. The residents will be physically disadvantaged in terms of mobility and accessibility.
> 2. They will also be economically disadvantaged, as they will generally be low-income earners.
> 3. This will mean that they will have poor nutrition/diet, as they will generally eat cheaper, more filling foodstuffs than traditional meat/fruit/vegetables.
> 4. They will be geographically disadvantaged because of the lack of choice of food stores in their area.
> 5. Local stores will only supply limited selection of foods, at higher prices than do larger superstores.
>
> (Guy and David, 2004: 223)

Much of this new wave of research emanated from the health and food science professions, and was driven by a long-standing concern for affordability of good quality food:

> It is well recognised that the problems of food poverty go beyond individual lifestyle factors: access to, availability and affordability of good quality food all contribute to food poverty. Whereas affordability has been the focus of much of the earlier research, either in relation to the adequacy of welfare benefits, or the price of food, more recently the issues of store location and access to food have been highlighted.
>
> (Reisig and Hobbiss, 2000: 138)

It was thus claimed that poor levels of access to sources of good quality food was exacerbating the poor levels of nutrition frequently observed in areas of social deprivation:

> [There is] considerable evidence that income and resources (including transport and access to a car) affect food behaviour ... There is little point in encouraging low-income consumers to eat more healthily if their district has inadequate local food suppliers and if shops which do offer a choice are located inconveniently for socially disadvantaged groups such as single parents, women, the elderly, disabled individuals and the poor who tend to have worst access to cars and transport.
>
> (Lang and Caraher, 1998: 203)

Unlike the earlier research by geographers which typically investigated shopping behaviour in space, and viewed lack of access to modern large-format retailing as an issue of social inequality, the new focus was on consumption of food – especially 'healthy' foodstuffs such as fruit and vegetables – and spatial variation in its availability within urban environments. Exercises carried out in London (Donkin *et al.*, 1999a; 1999b) and Sandwell, West Midlands (Dowler *et al.*, 2001) identified all points of sale of food products, including specialist food retailers, market stalls, small general stores and even petrol filling stations. Lists were made of the foods available and (sometimes) typical prices. In this type of exercise, detection of the presence of 'food deserts' is usually carried out by identifying areas of housing which lie more than a given distance (often 500 m) from any adequate source of food.

The incidence and nature of food deserts in British cities has recently been examined thoroughly in three separate studies. Two of these, the Economic and Social Research Council/J Sainsbury sponsored study of Leeds, Bradford and Cardiff, and the Department of Health sponsored study of Glasgow, examined accessibility to food shopping across these entire cities. In Leeds/Bradford and Cardiff, accessibility was generally poorest in peripheral local authority housing estates, as expected (Clarke (G.) *et al.*, 2002). However, low accessibility also typified some high-income areas. The Glasgow research showed that generally, low-income areas had better access to low-priced food than the average across the whole city, confirming previous research which showed that the density of food stores, both multiples and independents, was higher in low-income areas (Cummins and McIntyre, 1999; 2002a). A third study, carried out in Newcastle, showed that:

> A shop selling any five of the 33 surveyed food items was within easy walking distance (250 m) of almost all residential streets in the city. However, some parts

of the city were further than 1 km from a shop selling ten 'less healthy' food items or ten fresh fruits and vegetables. People who shop at local and convenience stores, and to a lesser extent discount supermarkets, appear to be the most disadvantaged with respect to availability of food items.

(Food Standards Agency, 2004: 2)

The findings in Newcastle and Glasgow match the wider analysis undertaken by the Competition Commission, which in its report on supermarket competition, concluded that

There is no systematic link between the locational strategies of supermarket operators and restricted access to groceries ... supermarkets are not systematically avoiding low-income urban areas, nor do they appear to be exacerbating any isolated problems of grocery access that might exist by withdrawing from those areas.

(Competition Commission, 2000a: vol.2, 314)

Research in Cardiff, which examined supermarket openings and closures over a 12-year period, suggests however that there was some tendency for closures to occur in the more socially deprived parts of the city. This process exacerbated the already existing differences between adequately and poorly provided areas. Closures tended to be in the smallest multiple-owned stores, several of which were in areas of deprivation. This appeared to be due to rationalisation of operations rather than any discriminatory action by the multiples (Guy *et al.*, 2004).

These studies all had the objective of examining possible relationships between poor accessibility to food shops, and incidence of unhealthy diets. In every case the authors have stated that this relationship, if it exists at all, is statistically weak. In the case of Newcastle, 16 per cent of the sample of households usually did their main food shopping on foot, and 'this group of individuals ... did have a relatively poor diet, including low fruit and vegetable consumption' (FSA, 2004: 2). However, even in this group, 'the main determinants of a healthy diet were dietary knowledge, age, lifestyle behaviours and socio-economic factors' (ibid.). Similar results were obtained in the Seacroft, Leeds investigation within the ESRC-funded study (Wrigley *et al.*, 2002b).

It has become clear from these studies and other research that 'physical access' – the ability to travel to shops where good quality food is available at reasonable prices – should be distinguished from 'economic access' – the ability to afford such food. Some 'healthy' food items – particularly where advised as part of a specialist diet – are seen as expensive; others may be rejected by family members with the result that food is wasted. 'Unhealthy' food is regarded as cheaper and more satisfying.

Food poverty thus appears to be associated with a combination of demographic and socio-economic factors, attitudes to diet and nutrition, and behaviour including amount of exercise and alcohol and tobacco consumption. Physical accessibility to food shops seems to be of minor importance in affecting rates of consumption of healthy foods. Analysis of the effects of the opening of a Tesco hypermarket in Seacroft, Leeds, during the study period shows that intake of fresh fruit and vegetables showed an improvement amongst those shoppers who chose to visit the new store and previously did not use a Tesco store for their main shopping (Wrigley *et al.*, 2003). However, a further study conducted along similar lines in Glasgow has failed to identify more than a very slight effect of this type (Cummins *et al.*, 2005a; 2005b). A study of elderly shoppers in Guildford, Surrey by Wilson *et al.* (2004) found no statistical association between the variety of types of food in their diet, and measures of shop type mainly used or of the perceived convenience of their main food outlet.

Other, more qualitative studies have reinforced the view that a combination of low income and attitudes towards diet and health are largely responsible for deficiencies in nutrition amongst households in socially deprived areas. These studies also confirm the view that most such households prefer to carry out most or all of their food shopping in supermarkets and superstores. In order to travel to these stores, people who do not possess a car often rely on lifts from friends and relatives, or use taxis. Small shops close to the home are often ignored as they are considered to be of poor quality (Whelan *et al.*, 2002; Wrigley *et al.*, 2004; Hitchman *et al.*, 2002). However, some differences occur between age groups with respect to both typical diets and the use of traditional shops. In the Leeds study, the elderly tended to visit the nearest district centre by bus, using both supermarkets and specialist food shops, rather than visit the nearest superstore (Whelan *et al.*, 2002). This recalls the findings of previous quantitative research (see above).

Much less research has been carried out into access to *non-food shopping* in areas of social deprivation. Physical access to shopping opportunities is perhaps less important than economic access. Research by Williams (C.) and Windebank (2000; 2002) indicates that many low-income families tend not to use shops at all for some goods, but obtain them through friends and relatives or through second-hand and charity shops. This finding was however disputed by Williams (P.) and Hubbard (2001) in their study of shoppers in Coventry.

Intervention in areas of deprivation: government and private sector initiatives

The government's interest in the research discussed above was initiated largely by the Independent Inquiry into Inequalities in Health, which found that people in lower socio-economic groups were likely to have poorer quality diets. One reason for this lay in difficulties in accessing good quality food, especially fresh fruit and vegetables:

> the increasing tendency to out of town supermarkets has led to the creation of 'food deserts' where cheap and varied food is only accessible to those who have private transport or are able to pay the costs of public transport if this is available.
>
> (Acheson, 1998: 65)

This report went on to recommend '... policies which will increase the availability and accessibility of foodstuffs to supply an adequate and affordable diet ... [and] which will ensure adequate retail provision of food to those who are disadvantaged' (ibid.: 65–6).

In response, the Department of Health stated that 'The Government wants everyone to be able to make healthy eating choices. Some deprived neighbourhoods are characterised by lack of easy access to shops that will sell food at reasonable prices' (Department of Health, 1999b: 29).

Research into access to shopping in areas of social exclusion was carried out as part of the Social Exclusion Unit's wider remit (see above). The report by the SEU's Policy Action Team 13 (PAT13), which included civil servants and outside experts, described the serious difficulties faced in some areas of social deprivation, by both retailers and shoppers. The recommendations addressed mainly the problems faced by retailers, particularly regulatory pressures and the fear of crime. It also suggested that local authorities should set up surveys to identify areas of poor access, and formulate 'local retail strategies' (Department of Health, 1999a). The full list of recommendations is summarised in Table 8.2.

Table 8.2 also lists several government initiatives which were begun after the report's publication, although some of them resulted from subsequent investigations, particularly the DTI's Retail Strategy Group (2004) report. It is noticeable that one key recommendation – establishment of a 'neighbourhood retailing task force' – does not appear to have been taken up. This is perhaps a symptom of a general lack of government support for the independent retail sector at local level.

Following the publication of PAT13, the 'food deserts' issue was mentioned in further government statements and Ministerial speeches:

> I want to see planners put more emphasis on developing local solutions to solve problems of social exclusion from services. This will involve defining the food shopping needs of local people within a retail strategy and identifying 'food deserts' – areas that lack retail services within say a 500 metre radius.
>
> (Hughes, 2000)

Table 8.2 Recommendations of PAT13 Report, and follow-up activity

Actions	Detailed recommendations	Follow-up activity
Explore potential of local retail forums in developing local retail strategies		Some instances in London boroughs and other metropolitan areas
Government should set out a more proactive approach to planning for community needs at the local level	Aim to regenerate local centres in deprived neighbourhoods, involving the community Range of services should be grouped together Discourage provision of large new food stores outside major centres Local authorities should promote mixed-use developments and residential use above shops Government should explore potential for use of Section 106 agreements Agencies should be established to refurbish local shops in poor condition	PPS6 (2005)
Give much higher priority to tackling neighbourhood retail crime		Home Office, Small Retailers in Deprived Areas Initiative (2001) Local Crime and Disorder Reduction Partnerships
Improve business support for small retailers		Small Business Service (2000) Better Regulation Task Force, Report on Small Shops (2001) Action Against Business Crime (2004)
Establish a scheme to provide guaranteed loans for retailing services of social strategic importance		
Ease business burdens on small retailers	Explore simplification of compulsory purchase order system Fiscal measures to help start-ups Encouragement of more supportive role of private landlords Flexible approach by local authorities where acting as landlords	Planning and Compulsory Purchase Act (2004)
Ease regulatory burdens on small retailers		Retail Policy Forum (2004)
Establish a neighbourhood retailing task force to champion the voice of neighbourhood retailing at a local, regional and national level		

Source: summarised from Department of Health (1999a: 13–19); DTI (2004)

Further such exhortations followed (see Wrigley, 2002; Wrigley *et al.*, 2003). However, the PAT13 report was not followed by further government investigation or detailed policy formulation; although the research projects mentioned above in Leeds/Bradford/Cardiff, Glasgow, and Newcastle all received direct or indirect funding from government sources.

The PAT13 report considered ways in which the private and voluntary sectors could initiate improvements in the quality of food shopping in areas of social exclusion. It recommended that the main initiatives should be directed towards improving local shops. The report recognised the generally poor quality of fresh food offered in such outlets, and the difficult conditions under which their owners traded. It recommended that locally based partnerships of private sector and voluntary organisations should be formed in order to set up better quality local shops which would supply an adequate range of fresh fruit and vegetables, as well as the usual convenience selection. The Co-operative and Mace retail organisations agreed in principle to help fund any such initiatives under the banner of Community Owned Retailing. Their belief was that:

> retail spend within even small communities is enough to support micro-economies and neighbourhood-based shops. The task is to ensure this spend is retained within the community by moving local retailing from the second division – the place for top-up, convenience or distress purchases – and make it a primary shopping destination.
>
> (Peters and Lang, 2000: 4)

However, despite support for this organisation in the PAT13 report and subsequent government statements, only two stores were developed by Community Owned Retailing. More significant have been several 'food co-ops', which are run by volunteers in areas of social deprivation, and aim to supply healthy foods at reasonable prices. It is not clear how many such projects have existed at any recent point in time, but earlier research suggests that many co-ops and other 'food projects' struggle to survive (McGlone *et al.*, 1999).

The PAT13 report virtually dismissed the role of major food retailers in assisting food poverty and poor levels of access. It stated that:

> Most of the bigger retailers we spoke to said that the size of the neighbourhood we were focusing on, around 3,000 to 4,000 households, was too small to commercially sustain one of their conventional supermarkets. Population density was generally too low, servicing access was often inadequate and there was generally insufficient customer parking space to attract significant custom from outside the neighbourhood. Nevertheless, all the major retailers we spoke to expressed a willingness to contribute expertise.
>
> (DoH, 1999a: 25)

This advice did not fully reflect efforts already being made by some retailers to establish large new stores within, or close to, areas of social deprivation. An early example was the development of an Asda superstore which was co-ordinated with the redevelopment of the Hulme estate in inner Manchester (Carley *et al.*, 2001: 58–62). There followed several redevelopments by food retailers of existing district centres in outer city housing estates, such as the Tesco Extra store at Seacroft, Leeds, and the J Sainsbury store at Castle Vale, Birmingham (Carley *et al.*, 2001). These are discussed further in Chapter 9.

In 2002 the Social Exclusion Unit was moved to the ODPM, and a new government-funded initiative – the Underserved Markets project – was set up in order to place major retailers and developers more in the forefront of social inclusion policy. Experience from North America had shown that some urban areas, although characterised by poverty and social problems, nevertheless showed scope for new retail and leisure development. In effect, commercial developers and retailers had negative perceptions of such areas and would not consider developing there without convincing evidence of their potential. The Underserved Markets project, administered and part-funded by the charitable organisation Business in the Community, investigated the possibilities for retail development within the 88 most deprived wards in England. Using methods pioneered in the USA, the retail analysis company Experian identified 12 local authority areas which demonstrated a wide range of demographic profiles and local authority attitudes to retail development. From this base, it was hoped to bring into being four pilot projects involving actual retail development. Rather than simply replicating the work of the food retailers mentioned above, these projects could involve more complex designs to include comparison goods retailing and possibly leisure and residential uses. In its preliminary report the project concluded that

> The freeing of future development sites for retail investment in deprived areas within the context of Government policy on town centres and the promotion of social inclusion is crucial to the success of the project. It depends largely upon a mutual understanding of the benefits retail can bring. Retailers must learn actively to promote the benefits they offer, beyond jobs, and the public sector to do more to promote and to encourage the potential of retail-led regeneration.
>
> (BITC, 2004: 3)

The project team investigated several possible schemes for improving retailing within the 12 areas. However, it became clear that the private sector could not be expected to carry out large-scale projects in deprived areas without support from local authorities or other public sector agencies. The second phase of the project – initiation of four 'investment pilots' – has apparently been delayed by difficulties in working with the relevant local planning authorities (Walker, 2005). These problems indicate that, while food deserts can be treated through one-off developments of either large food stores or local volunteer activity, a generally poor retail and leisure environment within an urban area is much more difficult to remedy.

Retail planning policy and social exclusion

From the 1970s onwards, official policy for retail planning recognised that many consumers would not easily be able to reach the new superstores and retail warehouses because of their lack of mobility. The first version of PPG6, while generally supportive of out-of-centre developments (see Chapter 3), warned that:

> not everyone has the use of a car … Their needs must continue to be catered for by easily accessible shops, especially those smaller shops that cater for a wide range of day-to-day needs among all sections of the community. Where possible, large new stores, especially those selling convenience goods, should be located where they can serve not only car-borne shoppers but also those who rely on other forms of transport.
>
> (DoE/WO, 1988a: para 6)

Also in 1988, the RTPI's Working Party identified two basic issues. The first was the difficulty faced by many elderly and/or mobility handicapped shoppers in entering and circulating within shops and shopping centres. They suggested that local planning authorities should monitor the situation and ensure that adequate arrangements were made in newly built stores and centres. The introduction, in 2004, of measures in the Disability Discrimination Act has now in effect made these recommendations mandatory. The Working Party also suggested that new retail developments should include adequate seating and toilet facilities.

The second group of recommendations related mainly to households without the use of a car. The Working Party recognised the advantages of modern large stores, but recommended that 'existing and proposed shopping areas' should include 'a full range of service uses and community facilities such as chemists, post offices, dry cleaners, health centres and libraries' (RTPI, 1988: 36). This would enable those without cars to obtain maximum benefit from their shopping travel.

These sentiments were reflected in subsequent versions of government guidance, which by 1996 required developers of new retail facilities to encourage access by public transport, walking and cycling. One of the four main objectives was 'to ensure the availability of a wide range of shops, employment, services and facilities to which people have easy access by a choice of means of transport' (DoE, 1996: para 1.1). However, there was no specific reference to areas of social deprivation in PPG6, or the corresponding Welsh and Scottish guidance.

The genesis of policy to address the plight of people living in 'food deserts' and other poorly served areas arose from the Cabinet Office and Department of Health (see above), rather than the Environment Ministry. The latter's first recognition of this issue appears to have been in a speech by the then Planning Minister Nick Raynsford:

> Tackling social exclusion is the next main task for retail planning policy – to provide access to shopping for all. ... The [PAT13] report ... highlights the need to change the way we plan for local shopping, and, in particular, the need for local retail strategies – a bottom-up approach, based on ensuring access to local shops. ... This will require a much more positive and proactive approach to local planning, with the policies and the local retail strategy being developed in partnership with the local community.
>
> (Raynsford, 2000: 5–6)

This was followed by a statement by the then Minister for Regeneration and Regional Development in the ODPM, at a conference relating to the Underserved Markets Project:

> To date, planning policy has mainly been seen as a regulatory tool – to protect existing centres and to stop out-of-centre development. Our sequential test in the planning policy on town centres and retail (PPG6) ... was too top-down and gives insufficient attention to the needs of local communities. A more positive approach is required to deliver the goods (literally) for deprived communities. Planning which will respond directly to communities' needs – finding local solutions in partnership with the private sector and all stakeholders.
>
> (Rooker, 2004: 5–6)

Lord Rooker also claimed that 'As yet very few development plans acknowledge the gaps in provision and the special needs of deprived communities' (ibid.: 6). Cannings (2001: 304) in a review article supported this view but also noted that PPG6 'contains little guidance on the importance of enhancing the vitality and viability of smaller neighbourhood centres'. The analysis of recent Local Plan and Unitary Development Plan statements, discussed in Chapter 4, found little evidence of the 'proactive' policies sought by ODPM. More typical are vague statements of 'support' for smaller centres, together with rather negatively worded development control policies which seem intended to prevent rather than stimulate change.

A further deficiency in the wording of PPG6 was that 'local centres' were not specifically protected through the sequential approach. This meant that if the impact of a new development would fall mainly on a local centre, the developer could argue that this was not contrary to planning policy. Also, a developer's proposal for new retail development which was in or close to a local centre could be interpreted as 'out-of-centre' by the planning authority, and refused on this basis. PPG6 classified local centres as 'small groupings' of 'small shops' (DoE, 1996: Annex A), thus implicitly denying possibilities for any upgrading.

However, the new emphases on social inclusion and underserved markets produced substantial changes to retail planning policy, bringing it more into line with mainstream government thinking on tackling disadvantage. It appears that pressure was placed on ODPM, between the draft and final versions of PPS6, to include several mentions of 'social inclusion' as a policy objective, and advice on actions that local authorities should take.[2]

Thus, one of the government's 'wider policy objectives' is now 'to promote social inclusion, ensuring that communities have access to a range of main town centre uses, and that deficiencies in provision in areas with poor access to facilities are remedied' (ODPM, 2005a: para 1.3). Local planning authorities are advised that, 'where deficiencies are identified in the existing network of centres, new centres may be designated through the plan-making process, with priority given to deprived areas' (ibid.: para 2.7). Furthermore,

> Deprived areas often have poor access to local shops and services. To tackle this problem, local authorities should work with the local community and retailers to identify opportunities to remedy any deficiencies in local provision. This is likely to be best achieved through strengthening existing centres or, where appropriate, proposing new centres.
>
> (ODPM, 2005a: para 2.56)

However, the term 'local retail strategy' does not actually appear within PPS6, despite its inclusion in Ministerial speeches. The policy remains that 'Local centres will generally be inappropriate locations for large-scale new development' (ODPM, 2005a: para 2.42). This reflects the importance of 'appropriate scale' as one of the main criteria for the location and size of new development (see Chapter 4).

At the time of writing, official Welsh and Scottish policy makes no explicit reference to social exclusion or to local retail strategies. The most recent Welsh guidance merely suggests that 'further allocation' of retail and leisure development could be justified if 'it would alleviate a lack of convenience provision in a disadvantaged area' (NAW, 2005: para 10.2.10).

There appears to be no published review of local authority planning policies which address deficiencies in access to retail goods and services. An internet search (made in November 2005) indicates that a few local authorities, mainly in conurbations, have attempted some form of local retail strategy. In the absence of government guidance, a publication by the Food Strategy Unit of the London

Development Agency gives probably the most detailed indication of the steps local planning authorities can take in these respects, although confined to food access rather than retail as a whole (see Table 8.3). These suggestions replicate to some extent existing practice and official advice, but are valuable in stressing the need to establish links with local health and regeneration agencies.

Discussion

Despite all the research findings discussed in this chapter, we still do not have a clear overview of problems of access to shopping. 'Food deserts' appear to occur

Table 8.3 Actions planners can take to improve food access

Consultation with residents and local businesses	• Consult the local community • Consult the retailers
Mapping and monitoring	• Identify food deserts • Monitor change • Assess food poverty • Liaise with health agencies to monitor health inequality
Support for existing and new neighbourhood food retail outlets	• Go into partnership with large retailers • Research and support street markets and farmers' markets • Get involved in crime reduction initiatives • Promote mixed-use developments • Protect neighbourhood shops from changes of use • Improve transport and physical access • Provide facilities for food co-operatives • Involve local businesses in surveys
Support for community food projects and educational activities	• Allow use of council-owned and vacant premises
Using Section 106 agreements	• Consider food access as an area worthy of support through agreements • Work in partnership with health and regeneration agencies • Identify infrastructure improvements

Source: summarised from LDA (2005: 18–31)

in many urban areas, although their geographical extent and significance for health policy may have been exaggerated (Cummins and McIntyre, 2002b). We also do not know to what extent the expansion of multiple retailing and large 'category killer' stores has made life worse (or better) for people in socially deprived areas who face difficulties in accessing routine shopping.

A second unanswered question is what sort of retail provision is most appropriate in areas where a significant minority of people find difficulties in their routine shopping trips. Basically, three possible solutions exist:

• Provide all-purpose supermarkets or convenience stores at regular intervals, so that they are accessible on foot from residential areas. This is the situation which usually exists in the relatively high-density areas developed in British towns and cities before 1914. This model of small centres located within walking distance was also applied in the early post-war New Towns and other residential developments (see Chapter 2). However, it is doubtful whether sufficient numbers of viable stores, large enough to sell a reasonable variety of fresh foods, can be developed today within modern low-density environments. Research carried out in a suburban area of Cardiff which does include several convenience stores shows that firstly, these stores have only a limited selection of 'healthy foods', often at high prices (Guy and David, 2004); and secondly, for many residents, no store is accessible within 500 m walk along the rather tortuous road system (Guy, 2004b). The result is that most of the area's residents use these stores relatively little and prefer to make longer trips to larger stores elsewhere (Rubin, 2005), a pattern also found in Seacroft, Leeds, prior to the opening of the Tesco Extra (Wrigley et al., 2002b).

• Develop large food stores on the Seacroft model, to serve deprived areas for all types of food requirements and some non-food. This solution undoubtedly benefits those residents living close to the store, and in the Seacroft and Glasgow cases was found to substantially reduce average trip lengths and increase walking trips, a desirable outcome in transport planning terms (Wrigley et al., 2003; Cummins et al., 2005a). However, some residents will live beyond a reasonable walking distance, and the new store may force smaller local stores to close (Clarke (G.) et al., 2002). This solution is likely to be more controversial in planning policy terms, as official guidance requires new development to be in 'scale' with the existing size and nature of the centre concerned (ODPM, 2005a: paras 2.41–2.42).

• Improve public transport, in order to make supermarkets or superstores outside the residential area more accessible. The PAT13 report did not discuss this possibility, apparently because 'transport' was outside its remit.[3] Many superstores already offer free bus services, although examples known to the author tend to run only in off-peak periods of the daytime, and in any particular residential area there may be only one service per week. The government expects local transport authorities to carry out exercises in 'accessibility planning' for deprived areas in their Local Transport Plans (Cabinet Office, 2005a: 110–11). This involves 'a systematic assessment of whether people can access local services' (ibid.). Transport authorities are also encouraged to consider 'innovative solutions' in this respect. There is no mention of such policies in PPS6.

Two further partial solutions, which lie outside the remit of local authority planners, but could co-exist with any of those above, should be discussed. The first is to develop 'local food projects', which may include food co-ops and various 'healthy eating' initiatives, usually developed by volunteers working within urban neighbourhoods or rural villages. As noted above, these can achieve good results in the short term, but tend to be fairly ephemeral in nature as they rely upon transitory funding mechanisms and the willing participation of local volunteers. It is unlikely that a national network of local food projects could be organised or maintained satisfactorily.

The second partial solution is initiate a programme to extend the use of internet shopping to deprived households. A survey shows that 52 per cent of all households in the UK had access to the internet from their homes in July 2005. Only 39 per cent of those aged 65 and over had ever bought anything online, compared with over 50 per cent in other age groups (ESRC, 2005). Another SEU report states:

> Financial savings can be achieved using ICT. According to research by UK online centres, over a third of the UK population is needlessly paying up to £283 per year extra for everyday goods and services simply because they are not using the Internet. A challenge undertaken in Northumberland to provide a family of four with healthy food, including fresh fruit and vegetables, on a budget of £35 a week found that even with delivery charges it was cheaper to shop online through a major supermarket than use local shops. However, this raises the issue that many people on lower incomes may not have access to debit or credit cards to make online purchases.
>
> (SEU, 2005: 32)

Despite this positive observation, there appears at the time of writing to be no official support for on-line shopping. The SEU report explains the barriers to use of on-line services typically faced by low-income and elderly people, including low educational attainment, lack of knowledge of computers, and inability to obtain credit or even banking facilities. A number of past initiatives which facilitated the use of early versions of on-line shopping and services were set up by local authorities with the assistance of multiple retailers, notably the Gateshead Shopping and Information Service (Davies, 1985). These all came to an end when public sector funding was eventually withdrawn. However, many public libraries now have portals which allow access to the internet.

Following pressure from retailing and urban regeneration interests as well as the food poverty lobby, retail planning guidance (in England) is now concerned with the improvement of access and choice within areas of deprivation. However, the role of local authorities remains unclear. They are expected to assess 'where deficiencies exist in the provision of local convenience shopping and other facilities which serve people's day-to-day needs' (ODPM, 2005a: para 2.58). But there is no official guidance on how to do this, nor is any imminent at the time of writing. The suggestions included in the LDA's (2005) report (Table 8.3) are sensible, but mainly represent potential rather than actual good practice, and would require substantial resources of staff time.

It is still not clear to what extent local authorities even consider social exclusion to be relevant to retail planning policy. The cautious reaction to the work of the Underserved Markets project (see above) shows that local authorities are not generally sympathetic to any expressed need for retail-led regeneration outside town centres. And, despite the advice in PPS6, few local authorities appear to be interested in consulting ordinary shoppers about deficiencies in their local retail system.

Conclusions

This chapter has reviewed issues relating to social exclusion and shopping. Concern for the 'disadvantaged shopper' existed long before the recent debates on food deserts. Research carried out by geographers in the 1980s and 1990s in low-income areas indicated a consistent pattern of reliance largely on district centres for main food shopping and some comparison shopping, together with frequent visits to local centres and corner shops for topping-up purposes. As the numbers of small local shops continued to decline, more and more shoppers who appeared to be disadvantaged through lack of personal transport nevertheless managed to shop at superstores, in order to take advantage of lower prices and a wider range of goods. However, many shoppers, especially the more elderly, continue to prefer smaller supermarkets and the traditional urban district shopping centre.

A widespread concern in the late 1990s over diet, health and nutrition attempted to establish a link, if rather tenuous, between public health policy and retail planning policy. It was felt that the increasing difficulties faced by some shoppers living in areas of disadvantage were partly responsible for the poor levels of nutrition which were found to be typical of such areas. The resulting research programme has made it clear however that offering better access to good quality food is only a minor contributor towards improving the levels of nutrition and health amongst the poor and underprivileged in our society. Nor is it reasonable to blame the expansion of multiple food retailing for the worsening of problems in some areas, or to assume that the answer lies simply in improving the small-shop sector. It has to be remembered that most shoppers living in areas of social deprivation welcome the growth of superstores and make every effort to do at least some of their shopping in them.

Most commentators now agree that improving diet and health in areas of deprivation requires a multi-sector approach, with local health boards leading the way. The contribution of land use planning to this endeavour is likely to be fairly limited. A more appropriate role for retail planning would seem to be the improvement of poor quality retail facilities generally, to the benefit of the surviving businesses and the local population. Current policy guidance is sympathetic to this ideal, but does little to assist local authorities to take steps in this direction. Certainly it is not sufficient simply to include vaguely worded policies in development plans which aim to 'support' local and district centres.

Chapter 9
Urban regeneration and retail policy

Introduction

This chapter explores the links between urban regeneration and retail planning policy. It does not attempt to describe in full the regeneration process or the physical outcomes of urban regeneration programmes where these have included a substantial retail component. The main emphases are firstly, to explain why urban regeneration has often been linked with large-scale retail development; and secondly, to discuss relationships between retail-led regeneration and broader retail planning policies, as presented in earlier chapters. Since most retail development associated with urban regeneration has been out-of-centre, according to the strict definitions used in retail planning guidance, the resulting tension between the official guidance and the regeneration imperative forms a major focus for this chapter. The question whether the social and economic benefits of retail-led regeneration are as significant as proponents claim is also examined.

'Regeneration', in the present context, means broadly the physical (re)development or 'renewal' of land already used for urban purposes: such land is usually termed 'brownfield'. There is a strong connotation of reviving the local economy and providing new jobs, through the development itself, through linkages with existing firms, and through stimulating further (re)development.

In the retail planning context, the term 'urban regeneration' has become increasingly used to describe almost any development project which uses land already developed, within or outside town centres. Such land may typically have been used for manufacturing industry, wholesale distribution or transport purposes, and is generally derelict or partially derelict, and often contaminated by the waste products of previous uses. Where outside town centres, physical access by roads and public transport may be of poor quality, and other infrastructure such as drainage or electricity supply may need improvement. Many parts of Britain still have so many such areas requiring regeneration that it is unreasonable to expect all activity to be funded by the public sector. In such circumstances, those responsible for regeneration will wish to attract occupiers who are prepared to undertake some of the physical remediation, or provide advance funding.

The experience of the last 25 years or so indicates that retail development has often taken place as part of an urban regeneration agenda, in some cases providing the initial input of capital which is required to upgrade sites for further development. Until recently, discussion of 'retail-led regeneration' referred mainly to sites lying outside town and district centres. In the 1980s and 1990s, retail innovations including regional shopping centres, retail parks and factory outlet centres all made good use of previously derelict urban sites. More recently, town centre redevelopment, whether of retail or non-retail sites, has often been termed 'regeneration'. While this type of regeneration is generally in compliance with retail policy, issues relating to the nature and size of such developments, as well as their broader economic effects, still need to be examined.

These trends have reflected the involvement of a widening selection of retailers in regeneration schemes, and the emergence of regeneration as a key issue in the retailers' public presence:

> The retail sector has an important role in helping to tackle deprivation and interlinked problems such as unemployment, poor skills, low incomes, poor housing, high crime, bad health and family breakdown. We can give socially excluded groups the chance of a living and working environment in which they can thrive. We can help create new markets and regenerate and revitalise towns and cities across Britain.
>
> (BRC, 2004)

The chapter proceeds as follows. The next section explains why retail development is often a key feature of urban regeneration schemes. This is followed by a discussion of the frequent incorporation of hypermarkets and other very large stores in such schemes. This in turn has identified a lack of clarity over the significance of 'regeneration' as a key element of retail planning policy. Regeneration schemes in town and district centres, which are generally more consistent with overall policy, are then briefly reviewed. The final sections discuss some controversies over the role of retail development in urban regeneration, and draw some conclusions for policy formulation.

Retail-led development in urban regeneration

Urban regeneration schemes take place for several reasons, including physical (improve the appearance of an area), economic (provide land for new or relocated economic activity), and social (provide employment opportunities and community facilities). Provision of new retail facilities is not usually a prime motive for regeneration: standard texts on urban regeneration (e.g. Roberts and Sykes, 1999) devote little attention to retail development as such. However, many regeneration schemes do include a substantial amount of new retail development.

Schemes involving retail development tend to be examples of what Turok (1992) has termed 'property-led urban regeneration'. He states that such schemes aim to create economic regeneration through property development, in five possible ways:

- Through construction activity, providing temporary jobs and household income;
- Through indigenous growth, whereby the new buildings accommodate expanding firms;
- Through inward investment, whereby property attracts incoming firms;
- Through neighbourhood revitalisation, in which physical improvement makes the place more attractive to residents and encourages further investment; and
- Through local economic restructuring, as a result of further investment and economic diversification.

These arguments were particularly attractive to Conservative politicians in the 1980s as they encouraged private sector developers to take an active part in regeneration. The Urban Development Corporations, set up in decaying inner areas of British conurbations, were particularly important in promoting property-led regeneration (Imrie and Thomas, 1999). Within such schemes, retail development often assumed a leading role. The basic reason for this tendency lies in land and property values. Retail uses usually provide the largest uplift in land values, reflecting an overall scarcity of available space compared with other employment uses, especially manufacturing industry, where a surplus of land is more likely to be the case. According to the Competition Commission (2000a), land with planning consent for retail use in the late 1990s was typically valued at between £1m and £3m per hectare, compared with well under £1m for residential or industrial use (see Table 9.1).

A second reason is that funding for retail development is usually readily available, either from a major retailer's cash flow, or from financial institutions in cases where development is carried out by property companies (Guy, 1994a). Retail park development in particular has been very attractive to developers in the last 15 years or so, because of increasing planning restrictions on such development (see Chapter 4). This availability of funds means that a retail development is often used to 'kick-start' broader regeneration schemes: for example in the former Cardiff Bay Development Corporation area, as summarised in Table 9.2. In each case, the retail component was the first to be developed on site, and the developer either purchased their site outright or paid for infrastructure improvements, leading to further office and residential development in the Tesco examples (Wrigley *et al.*, 2002a: 2106).

Table 9.1 Comparison of land costs in UK (£'000 per hectare)

Land use	Land cost
Food store (Asda, Safeway, Sainsbury, Tesco, Waitrose)	1,500 – 3,300
Food store (other leading multiples)	500 – 2,000
Retail warehouse	1,100 – 2,700
Industrial use	180 – 520
Residential use	330 – 800

Source: Competition Commission (2000a: Table 12.25)

Table 9.2 Retail developments in Cardiff Bay

Name of scheme	Type of development	Date opened	Total floorspace (gross, m²)	Distance from nearest town or district centre (km)
Penarth Haven	Tesco superstore	1994	4,036	1.2
Cardiff Bay Retail Park	Asda superstore	1997	8,361	2.1
	Retail park Phase 1	1997	11,613	2.2
	Retail park Phase 2	1998	5,574	2.5
Pengam Green	Tesco superstore	2001	7,572	2.0
Sports Village	Retail (superstore, DIY store, sports-related), leisure, sports	Under construction	25,083	1.2

There appear to be no published reviews of long-term trends in retail development associated with urban regeneration. A reading of the practice literature suggests that the development process may take place in two ways. The first occurs when a developer purchases a derelict site (perhaps very cheaply) and seeks to develop retail or retail and leisure uses. This would not be related directly to any ongoing public sector regeneration programmes although the regeneration benefits of the development would of course be stressed. This type of opportunistic scheme typifies the early days of retail development on non-central brownfield sites, and an outstanding example would be the Metro Centre in Gateshead, developed by Sir John Hall from land used for dumping ash at a former power station (Guy, 1994b).

A second type of development process, which is probably now more typical, is where a public sector agency organises a programme of renewal across a large area, purchasing land where possible. Here, the sale of some of this land to a retailer or retail developer in advance of development provides funds which can be used for land clearance and infrastructure provision on other sites. The retail developer may even enter into a formal partnership arrangement with the public sector agency and possibly other private sector interests. The developments in Cardiff Bay listed in Table 9.2 are of this type, as typically are case studies discussed in recent reviews such as Carley *et al.* (2001) and Hooper (2002).

The 'partnership' mode of development may take longer to realise, but carries some advantages for the developer. First, there may be some financial support provided (usually in kind) by the public sector, for example provision of road access to the site. Second, risk may be shared between public and private partners instead of being carried solely by the developer. Third, the developer gains support from the public sector agency when applying for planning consent to the local authority. Fourth, a successful development earns the developer good publicity in terms of corporate social responsibility, as discussed in the following section.

Since the mid-1990s, partnership-based regeneration schemes have become the norm. Although no comprehensive review is available, the impression is that such schemes have generally become larger, more complex, and are now developing a mixture of land uses rather than simply commercial. However, a retail component is still crucial in many schemes:

> Some supplemental enquiries with a sample of leading Scottish regeneration agencies/companies brought the role of retail/commercial development to the fore, in regeneration projects. Most felt that the 'early phase catalyst' was a positive effect of retail with higher land values assisting with the strain of a deficit cash-flow, often affected by decontamination and land assembly/infrastructure costs. However, others suggested that the inclusion of retail centres could conversely be seen as a later phase complementary service to an established new urban quarter and some comments referred to the possibilities of lower decontamination costs if a simple retail car park was required, as opposed to a use such as residential. But the general view amongst regeneration specialists was positive towards commercial/retail development as a focus and catalyst for further renewal and higher density development.
>
> (CBRE, 2004c: 78)

Urban regeneration and large-format retailing

Although no comprehensive data are available, most of the retailing in urban regeneration schemes appears to be in the form of superstores/hypermarkets and retail parks. This reflects two rather different influences. First, hypermarket and retail park development are relatively straightforward in terms of design and attraction of tenants. They can be quickly developed compared with more complex shopping mall or mixed retail/leisure schemes. Second, these developments have generally been more acceptable to local authority planners than larger-scale developments, and urban regeneration agencies are often able to secure some relaxation of planning policy. In contrast, those regional centres which have been developed in brownfield locations all received outline planning consent before the tightening up of policy in 1993. The two likely to be developed in London at the time of writing – White City and Stratford – could be argued to be in edge-of-centre locations although they are both associated with major regeneration schemes (see Chapter 4).

Hypermarket and retail park developers have not been slow to make a virtue out of necessity. Typically they present 'regeneration' as a major motivation for new development, for example: 'We prefer to build our stores on previously developed sites that have been identified for regeneration ... making a valuable contribution towards improving the environment ... cleaning up contaminated land, undertaking massive ground works and substantial infrastructure improvement' (Asda, 2005); and:

> In the year 2000, B&Q began working with local government regeneration programmes which focus on areas in need of development. Based on its learning from three initial case studies, it has continued to form partnerships across the country, working with local people to identify individual community needs and where possible offering employment, skills and training, marketing expertise and support to local projects.
>
> (Kingfisher, 2002: 24)

> Land Securities' extensive redevelopment programme aims to regenerate major towns and city centres across the UK which, in addition to providing new commercial and residential floorspace, also provides an opportunity to upgrade existing infrastructure and to improve the public realm through the creation of aesthetically pleasing open squares and spaces. By virtue of its Section 106 obligations, the Group is able to deliver a wide range of local amenities to support the commercial content of its developments. Examples include the provision of public art, affordable housing, park and ride facilities, community/heritage centres, libraries etc.
>
> The Group recognises the need to deliver schemes which are both economically and socially viable. In this regard strong communication and support from the local community and stakeholders plays an integral role in the successful planning and implementation of development projects. Public engagement is a process which is initiated at the feasibility stage and carries on through the construction programme.
>
> (Land Securities, 2004: 18)

The most extensive programme of regeneration led by a major retailer has been the Tesco Regeneration Programme (Tesco, 2005; BITC, 2005). The company have entered into partnerships with public sector agencies including local authorities, training providers, the Government's Employment Service and Basic Skills Agency, and local community representatives:

> The basic idea is to create opportunities for people through jobs and training that in turn generate the potential for improved wealth right across the broader community. ... The measurable outcomes include over 880 people back in work, or working for the first time, with knock-on benefits for many families and very high success rates for the training programs compared with other work-based schemes.
>
> (BITC, 2005)

These training programmes are based around the stores themselves, but also extend to other parts of the urban areas concerned (ibid.). In mid-2005, Tesco had opened six stores, creating 2,200 new jobs, and a further seven partnerships of this type were under way (Tesco, 2005: 1). The programme will also lead to the reclamation of 98 acres of derelict land (ibid.: 14).

Tesco have understandably tried to justify this programme in altruistic terms. According to Lucy Neville-Rolfe, Group Director of Corporate Affairs:

> How did we develop our approach to regeneration? We looked at the social exclusion agenda and at our own property programme and identified what we believed would be a win/win for communities, customers and business. Our approach to corporate social responsibility is built on a long tradition of understanding and meeting the needs of all sections of society. No neighbourhood is a no-go area for investment or for serving customers.
>
> (Tesco, 2005: 2)

This clearly links their programme to the 'social inclusion' and 'under-served markets' agendas discussed in Chapter 8. However, another motive for the programme would appear to be Tesco's desire to maintain their store development programme, particularly of Tesco Extra hypermarkets (Guy, 2002b; Wrigley *et al.*, 2002a; Wood *et al.*, 2006). In the words of one commentator:

> Tesco is the first major UK company to recognise the importance of confronting the complex social and economic issues raised by long-term unemployment. Its approach is to work in partnership with local authorities, government agencies and community groups to produce a co-ordinated strategy in some of the country's worst unemployment black spots. The bottom line, says Tesco, is to help put more

people into work. Cynics may say it's just a clever device to get new stores built and passed by the planners.

(Scotsman, 2000)

It is difficult to establish how significant the regeneration agenda has been in recent large store development programmes. Certainly the retailers make every effort to justify proposals for new stores in terms of employment creation and property-led regeneration. This represents a major change from the 1980s, when new stores and retail parks were justified largely on grounds of competition, innovation and convenience for shoppers. However, it is arguable that many recent developments have been designed to comply with overall planning policy, fitting the store's size and site layout into central or edge-of-centre sites (Guy and Bennison, 2006). Developing new stores in off-centre regeneration schemes is a more risky alternative, as the next section explains.

Urban regeneration and retail planning policy

It should be clear by now that much of the retail development in regenerated brownfield areas also constitutes out-of-centre development. For example, all the schemes in Cardiff Bay, listed in Table 9.2, are at least one kilometre (as the crow flies) from the nearest town or district centre. This point is usually omitted in statements by developers or public sector regeneration agencies. Nevertheless it appears that many out-of-centre schemes have been assisted by their incorporation into regeneration projects. In planning terms, the regeneration imperative becomes a 'material consideration' which in the local planning authority's view, might outweigh the normal policy stance.

There has also been plenty of anecdotal evidence that off-centre development is more likely to be approved in areas of economic and social stress. The 'effectiveness' review in England concluded that:

> In the convenience sector, there is mixed evidence of the effectiveness of PPG6. Overall, there is evidence of an increase in openings of town centre stores and neighbourhood stores, and a significant decline in the pipeline of out-of-centre stores. However, this trend has been by no means universal. Superstore operators have found it easier to develop large stores in the north, where employment and regeneration considerations have carried more weight.

(CBHP, 2004: 12)

It is widely felt, despite a lack of firm quantitative evidence, that retail development generally has benefited more from the regeneration imperative in areas outside the south-east of England, particularly in parts of northern England,

Wales and Scotland. Many inner areas of cities and conurbations also have examples of retail-led regeneration schemes completed in out-of-centre locations.

The question whether regeneration needs should be part of retail planning policy was for many years ignored in official guidance. In the 1996 version of PPG6, it was however made clear that retail development should not occur on land zoned in an approved development plan for other employment-generating purposes (DoE, 1996: para 3.23).

In addition, the regeneration potential of retail development was given little support:

> Retail development should not be used simply as a mechanism to bring vacant or derelict sites into development, unless it would help to support the vitality and viability of existing centres. Developments, especially those out of centre, may compete with town centres which may need investment for their own regeneration.
>
> (DoE, 1996: para 3.24)

and:

> The local job creation benefits from retail proposals should be carefully assessed as there may be off-setting losses elsewhere in the area when trade is diverted and, as in the case of food retailing, losses in other sectors, such as processing, packing and distribution.
>
> (ibid.: para 3.25)

In the Scottish guidance, no such advice is provided. There is a general statement that 'the Government has adopted planning policies which promote sustainable development by supporting the regeneration of urban areas, particularly town centres' (SODD, 1998: para 5).

Despite (or perhaps, because of) this vagueness in NPPG8, only 31 per cent of retail applications submitted in Scotland in 2002, and 39 per cent of approvals, were related to areas allocated as retail in approved local plans (SEDD, 2004: Table 12). About one-third of all retail applications, including one-quarter of total floorspace, approved in 2002 were on out-of-centre brownfield sites (ibid.: Tables 16, 17).

Urban regeneration emerged as a major issue (and cliché) in land-use planning in the late 1990s. Various interests, including retailers, property developers, and regeneration agencies put pressure on those responsible for policy preparation to recognise that retail development was an important part of urban regeneration. In 2003, the Neighbourhood Renewal Unit of ODPM published, together with the British Retail Consortium, a 'good practice' guide relating (in part) to retail development in deprived areas (ODPM/BRC, 2003). Case histories included stores operated by B and Q, Tesco, the convenience retailer Morning Noon and Night, and the West Quay shopping mall in Southampton. Another ODPM initiative was the Underserved Markets project, discussed in Chapter 8.

At around this time, it became more common for proponents of out-of-centre schemes to stress the regeneration benefits of their proposals. The interest group British Council for Out of Town Retail (BCOTR), subsequently re-named as Accessible Retail, has produced a 'Planning Newsletter' since November 1999. This summarises appeal and call-in decisions affecting large-format stores. In the sixth such newsletter, published in March 2002, 'Regeneration of Sites' became for the first time a focus of attention, with five out of seven such schemes proving successful at appeal. It was noted that if a strong regeneration case could be made, it appeared that the sequential test would not carry as much weight as usual (Bowhill, 2002).

Some proposals which have been called in by Secretaries of State have also been allowed, while others which one would have expected to have been called in as departures from development plan policy were not called in at all. In each case there were clear overall regeneration benefits and it seemed likely that other development would follow. Two such examples were the development of a new district centre incorporating the largest Asda/Wal-Mart in the UK, in East Manchester, and the development of a large retail park on the edge of Cardiff (Guy, 2004c). In these two cases, new sporting facilities were the main justification.

This new emphasis was inconsistent with the lack of treatment of retail-led regeneration in PPG6 and NPPG8. However it became an issue in ministerial speeches at around this time. For example, Lord Falconer, the then Minister for Planning, said in a conference speech:

> Some of our towns and cities are in desperate need of the investment and prosperity which well-planned, appropriate retail development can bring. Left to its own devices, however, the market may simply ignore these places, or else use them cynically for cheap land under the pretence of regeneration. It is clear that our aims for urban regeneration and neighbourhood renewal will not be achieved by leaving it entirely to the market. I believe retail development can help make communities across the country more sustainable, prosperous and successful, but developers and retailers need a clear steer to make this happen. That means a policy that delivers a positive framework for development, regeneration and neighbourhood renewal. In the past the debate about PPG6 was too often conducted in negative terms – it was seen solely in terms of stopping out-of-town developments. But what I am trying to achieve is entirely positive planning – promoting an urban renaissance, tackling social exclusion and promoting a more sustainable pattern of development.
>
> (Falconer, 2002)

The position in England thus became clearer on revision of PPG6. The introduction to the definitive version of PPS6 quoted regeneration as a relevant element of government policy:

> The following of the Government's wider policy objectives are also relevant ...
> - to encourage investment to regenerate deprived areas, creating additional employment opportunities and an improved physical environment;
> - to promote economic growth of regional, sub-regional and local economies.
>
> (ODPM, 2005a: para 1.5)

The inclusion of regeneration as an element of policy had two implications. First, a local planning authority could designate land for new retail development in an area where regeneration is required, provided that other elements of policy were taken into account. The guidance states that:

> Considerations to be taken into account in drawing up plans include:
> - Physical regeneration: the benefits of developing on previously-developed sites which may require regeneration;
> - Employment: the net additional employment opportunities that would arise in a locality as a result of a proposed allocation, particularly in deprived areas;
> - Economic growth: the increased investment in an area, both direct and indirect, arising from the proposed allocation and improvements in productivity, for example arising from economies of scale; and
> - Social inclusion: this can be defined in broad terms and may, in addition to the above, include other considerations, such as increasing the accessibility of a range of services and facilities to all groups.
>
> (ODPM, 2005a: para 2.51)

These 'considerations' would appear to be relevant in three instances, although these are not spelt out clearly. First, extension of a town centre involving redevelopment of under-used or derelict sites; second (and unlikely to occur in most development plans) meeting quantitative need through provision of out-of-centre development, using the sequential approach; and third, 'designation of new centres' in 'areas of significant growth, or where there are deficiencies in the existing network of centres' (ODPM, 2005a: para 2.53).

'Designation of new centres' may become a more prominent issue in the years to come. A recent example has been the controversial new Ravenscraig town centre development on a former steel works site (see Chapter 4).

The position concerning the appraisal of private sector planning applications by local authorities is no clearer than previously. Regeneration is stated as a 'material consideration' (ODPM, 2005a: para 3.28), not an element of 'need'. No further guidance is given here. It is thus not clear to what extent material considerations can be more important than either an approved development plan or government policy in determining the outcome of any planning application. Analysis of planning inquiries suggests that this can occur, if only rarely (Bowhill, 2002).

A survey of unitary local authorities in England, carried out in 2002, suggested that the majority of retail proposals of over 1,000 sq.m. were seen to have regeneration benefits, particularly site improvement and employment gains (Baker, 2002). However, almost all authorities felt that regeneration needs should not override established planning policy, particularly the sequential approach. More recently, the Underserved Markets Project has found problems in persuading local authorities to take part in regeneration schemes with a substantial retail component (see Chapter 8). It seems that there is reluctance to use compulsory purchase powers, and an attitude that retail jobs are somehow inferior to other types of employment.[1]

The position which seems to be emerging is that regeneration needs can sometimes justify a retail proposal in an edge- or out-of-centre location, as long as these needs are important in themselves, and if the proposal meets a quantitative need and does not pose a significant impact threat. The position may become clearer in England as a result of appeal or call-in decisions. In Scotland and Wales, regeneration needs seem to occupy a stronger position.

Regeneration in town and district centres

As noted above, the term 'regeneration' has become widely applied to retail or mixed-use schemes within city, town and district centres. Such schemes may involve large-scale redevelopment of outdated prime retail areas, as in the Birmingham Bullring scheme completed in 2003, or perhaps more commonly, redevelopment of areas comprising retail and other uses, in order to modernise and extend the prime retail area. Schemes of this type are currently proposed in several cities, including Bristol, Sheffield, Leeds, Nottingham, Chester and Cardiff.

Such major redevelopment schemes include some characteristics which differentiate them from the shopping mall developments typical of earlier periods (see Chapter 2). These are summarised in Table 9.3.

The table shows that recent schemes have been more complex, both in terms of the mixture of built forms and land uses, and in the processes of planning and development.

A further characteristic of most recent town centre schemes is that they have been promoted and justified in regeneration terms, which include both the conventional aspect of job creation and a more recent emphasis on the more intangible publicity gains from such developments. For example, in Southampton,

Table 9.3 Large-scale retail-led schemes in town and city centres

Characteristic	1970s schemes	2000s schemes
Identity of developer	Single property developer	Consortium of developers
Role of local authority	Passive or encouraging	Included in planning process and (possibly) consortium; may use compulsory purchase powers
Land uses	Retail, car parking	Retail, leisure, residential, car parking
Physical layout	Enclosed shopping mall	Shopping mall plus open areas

the West Quay shopping mall was justified partly on its ability to raise the city's profile in general, as well as a shopping destination (Lowe, 2005). This scheme also featured in the ODPM's 'good practice' report for its recruitment policies (ODPM/BRC, 2003). In other cases, Urban Regeneration Companies, set up to regenerate a town as a whole, have been heavily involved in town/city centre redevelopments. This involvement may include membership of a partnership which organises the redevelopment, and/or use of compulsory purchase powers (Jones *et al.*, 2003).

In smaller town centres, mixed-use schemes involving a superstore or hypermarket as the main anchor are becoming more common. An early example was the St Elli Centre in Llanelli, anchored by an Asda superstore. Research shows that this development increased footfall in the town centre as a whole, reversing previous trends, but it does not appear that the superstore generated extra trade for non-food stores in the town centre as a whole (Bromley and Thomas, 2002; Thomas and Bromley, 2003). There is clearly a danger that this kind of development will simply draw in more motorised traffic to the town centre, since most if not all superstore shoppers wish to travel by car (see Chapter 7).

Several recent schemes include residential uses as part of a superstore-anchored scheme. Retailers, including Tesco, Asda and Ikea, have designed these schemes in order to be able to continue building large stores, while at the same time adhering to official guidelines on the desirability of mixed uses in town centres (Guy and Bennison, 2006). It is clear from discussions with retailers that such schemes are seen as more costly and less efficient than the stand-alone superstore (see Chapter 6); however, they are keen to publicise such schemes where this will benefit the public image of the company concerned.[2]

Recent programmes of redevelopment of district shopping centres have shown some similar characteristics, such as the creation of partnership arrangements and the use of economic arguments to justify proposals. Again, redevelopment has tended to involve hypermarket developments rather than shopping malls. Two well-known examples have been at Seacroft, Leeds (Wrigley *et al.*, 2002a), and Castle Vale, Birmingham (Mitchell and Kirkup, 2003); both of these and other schemes are also reviewed in Carley *et al.* (2001). District centres comprising a supermarket and several small shops and service businesses had been developed in the 1960s, in local authority housing estates on the periphery of these cities. The centres had gradually become dilapidated and were largely vacant at the time the decision was made to redevelop. Tesco and Sainsbury, respectively, agreed to enter a formal partnership with the local authority, employment agencies and local community interests. The new district centres are dominated by the hypermarket but also include smaller stores.

While such developments would appear to be consistent with official policy, and obviously comply in principle with the sequential approach, they have nevertheless proved controversial. In order to be viable economically, the superstore or hypermarket concerned needs to draw upon a catchment population larger than that of the previous district centre, which would have been largely the residential population within walking distance. Mitchell and Kirkup (2003: 457) comment that 'A retailer needs to have confidence that his investment will attract customers from outside, as well as within, the regeneration area.' In this example, Sainsbury's catchment area extended some four miles from the centre (ibid.: 456).

This has raised suspicions that the retailers are using the regeneration agenda as a means to continue building large-format stores which are out of scale with the needs of the local population for which regeneration is intended (Guy, 2002b: 327–8; Wrigley *et al.*, 2002a: 2110–11). Such fears were voiced in 2000 by a government minister:

> Some are now experiencing the problem of large supermarkets seeking to piggyback on a local centre, arguing that they are in a town centre but in practice having all the characteristics of a free-standing superstore, relying predominantly on car-borne shoppers diverted from other out-of-centre stores.
>
> (Raynsford, 2000)

It is not clear whether this advice related solely to 'local centres', as designated in local authority development plans, which would lie outside the sequential approach, or included (by implication) district and town centres. The advantages and disadvantages of large store development in areas of social exclusion and poor access to retail facilities are discussed further in Chapter 8.

Advice in PPS6 is that 'the scale of development should relate to the role and function of the centre within the wider hierarchy and the catchment served', and 'local centres will generally be inappropriate locations for large-scale new development' (ODPM, 2005a: paras 2.41–2.42). The intention is that local authorities should designate a hierarchy of centres, ensuring that new development is of 'appropriate scale' for each centre, and setting out upper floorspace limits for this purpose.

This advice also applies to the insertion of large stores into existing district centres, without redevelopment. Whysall (1995) has shown that the development of an Asda superstore in an inner suburban district centre in Nottingham appears to have given little benefit to the rest of the centre. The Asda store attracted relatively few shoppers who also visited the pre-existing centre; and:

> rather than regeneration having been stimulated by positive spin-offs from the superstore, ... any benefits have arisen as a result of the traditional traders innovating to compensate for the negative impacts of the superstore on their trade. Such traders would not see this as regeneration but as a strategy for survival.
>
> (Whysall, 1995: 11)

Whysall concludes that

> Often the problem of inner city shopping areas is an excess of supply of retail properties over a declining level of local demand, set in an increasingly competitive context. To respond to this by adding more attractive floorspace is surely a high-risk strategy.
>
> (ibid.: 12)

Most local authorities appear to support the view that development of a superstore in an inner urban district centre will benefit the centre as a whole (Cannings, 2000). However, they wish to see an element of competition between the superstore and smaller shops, and are forced into difficult decisions when a superstore operator wishes to extend or relocate a district centre store (ibid.). Carley *et al.* (2001) present case studies which suggest that it is possible to regenerate a failing district centre without developing a superstore. Methods include provision of smaller-scale supermarkets, and integration of the centre with community facilities, in order to encourage multi-purpose trips.

Discussion

The issues discussed so far in this chapter are particularly difficult to assess. There is little quantitative evidence as to how significant retail-led regeneration has been, and to what extent it has conflicted with mainstream retail planning policy. Two main questions need to be considered. First, how effective is retail development in securing regeneration benefits? And second, what conditions should be placed upon retail-led regeneration in order for it to be acceptable within overall retail planning criteria?

Does retail development provide employment gains?

The first question itself has two main components. Retail-led regeneration is usually supported on grounds of job creation, and its ability to engender other developments through infrastructure improvements and environmental upgrading. However it has to be asked whether new retail development does actually provide net gains in employment, or, if not, does it improve in some way the quality of jobs?

As is often the case in retail research, most of the empirical work on this topic has been carried out in connection with food superstore development. Unfortunately, the conclusions are unclear. There are two broad principles which are inconsistent. On the one hand, a new superstore provides several hundred jobs which did not previously exist. On the other hand, superstores are the most productive form of retail development (see Chapter 6), benefiting from economies of scale and efficient deployment of labour. Thus, a town served entirely by superstores would be expected to have fewer people in full-time equivalent (FTE) retail employment than a town served by traditional small stores.

Between these two extremes, almost all towns in Britain possess both superstores and small traditional stores, as well as supermarkets, discount stores, etc. It was shown in Chapter 5 that the trading impact of superstores is difficult to determine from empirical studies, although clearly the rise in number of such stores has taken place at the same time as a pervasive loss of small stores. Thus, 'gains' from employment in new superstores occur at the same time as employment losses when small stores are closed down. This has led most researchers to conclude that the long-term employment impact of superstores tends, in simple numerical terms, to be zero or negative. This was the conclusion reached by two studies carried out for the National Retail Planning Forum (NRPF) in the late 1990s (Porter and Raistrick, 1998; Thorpe, 1999), as well as an analysis of changes in convenience retail employment over a 30-year period in Greater London (Webber, 2004).

However, these findings have been disputed in another study carried out for NRPF and funded by Tesco (Fell, 1999). A further research exercise which attempted to relate Tesco and Sainsbury store openings to overall retail employment trends in labour market areas also concluded that the store openings had positive effects upon total employment (Guariglia, 2002).

These disagreements arise for several reasons (Sparks, 2000; see also Dixon and Marston, 2003: 64–70). First, many of the new jobs provided in superstores are part-time or casual. Hence, there can be an overall increase in number of jobs in the locality, at the same time as an overall loss in FTE jobs. Second, deficiencies in employment data for small areas, particularly for the self-employed and for small firms, make analysis of changes over time very problematic. Third, findings can depend upon the size of the geographical area examined. There tend to be net gains close to the store, but net losses if a wider area is examined. This is because the trading impact of a superstore, and hence an eventual effect upon employment, reaches out into areas at least 20 minutes drive time from the store.

Proponents of superstore development would argue that providing part-time employment meets a demand from those who are seeking secure part-time employment close to the home. They also emphasise the security of the new jobs provided and their suitability for those who have been out of the workforce for some time. It is difficult to disagree with their claims that superstore development can improve economic and social circumstances within the immediately surrounding area. A sensible conclusion is that:

> Superstores … concentrate employment and modernise facilities through their efficiency and approach. The modernisation aspect is surely the most important point at this time and it is understandable if some local authorities and retailers seek to develop such stores in particular areas to improve the locality and to provide a local job focus. They have to recognise however that there will be both positive and negative consequences of this decision.
>
> (Sparks, 2000: 15–16)

A further question concerns the indirect employment effects of new development. A study of six town centre shopping malls developed in the early 1990s showed that 'During a period of recession and overall job losses, shopping centre developments in our six centres appeared to create jobs against the trend' (Dixon and Marston, 2003: 126). They suggest that on average, provision of 400 FTE jobs led to another 80 jobs through the effect upon suppliers, and another 120 jobs through 'induced demand' created through household expenditure by those employed in the shopping centres.

However, such gains seem less likely in the case of superstores or retail parks. Indeed, it is claimed that superstores can have negative effects on local economies, by using fewer local suppliers of goods and services compared with smaller food shops (NEF, 2003).

Does retailing generate further development?

The second broad issue is whether retailing can help bring about wider regeneration benefits to areas of urban decay. The retailers are keen to stress the wider benefits of new development:

An ASDA development is also able to act as a catalyst for other forms of investment and further regeneration. The footfall created by a new store creates business opportunities for others. Many of our new stores are quickly joined by other forms of development, such as residential, leisure, retail, commercial etc. In isolation, none were able or prepared to invest until ASDA had shown a commitment and given credibility to a difficult area, through the careful handling of a multi-million pound development.

(Asda, 2005)

However, academic commentators are unable to agree. Referring to retail and mixed-use schemes including the regional centres at Meadowhall, Metro Centre and Merry Hill, Turok (1992) considers that

It is debatable whether the results amount to economic regeneration. Few additional jobs have been created overall, because of trade displacement from existing outlets and higher labour productivity in the new stores ... the retail and leisure sectors provide a weak base for sustained growth because they are concerned with distribution and consumption rather than the production of income and wealth.

(Turok, 1992: 374–5)

However, Colin Williams (1996; 1997) develops an argument in favour of retail and leisure development as a method of economic regeneration. Rather than emphasising employment provision, as has tended to be the case with retailers themselves, he concludes that:

consumer services can play an important additional role in encouraging economic growth. They prevent leakage of spending out of the local economy. This occurs in two ways. First, consumer services can hinder the leakage of money from the locality by providing facilities that offset the need and desire of people to travel outside the area to acquire that service. Second, locally provided consumer services can change local people's expenditure patterns by raising the proportion of total local spending on consumer services.

(Williams, 1996: 55)

The first of his arguments raises the familiar paradox, already confronted in the discussion on employment gains and losses. New development not only employs people, but is also likely to widen the population catchment of its local area and to reduce expenditure flows out of the area. However this increased trade is likely to be at the expense of surrounding shopping facilities – the familiar impact question discussed in Chapter 5. Most commentators feel that at sub-regional level, there is no net gain in shopping expenditure or employment: indeed, this assumption is at the heart of retail impact assessment methods. Williams' second argument disputes this commonly held assertion: however, he provides no convincing evidence in support.

The extent to which retail-led regeneration has brought about further property development and economic improvement is again hard to determine. There are many examples of retail development apparently attracting further employment opportunities and/or housing, not least in the Urban Development Corporation areas set up in areas of industrial decline in the 1980s.

The regional shopping centres given consent in the 1980s have not been studied thoroughly in this respect. Williams (1997) argued that the Metro Centre has attracted not only further retail uses, but also offices and a hotel: 'When it displayed that it could successfully trade in the locality, it demonstrated to other businesses that firms could succeed and gave them greater confidence to relocate than would otherwise have been the case ...' (Williams, 1997: 215). Lowe (2000) supported this argument, and also showed how Merry Hill regional shopping centre became the focus for a mixed office, leisure and residential development which is still expanding (Hunt Dobson, 2002). However, casual observation of other regional centres, including the Trafford Centre and Cribb's Causeway, suggests that these centres have only attracted further consumer services to the locality. Overall, it is doubtful whether any retail or retail/leisure development in Britain can compare in size with the North American 'edge cities' identified by Garreau (1991).

More generally, however, there is increasing evidence that property-led regeneration can be maintained after the initial stimulus. Adair *et al.* (2005) find that total returns on all types of commercial property developed in regeneration areas outside town centres or other prime locations have been at least as good as returns from prime locations. This is mainly because of a more rapid decline in investment yields, indicative of a rapid rise in site values. In other words, the initial investment (typically seen as risky by established property interests) becomes profitable because it leads to further developments, which improve the status of the area. This is particularly the case for retail developments (ibid.: 18).

Regeneration versus retail planning?

The final issue is to what extent retail development carried out under regeneration policy is consistent with other elements of policy. Clearly, many of the schemes mentioned in this chapter have been designed to improve access to modern retailing in areas of social deprivation (see Chapter 8), as well as providing employment and other regeneration benefits. This is especially the case with some superstore developments, including redeveloped district centres such as Seacroft. However, anything larger than purely local convenience shopping provision outside town centres is not generally consistent with overall planning policy. And a new modern superstore will attract car-borne traffic from outside the area for which regeneration is intended, as shown at Castle Vale (Mitchell and Kirkup, 2003). This appears to contravene the official guidance on reducing car travel (see Chapter 6), as pointed out by Carley *et al.* (2001: 12).[3] Several of the schemes recently developed under regeneration initiatives have also been criticised for including large car parks, which separate the shops from the surrounding residential areas and make pedestrian access more difficult (Carley *et al.*, 2001; Hooper, 2002).

Generally, official guidance does not make clear under what circumstances regeneration and/or social inclusion arguments should override the sequential approach or the assessment of need. One suspects that the resolution of this question is being left to the 'case law' built up through planning inquiries, as has often been the case in retail planning.

Regeneration within town or district centres is encouraged by all sides and does not have to be supported by arguments over 'need' or predictions of impact. This carries a danger that retail or mixed-use proposals which have been determined by the developer's assessment of market demand will be out of scale compared with the current role and nature of the centre concerned. Whether this matters is another issue which needs further discussion.

Conclusions

Urban regeneration has become an important issue in retail planning, but the policy debate has not been clearly focused. Retailers, property developers and the public sector have used the term indiscriminately, at times to support almost any proposal. Much of the literature on property-led regeneration unquestioningly supports retail development. This is because it can 'kick-start' the remediation process and instantly supply hundreds of relatively secure jobs in areas of high unemployment. In some cases 'regeneration' has been used to justify development in areas where mainstream policy would not normally support it. However retail planning policy has tended to downplay or ignore this question.

Policy favours the regeneration of town and district centres, but without making it clear what type of retail development is most likely to succeed in this aim. Lord Falconer in his speech to the British Urban Regeneration Association stated that:

> a retail-led renaissance is not about building big boxes in deprived areas for the better off to drive to. In some places, hypermarkets – stores of 10,000 square metres or more – are being plonked down in or close to deprived neighbourhoods, as part

of the further roll-out of a coarse network of stores. They are Trojan horses – the jobs they bring are seductive, but they can spell death to local shopping for miles around. Local communities need to look carefully at the gifts they are offered.

(Falconer, 2002)

This statement sums up many of the concerns raised in this chapter. However, Falconer did not explain why these drastic consequences would not happen if these big stores were 'plonked down' in an existing town or district centre, in line with general policy.

If indeed the prime motive for retail-led regeneration is the improvement of retail provision and employment opportunities for those living in socially deprived areas, then one could argue that such development should be encouraged. However, sites outside existing town or district centres are generally cheaper than those within centres (and may even have negative value before remediation), and there are usually fewer problems over ownership patterns and availability for development (Adams *et al.*, 2002). Does this mean that out-of-centre development is justifiable? It is noticeable that a report on retail regeneration and under-served markets in Greater London, while supporting the case for new provision in under-served areas, does not discuss at all whether it should be confined to town and district centres (GLA, 2005).

Another unexplained feature of government advice, and much of the literature (e.g. Carley *et al.*, 2001) is the constant linking of 'regeneration' and 'sustainability'. Reclamation of a derelict and polluted urban site involves substantial use of energy and materials, compared with the more straightforward preparation of an edge-of-town greenfield site. Nor is it clear that the reclaimed urban site will generate less car travel in total than would the greenfield site.

We end this chapter with some unanswered questions, which stem from the debates reviewed above. Should the term 'regeneration' be used at all in the context of retail (re)development within town centres? When should a case for regeneration over-ride the key policy tests of impact, need and the sequential approach? Should more retail-led regeneration be encouraged in areas of high unemployment? Are regeneration arguments the same as those used to support development to relieve 'social exclusion'? Retail planning policy needs to face these questions and provide more consistent and detailed guidance.

Chapter 10
An evaluation of retail planning policy

Introduction

This chapter attempts to summarise the events and issues discussed in this book, and examines some key questions concerning the recent history and possible future path of retail planning policy and practice. It begins by reviewing the main themes in retail planning and how these have changed since the 1960s. This is followed by an analysis of some of the main developments in policy, and their impacts.

The focus then changes to a critical evaluation of the main elements of current retail planning policy. Some weaknesses in policy formulation, often resulting from lack of a soundly conceived basis of empirical evidence, are identified. This leads on to discussion of some unresolved questions in retail planning, and finally some suggestions for policy refinement, simplification and improvement.

How has retail planning policy changed over time?

The account in Chapters 2, 3 and 4 attempted to explain changes in retail planning policy in terms of reactions by political and environmental interests to two major trends: first, changes in retailing methods and locations, and second, the development of principles concerning broad planning objectives and the role of government.

The most important trends in retailing have resulted from multiple retailers' strategies for maintaining or increasing market share. Prominent amongst these strategies have been physical expansion into new territories, and realisation of economies of scale. These have led to intensive pressure for development of new stores and centres, often of much larger size than was anticipated in the 1960s. This in turn has taken retail development into suburban or edge-of-town locations based upon access by road, rather than access by foot. At the same time, there has been a steady decline in the independent retail sector, in town centres and elsewhere.

Retail planning policy has struggled to adapt to these trends, and has often seemed to some private sector interests to be over-protective of existing retail systems. However, policy itself has broadened in scope through the introduction of new principles, reflecting parallel developments in social, economic and environmental policy. In the 1960s, retail planning attempted mainly to control negative externalities, especially the trading impact of new developments. The 1970s saw a movement towards correcting market inadequacies, so that new developments should cater more adequately for non-car users. In the 1980s, reflecting the philosophy of a more right-wing political regime, the emphasis was on allowing or even promoting competition between methods of retailing. This experience showed however that a lack of coherent retail planning policy caused problems to private and public sectors alike. There grew a consensus that comprehensive, fair and clearly worded policies were necessary, and that central government should take a leading role in preparing such policies. This challenge has to some extent been met.

The 1990s also saw a new emphasis in promoting sustainable development. This encouraged policy makers to support town centres as the principal location for new retail development, in the belief that they are generally the most accessible location for most types of shopping trip. Impact assessment became more rigorous. Recently, policy has emphasised links between retail development and both social inclusion and urban regeneration. It is conceivable that future policies will take some note of environmental concerns over 'food miles', and the need to support small-scale retailers and other related businesses.

Over time these ideas have altered in nature as well as in their significance in the retail planning process. The early concerns over the trading impact of new retail development led eventually to a requirement that developers should demonstrate a 'need' for the scheme. The early concern over 'disadvantaged consumers' eventually became a more general statement that symptoms of 'social exclusion' could include a poor level of access to everyday retail facilities. The early concern that new developments tended to respond to the needs of car users rather than those without cars became part of an overriding policy of 'sustainable development' in retail planning.

During these 40 years or so, retail planning policy has become increasingly long and complex. Table 10.1 show how the sheer length of government policy statements applying to England and Wales, and then England, have increased since the first version of PPG6 in 1988.

Table 10.1 Length of English retail policy statements, 1998–2005

Policy statement	Year	Number of paragraphs
PPG6	1988	24
PPG6	1993	48
PPG6	1996	103
PPS6	2005	109

Note: Ministerial 'clarifications' and 'daughter documents' are not included.

It is also the case that the guidance in the English statements is much more detailed than in the equivalent statements issued for Wales and Scotland (see Table 10.2). Since development pressures and the planning system are very similar in these three countries, it is not clear why the English policy guidance should be so much more detailed.[1]

A third feature of retail planning policy has been its cyclic tendency over time. In the earliest period, retail planning was (in theory at least) carried out largely by local authorities, who would try to predict future requirements for retail space, quantified in terms of floorspace, and would allocate these requirements to a limited number of existing centres. During the 1980s this procedure was in effect rejected by the government, and replaced with a 'laissez-faire' system in which local authorities were expected to assist retail developers but not to direct their proposals. More recently, a system rather like the former 'future requirements' exercise has been put in place, with the additional complication that both regional and local authorities should contribute to the planning of retail growth and change. The difficulties found in implementing this type of planning, discussed in Chapter 2, may thus recur. In other respects, a return to the 1970s has been moderated by the increasing influence of central government over local authority decision-making and policy formulation (see Table 10.3).

Some elements of policy have remained more consistent over time. Estimation of the trading impact of new development upon existing centres has always been an important feature of retail planning, and the methods used have not changed greatly since the 1970s. Several other elements of policy have grown in importance, including sustainable development and the reduction of car travel; physical design and 'good neighbourly' relations with existing development; the need to improve retail quality in areas of social deprivation; and the demonstration of quantitative need in retail proposals.

Finally, it is clear that the operation of retail planning policy has become more centralised, especially in England. This is evidenced through the large number of Ministerial call-ins of planning decisions in recent years. There seems to have been a determined attempt by the Department of the Environment and its successor ministries to ensure that retail planning policies, and decisions on

Table 10.2 Length of recent retail policy statements

Policy statement	Country	Year	Number of words
PPS6	England	2005	12,028
SPP8 (draft)	Scotland	2005	4,525
Planning Policy Section 10 (revised)	Wales	2005	3,507

Note: TAN4 (Wales) and English 'daughter documents' are not included.

Table 10.3 Retail planning policy development, 1960–2006

Policy stance or issue	Early Days: 1960–1980	A Free for All? 1980–1990	Tightening Up: 1990–2006
Retail planning policy generally	Active	Reactive	Active
Responsibility for planning location of new development	Local government	Retailers and developers	Central and local government
Responsibility for planning amount of new development	Retailers and developers; local government	Retailers and developers	Central and local government
Responsibility for design of new development	Local authorities	Retailers and developers	Local authorities; retailers and developers
Stance of central government	Pro-town centres	Pro-developer	Pro-town centres
Assessment of need and impact	Local authorities	Local authorities	Local authorities; retailers and developers
Other government objectives incorporated into policy	(none?)	Encouragement of competition	Encouragement of competition; sustainable development; urban regeneration; social inclusion

applications for major development, are formulated in accordance with central policy. The battle between the opposing forces of 'flexibility' and 'consistency' in planning (see Chapter 2) has thus been resolved in favour of the latter. In contrast, in Scotland and Wales there have been very few call-ins relating to retail proposals, and although central guidance is similar to that issued by ODPM and its predecessors, there seems to be more willingness to allow local authorities to use their own judgement.

Who determines policy?

A more difficult question to address is how and why policy initiatives occur and become established in retail planning guidance. As explained in Chapter 1, central government guidance has a strong influence on the development plan policies produced by local authorities, and on the authorities' decisions regarding proposals for development. Broad policies are (in theory) devised by government ministers, reflecting to some extent political pressures, although constrained by existing legislation in respect of town planning, competition regulation and other matters. The detailed wording of guidance is of course written by civil servants within the responsible government ministry or department. Draft versions of new guidance are subjected to an extensive process of consultation with other government ministries, various organisations representative of private sector interests and local authorities, and any other organisations or individuals who wish to participate. This process is summarised in Figure 10.1. The rather passive procedure of allowing organisations and individuals to comment on draft publications may be preceded by 'Chatham House Rules'[2] meetings with at least some of these organisations, in order to hear their opinions, review the effectiveness of current policy, and (perhaps) agree a broad list of policy initiatives or amendments. In England, the National Retail Planning Forum and the Oxford Retail Group (linked to the Oxford Institute of Retail Management) have hosted several such meetings.

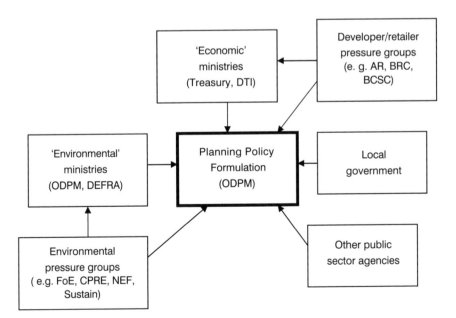

10.1 Current influences on retail policy formulation in England (Source: based upon Guy, 2006a: Figure 1)

Figure 10.1 also indicates that pressure groups may attempt to use 'sympathetic' government departments to further their cause.

The nature of this process suggests that changes to policy are likely to be incremental rather than basic, since the discussion tends to concern details of existing policy of particular concern to vested interests, and which are perceived as unfair, ambiguous or ineffective (for a case study see Pal *et al.*, 2001). In recent years the ministries concerned in England and Scotland have also commissioned more wide-ranging reviews of planning guidance. These have eventually been published, although in each case it was made clear that the basic policies were not under question. No such reviews however took place during the formulation of any versions of PPG6, nor of NPPG8.

The several examinations of policy by Parliamentary Select Committees, discussed in Chapter 4, could have been opportunities for a more fundamental exercise. The first of these, in 1994, seems in retrospect to have been the most significant of these, as it served to ground policy more firmly within the 'sustainable development' ethos. More recent inquiries have done little more than recommend ways of making Ministerial policy more effective.

Government policy-making seems receptive (to some extent) to the views of retailers and developers, as expressed through their representative organisations. For example, guidance on using retail development to alleviate social exclusion was strengthened in the preparation of PPS6, following pressure from the British Retail Consortium. Advice on the wording and procedures for implementing policies may also be heeded when given by local government or town planning organisations. However, little notice seems to be taken of the views of shoppers, reflecting their lack of organisation for lobbying purposes. During the whole period covered by this book, no government department has commissioned a survey of the views of ordinary shoppers about retail development and planning.

Although politicians with responsibility for retail planning change identity fairly often, there is an underlying continuity, in terms of local authority planners, planning inspectors, civil servants and planning consultants. These all participate in the implementation of policy in various ways. Such activity includes research reports and 'best practice' guidance, as well as input to statutory planning procedures such as public inquiries. This process has had an important role in exposing some unclear or ambiguous areas of policy. However, its outcome is that, as noted above, radical reform of policy is unlikely: incremental changes which build upon ('refine' or 'clarify') previous guidance are much more likely to occur.

What have been the main impacts of retail planning policy?

One of the most obvious impacts of policy is shown in statistics of out-of-centre development. Chapter 3 describes the obvious 'booms' in both retail parks and off-centre shopping malls in the late 1980s, a period following relaxation of control over such development. A second boom in retail park openings followed in the mid-1990s, but rates of development rapidly decreased following the introduction of 'town centres first' policies and the sequential test (CBHP, 2004). This decrease has not been due to lack of demand from retailers; commentators agree that planning policy has made the development of retail parks much more difficult, especially as this form of development is not suited to town centre sites.

The 'town centres first' policy has also reduced the volume of so-called 'out-of-town' completions and proposals since the late 1990s. Of all shopping centre developments in the pipeline (proposed, with planning consent and under construction), 78 per cent were located in town centres by mid-2005, compared with 66 per cent in 1990 (CBRE, 2005a).

In examining impacts of planning policy upon retail development, one should be aware of other possible causes of development trends. Table 10.4 summarises possible links between off-centre retail development trends, planning policy and market forces.

The table suggests that planning control since the mid-1990s has substantially affected the numbers of retail parks and regional centres completed in this period, and the location of food stores. There has also been a less pronounced effect upon the size of food stores, and locations of retail parks and outlet centres. Other influences upon rates of development have included saturation of local markets (mainly for food stores), and saturation of supply sources for outlet centres (Guy, 2002a).

Table 10.4 Recent influences on off-centre retail development

Influences	Food stores	Retail parks	Regional centres	Outlet centres
Market saturation	X	X		
Supply saturation				XX
Retailer demand		XX		
Planning control (size and numbers)	X	XX	XX	X
Planning control (location)	XX	X		X

Note: X X = major impact; X = minor or uncertain impact

Government ministers have nevertheless claimed on several occasions that policy is 'working'. For example, the release of data of the broad location of retail development during the period 1971–2003, based upon the ODPM's Town Centres Statistics Project, prompted the observation that 'emerging evidence suggests that since the mid-1990s national planning policy has had a significant impact in terms of increasing the proportion of retail development locating in town centres, reversing the trend of the previous 20 years' (ODPM, 2005d: para 1.5). However, a detailed examination of the data reported therein shows that only around 40 per cent of new retail floorspace was built within or close to town centres in the years after 1999.[3]

As reported in Chapter 4, local authority planning policies for retail development tend to reflect closely government advice. However, analysis by Jackson and Watkins (2005) suggests that while the impact of 'negative' development control policies on local retail property markets is difficult to determine statistically, 'proactive' planning policies which encourage development can lead to increased demand by investors and occupiers. Similar claims have been made in reports on the effectiveness of town centre management schemes (e.g. Lockwood, 1999).

One effect of policies which are increasingly restrictive on out-of-centre development has been a shortage of good quality space, particularly in retail parks, for retailers wishing to expand geographically. This has created a heavy demand for retail parks by financial investors, such that retail warehouse and retail park values and rents have grown more rapidly since the 1980s than has been the case for any other type of property (see Table 10.5). This in turn has led to 'active management' by retail park landlords, which has made them more efficient in their use of premises, and more attractive and convenient for the shopper. Hence, retail parks, particularly those with open A1 consent, have proved in some areas to be powerful competition with high streets (Guy, 2000).

More generally, land prices for retail development in Britain are much higher than in most other developed countries. For example, the analysis carried out by the

Table 10.5 Rental trends for types of commercial property

Type of property	Rental index in 2005 (Base = 100 in 1980)	Growth in rental value p.a. 2000–5 (%)
Shops	172	2.3
Retail warehouses	326	3.4
Offices	144	1.6
Industrial	171	2.4

Source: CBRE (2005b)

Competition Commission (2000a, Vol. 2: 288–9) showed that land with planning consent for supermarket development in the UK was typically up to six times as expensive as equivalent land in continental Europe. However, this difference was not held to be due entirely to the effects of planning policy in Britain.

Research on the impacts of retail planning policy has been almost entirely aimed at establishing its development effects. Some of the more basic objectives, such as promoting sustainable development, have not been evaluated in a comprehensive manner. This suggests that policy needs to be assessed in a thorough way which goes beyond examination of the extent to which a few easily measured policy outcomes are attained.

How should policies be assessed?

In assessing elements of retail planning policy in a more fundamental way, five main criteria suggest themselves: use of empirical evidence; balance of costs and benefits; feasibility; transparency; and consistency. This section cannot make a full evaluation of past or present policy according to these criteria. It can at most refer to appropriate research findings, where these exist, and indicate ways in which the evaluation might be attempted.

Use of evidence

There has been much discussion recently of the need for 'evidence-based' policy in the public realm. The Government's White Paper *Modernising Government* stated a need for 'policies that really deal with problems, that are forward-looking and shaped by the evidence rather than a response to short-term pressures; that tackle causes not symptoms … policy making must also be a process of continuous learning and improvement' (Cabinet Office, 1999: 15). In response, the ESRC set up an Evidence Network which co-ordinates research and information on the use of evidence-based policy and practice.

A relevant question therefore is to what extent retail planning policy has been based upon research evidence. Such evidence is needed in order to examine both the effectiveness of existing policy, and the validity of any underlying assumptions about the workings of the retail sector (in its broadest sense). The effectiveness of policy has been examined in both England and Scotland in recent years (CBHP, 2004; CBRE, 2004c), although in both cases it was made clear to the research teams that basic policy or its underlying assumptions were not to be questioned. This recalls the earlier comment by Delafons (1995: 83) that:

> In practice, the kinds of research commissioned by government tend to be strictly utilitarian and directed more at validating existing policies than at clarifying the

needs and problems with which planning purports to deal, so as to provide a firmer basis for future policy development.

Similar conclusions have been drawn more recently by Solesbury (2002) and Healy (2002), despite the government's new commitment to 'evidence-based research'. Thus, research commissioned by the DETR on the impact of large food stores on market towns and district centres (CBHP, 1998) did not examine the impact of any stores built *within* town centres, as these were acceptable in virtually all circumstances under current policy. Similarly, research into the sequential test (CBHP, 2000) examined ways of making the test more effective and consistent, rather than any basic arguments for or against.

Nor has independent research by academics or practitioners thoroughly addressed the questions which need to be posed concerning the basic objectives and assumptions of retail planning policy:

> Research within planning has not produced the necessary research findings for planners to build up a bank of expertise on the impacts of different policies or applications of policy ... Major research studies in planning journals of the impacts of retail change ... are missing from the literature.
>
> (Findlay and Sparks, 2005: 13)

In addition, a search in the ESRC's Evidence Network's on-line bibliography[4] does not reveal any published research which appears to relate directly to the retail planning policy issues discussed in earlier chapters. This raises the question as to what extent existing government policies are based upon sound empirical evidence. If such evidence is lacking, it could be the case that opinions, uncertainties and even myths dictate retail planning policy.

Table 10.6 summarises an attempt to portray (cynically, perhaps) the assumptions about retail competition and shopping behaviour which appear to underlie current retail planning policies, particularly those regarding shopping travel and retail impact. The table suggests some counter-assumptions, some of which are supported by empirical evidence, and the further evidence which appears to be needed to clarify the issue.

Costs and benefits

This criterion for evaluating policy can itself be sub-divided. The first question is what resources (data, information, staff etc.) are needed in order to implement policy. The problem here is that as policy becomes more complex and detailed, greater staff resources and degree of expertise are required. This problem is made worse where detailed policy guidance emphasises the importance of 'experience'

Table 10.6 Assumptions in retail planning policy, and evidence required

Policy	Assumptions	Counter-assumption	Evidence available or required
Identification of hierarchies and networks	Hierarchies and networks exist and are useful concepts	Hierarchies and networks are artificial constructs and do not take account of off-centre retail	Studies of the use of these concepts in policy making, and their effects upon planning decisions
Reduction of car travel	Building more off-centre stores will increase car travel	Travel will decrease, if shoppers visit their nearest store	Cairns (1995) CBHP (2002)
	Concentrating new retailing in town centres will reduce car travel	Congestion and pollution in town centres will increase	Energy consumption and emissions from shopping travel in various locations
	Public transport, walk and bicycle are adequate for shopping trips	Car use is essential for some types of shopping trip	Ibrahim and McGoldrick (2003)
Assessment of need and impact	Impact of any development located within a town centre is irrelevant	Town centre development can have significant impacts on the town centre itself or other town centres	Research into impacts of town centre developments
Compliance with sequential approach	The sequential approach is well understood and effective	The sequential approach increases development costs and restricts competition and innovation	CBHP (2000) Guy and Bennison (2006)

and 'judgement' in carrying out, for example, assessment of need and impact. And the recent requirement (in England) for regional planning agencies to be involved in forward planning of major development indicates extra staff costs because of the negotiation processes likely to occur.

The second question refers to the distribution of costs and benefits arising from various policy elements. As well as the classic 'who gains, who loses' issues, we need to assess how much the procedures involved add extra costs to the development process. This may lead to costs for consumers, particularly in the form of reduced choice and higher prices. In summarising this issue, Table 10.7 makes use of research findings discussed in Chapters 5, 6 and 7.

Government departments and ministries are now expected to produce explicit justification for new or revised policies. For example, the draft version of PPS6 included a 'Partial Regulatory Impact Assessment' (ODPM, 2003: Chapter 3), in which the preferred policies were compared with two alternatives: 'current policy retained', and 'revert to 1980s – no planning, limited controls'. The assessment is summarised in Table 10.8. It should be noted that the draft version of PPS6 emphasised the potential of edge-of-centre sites for large-format retailing, a policy which was watered down in the final version of the guidance (see Chapter 4).

The analysis in Table 10.8 should be welcomed for providing a broad justification for ODPM's policy stance, but does not turn to the more basic questions raised in Table 10.7. It also clearly illustrates the way in which policy revision takes place in incremental fashion, as discussed above.

Table 10.7 Summary of benefits and costs of policy elements

Policy	Benefits	Costs
Reduction of car travel	• Environmental	• Inconvenience for car users • Restriction of large new stores, limits competition and may lead to higher prices
Assessment of need and impact	• Strengthens town centre vitality and viability	• Delays development • Adds to development costs through employment of consultants
Compliance with sequential approach	• Strengthens town centre vitality and viability • Maximises access for non-car users	• Town centre 'cramming' and congestion • Trading impact on established town centre retailers • Additional development costs • Failure to realise economies of scale; higher consumer prices

Table 10.8 Partial regulatory impact assessment of draft PPS6

	Retain PPG6	Adopt PPS6	Revert to 1980s
Benefits	• Continuity for local authorities and businesses	• Guidance streamlined and clarified • Needs of retailers recognised • Needs of socially excluded communities recognised • More equitable distribution of development across centres	• Multiples able to develop large-format stores more freely and cheaply
Issues of equity and fairness	• Benefits of PPS6 lost	• Increased competition and choice	• Reduced access to shopping for those without cars • Strengthened market power for largest retailers
Costs for businesses	• Large-format retailers find difficulty in developing new sites	• Needs of all types of retailers are recognised	• Fewer constraints on development, but greater uncertainty and risk of excess supply
Other costs	• No change	• Local authorities need to negotiate more with private sector and the community • ODPM needs to provide additional good practice guidance	• Environmental costs – loss of open land, greater use of cars for shopping

Source: summarised from ODPM (2003: Chapter 3)

Feasibility

Policies should be feasible, in that the main objectives should be achievable. This in turn raises two main issues. The first, already discussed, is whether sufficient resources, particularly staff time and expertise, are available to carry out policy.

The second more basic issue relates to the limitations of the planning system. This in itself can do little to prevent (or encourage) changes in retailing methods, or the mix of goods and services available, or the closure of existing stores. Planning control applies basically to development of new premises, and subsequent external alterations such as erection of advertising material. Unless specific conditions are attached to the original planning consent, changes of goods sold or internal alterations are not subject to planning control. This has implications for the effectiveness of certain types of planning policy. For example, the vitality and viability of town centres can be affected significantly by store closures or changes in ownership of key properties, neither of which are subject to planning control. More basically, policies which aim to reduce shopping travel cannot be implemented directly. They rely upon consumer response to changes in the retail environment. As discussed in Chapter 7, this response tends to be complex and unpredictable.

Transparency

Planning guidance and policies should be clearly worded and unambiguous, no matter whom the intended recipients. Transparency provides more certainty for developers about which types of and locations for new development are likely to be acceptable to planners. It also makes the process of decision-making by planners more straightforward: a clearly worded government policy should explain to local authority planners not only what policies and decision criteria are acceptable, but how much freedom the authority has to diverge from policy guidelines where there may be special circumstances.

In retail planning however, there has been a long history of debate at public inquiries into issues such as the significance of a certain level of trading impact, the interpretation of the sequential test, and the definition of 'edge-of-centre'. It can be argued that these debates arise from unclear wording in planning guidance: the 'effectiveness' reports identified several such problems. It also seems to be that compromises between different interests have at times led to unclear or even contradictory wording: the advice in PPS6 concerning 'flexibility' and 'disaggregation' is a recent example (Guy, 2006a).

The weight given to policy elements is to some extent unclear in current government guidance. Criteria which are 'wider government objectives' although not central to retail planning include social exclusion, retail innovation and regeneration. It is not clear whether, and if so, under what circumstances, these should override the main objectives, particularly the need to protect and enhance town centres.

Consistency

One likely effect of basing a set of policies on several different objectives is that the objectives will not always be compatible. For example, the 'town centres first' policy leads to a situation in which large food stores can be developed within town centres. This does not fit in easily with policy aimed at minimising the impacts of car travel, as discussed in Chapter 7. A second example is where retail development which would support social inclusion by offering much improved facilities in peripheral suburban areas is not acceptable in terms of the sequential approach. Table 10.9 attempts to show relationships between the stated objectives of current retail planning policy in England. In one case there seems to be a fairly clear conflict between policies to favour town centres, and encourage competition and innovation. This is because research has shown that some of the largest and most innovative retailers face reduced opportunity and increased costs because of the insistence on 'flexibility' in new development (Guy and Bennison, 2006). In several other cases, pairs of objectives can be both mutually supportive and in conflict, depending upon circumstances. For example, concentrating development in town centres supports regeneration of

Table 10.9 Compatibility of policy objectives

Policy or objective	Town centres first	Maximise accessibility	Reduce car travel	Encourage competition, innovation	Assist regeneration	Assist social inclusion
Town centres first	✓	?	✗	?	?
Maximise accessibility			?	?	?	✓
Reduce car travel				?	?	?
Encourage competition, innovation					✓	✓
Assist regeneration						✓

town centres themselves, but makes it more difficult for out-of-centre brownfield regeneration to take place (see Chapter 9).

Unresolved questions in retail planning policy

Several issues have been discussed in preceding chapters, which appear to be relevant to retail planning practice but do not enter clearly into policy either at national or local level. Some consideration of these issues, based upon sound empirical research as well as full consultation with appropriate interests, would improve the quality of both government guidance and local authority decision-making in the future. The first three of these call into question the 'town centres first' policy, arising from the view that this policy, as implemented through the sequential approach, is not effectively fulfilling most of the other objectives of policy:

- Should retail development proposals located in town centres be subject to the same criteria of need and impact as off-centre proposals?
- Retail planning policy does not discriminate between types of retailer, methods of retailing or types of store, except in relating the 'scale' of a proposal to the size and function of the centre within which it would be located. Does this give large retailers an unfair advantage? Should local authorities be allowed (or even encouraged) to give explicit support within policy statements for 'small' retailers and/or locally based suppliers of food and possibly other goods?
- Should the transport-related elements of policy focus on the *effects* of car use (including noise, delays to other traffic through congestion, atmospheric pollution as well as production of greenhouse gases)?

Four questions relate to the wider social context in which retail development has increasingly been placed:

- Should local authorities be allowed to discriminate for or against named retailers, in the interests of encouraging competition?
- Is retail development an essential and appropriate element of urban regeneration outside town centres? Does it act effectively to 'kick-start' further developments which are beneficial to the community?
- In what ways does new retail development change employment patterns? Are the outcomes of this process desirable socially?
- What is the most effective way to improve access to retail facilities in areas of social exclusion and/or a poor quality retail environment?

Two final questions relate to policy implementation, and have implications for the future revision of policy:

- Do the data and expertise exist to do retail planning (as presently conceived)? If not, what needs to happen?
- Can retail planning be made simpler, while at the same time fulfilling its essential purposes?[5]

Improving the policy-making process

This final section does not suggest any definitive reforms in retail planning policy, given that further research is needed into the evidence base for policy. Instead, three broad suggestions for the design of future policy are put forward.

- Policy, especially at national level, should be less detailed, less contradictory and more clearly worded.[6] The level of detail in forward planning, at all spatial scales, should be reduced, given that the pace of change in retailing is much more rapid than the development plan preparation cycle. Methods of assessing need and impact in development control should be made more straightforward.[7]
- The process of policy formulation and revision (at national and local levels) should be more thorough. Assumptions should be tested through empirical research. Discussion with interested parties should be more open. Shoppers' views should be elicited.
- There should be more freedom for local authorities to draw up policies and implement them as they see fit, within broad guidelines set out by central government. The difficult process of weighing up the advantages and disadvantages of (say) an out-of-centre regeneration scheme could be left to the local authority to determine, as has generally been the case in Scotland and Wales.

It seems inevitable however that retail planning policy will remain complex, partly because the retail sector is complex, partly because there are many basic issues and points of view involved, and partly because the planning system itself is complex and allows discretion in its application. The course of events, as well as efforts by vested interests, serve in time to render elements of policy obsolete or inadequate. Policy wording cannot be both concise and fully comprehensive. It is hoped that this book has helped the reader to understand at least some of these issues, points of view and events, and how they have (or have not) been translated into retail planning policy in Britain.

Notes

1 Introduction

1 This book does not cover retail planning in Northern Ireland.

2 Early days

1 These definitions of superstores and hypermarkets follow normal UK practice at the time. In most continental European countries, the term 'superstore' is little used, and 'hypermarkets' are defined with a lower limit of 2,500 sq.m. (26,910 sq.ft.).

2 Stephen Crow, personal communication

3 This and other such publications, up to the mid-1990s, were jointly produced by the DoE and the Welsh Office. However, it is generally the case that they were very largely written by officials in the DoE.

4 Peter M. Jones, personal communication

5 In the early part of this period, some planners thought that Class X of the then Use Classes Order, 'Use as a wholesale warehouse or depository' included premises used as a 'retail warehouse': thus an existing storage warehouse could be converted to retailing without the need for planning permission. This matter was clarified by guidance from the DoE/WO (1974), which made it clear that a warehouse style building selling goods direct to the public should be treated for planning purposes as a retail use.

3 A free for all?

1 Analysis of appeal and call-in decisions has become one of the principal ways of examining government policy on property development. Decisions are based upon the recommendations of the inspectors who are appointed to chair planning inquiries. The inspector in his/her 'decision letter' must summarise the arguments presented at the inquiry, and give his/her recommendation as to whether the development should be allowed. However, the final decision rests with the Secretary of State, advised by civil servants (usually professional

planners) employed by the government department concerned. In minor cases, the inspector's decision is final.

Inspectors' and Secretaries of States' decisions are intended to be made on the basis of general government policy in the area concerned, but in practice the policy is not always clear, and certain issues related to particular developments can sway the balance. Previous decisions are often quoted as 'precedent' during the course of inquiries, and in this way a kind of case law develops, with decisions made on a basis which is claimed to be consistent with previous decisions by other inspectors. However, analysts have on many occasions detected inconsistencies between successive decisions. These may reflect peculiar circumstances in individual cases, differences in attitude between individual inspectors, or even inconsistency amongst civil servants (for example between different regional offices).

2   The misleading term 'out-of-town' is not used in this chapter, except in quotations from the literature.

3   Up to 1988, the vast majority of cases were decided by Secretaries of State (i.e. in most cases, civil servants). The procedural rules were changed in 1988. In the period 1988–90 inclusive, 53 out of 95 superstore proposals (56 per cent) were determined by inspectors, compared with only 10 per cent in the previous period (Lee Donaldson, 1991: 44). However, a larger proportion of retail warehouse cases were determined by inspectors (Gibbs, 1986: 2).

4   Defined as 'a group of retail outlets designed and built as a unified whole under one roof ... supported by car parking facilities' (SDD, 1986: para 3).

5   There is some overlap between the two samples, but the Lee Donaldson sample of 50 cases is restricted to planning inquiries, whereas the Gibbs sample of 122 cases is over a shorter period (1981–85) but includes cases decided by written representations.

6   The RTPI Working Party were concerned enough about this issue to print a map of regional shopping centre proposals on the back cover of their report (RTPI, 1988).

7   Enterprise Zones with no control over retail development were more rare than is usually acknowledged. In most cases the development of food retailing above a size limit was subject to planning consent. In Swansea EZ, consent was required for any individual development of over 45,000 sq.ft. (Guy, 1994a: 174).

4 Tightening up

1   Under Section 121 of the Government of Wales Act 1998.

2   It should be made clear that government policy has prioritised central, rather than brownfield, sites for retail development.

3   For a brief history see http://sdgateway.net/introsd.

4   The term 'town centres' is intended to include city centres and district centres, except where otherwise indicated.

5   This was reduced from a proposed 5,000 sq.m. in the draft guidance.

6   A more detailed review of problems in interpretation of PPG6, and consequent modifications of the guidance, can be found in CBHP (2004: Chapter 2).

7   Michael Bach (personal communication) has explained that 'The brief was to assess the effectiveness [of PPG6] in achieving its objectives, not to question the policy or [to] rewrite – that is a matter for the Secretary of State'. See Chapter Ten for further discussion of this issue.

8   In the Planning and Compulsory Purchase Act of 2004, regional spatial strategies were given the status of statutory documents which would 'guide' the local development frameworks produced by local authorities.

9   This may be partly because Government Regional Offices scrutinise local plans for conformity with national policy.

10 Note however that a survey of major food retailers and local authorities indicated that 77 per cent of all applications for new food stores and extensions which were out-of-centre or out-of-town were approved between 1996 and 1999, compared with 80 per cent in edge-of-centre locations and 89 per cent within town centres (Competition Commission, 2000a: Vol.3, 467).

11 Defined as over 1,000 sq.m. gross floor space or where site area is 1 hectare or more.

12 Of over 5,000 sq.m.

13 Analyses of short-term series of decisions have been published by property consultants (e.g. DTZ Pieda, 2000; Drivers Jonas, 2003); and in the series of Planning Newsletter at www.accessibleretail.co.uk/newsletters.html.

14 Note that the 'out-of-town' floorspace did not include free-standing superstores and retail warehouses, or extensions to existing such stores.

15 The fourth major food retailer, Asda, built few new stores at this time because of financial difficulties following the acquisition of a parcel of existing superstores in 1989 (Wrigley, 1992).

16 Ironically, B and Q have (unsuccessfully) lobbied the government to prevent fashion retailers from occupying retail parks, in order to keep rents at an affordable level (Cockram, 2003).

17 Gross lettable area, including A3 uses. Source of information: BCSC (2005).

5 Demand, need and impact

1   The value of x was never officially set, but in practice has varied between about 5 and 15 per cent.

2   Some commentators would agree that this remains the case.

3   The equivalent of the planning inspectors in the English and Welsh systems.

4   Source: *WordNet ® 2.0, © 2003 Princeton University.*
5   Strictly speaking, trading impact expressed as a percentage of sales at an existing store might be high, but the store would remain viable.
6   For further discussion, see Guy (2006b), and ODPM guidance on Assessing Need and Impact of New Retail and Leisure Development, which was due to be published in 2006.

6 Innovation, productivity, competition and retail planning

1   In hindsight, this view seems exaggerated. Some shoppers are well aware of price differences between stores, and will 'cherry-pick', buying only those items which are seen as especially good value for money.
2   At that time, minimum wage legislation existed in France but not in Britain.
3   Subsequently, an investigation of this and other related issues was begun by the Competition Commission.
4   In evidence to the Competition Commission (2000a: paras 2.27–2.32), both Tesco and Sainsbury disputed the Commission's 'two markets' analysis. This of course preceded their move into convenience store retailing.

7 Sustainability, shopping travel and retail policy

1   Other aspects of sustainability, for which retailers are often criticised, include packaging, waste disposal, and 'food miles' incurred in sourcing goods from remote places (for a summary of retailers' responses, see BRC, n.d.). These are however outside the scope of retail planning as defined in this book.
2   This latter argument is discussed in Chapter Eight.
3   A survey carried out at a retail park in Sheffield found that on average, fewer shoppers arrived in each incoming bus than in each car (MORI, 2000). Another survey at Meadowhall Regional Shopping Centre recorded zero arrivals by bicycle (Ibrahim and McGoldrick, 2003: 72).
4   Thanks are due to David Bennison and Tesco Stores Ltd for allowing access to this unpublished information.
5   This may include some other shopping in premises adjacent to out-of-centre stores.
6   In support of this argument, a survey of shoppers at Somerfield stores found a high proportion of linked trips in town centres, with 46 pence spent elsewhere for every pound spent in the Somerfield store, compared with 21 pence for edge-of-centre stores and 10 pence for out-of-centre (reported in OXIRM, 2004: 14). Somerfield stores are generally much smaller than those operated by Tesco, Safeway or Sainsbury.

7 This is often concealed in official statistics: for example, until recently, the National Travel Survey did not record walking trips of less than one mile.

8 Social exclusion, access to shopping and retail policy

1 The date for this commitment has been revised to 2021, in a follow-up report (Cabinet Office, 2005b).
2 Source: Mark Bradshaw, personal communication
3 Recommendations for improving transport in areas of social exclusion were however presented in the *Making the Connections* report (SEU, 2003).

9 Urban regeneration and retail policy

1 Source: Mark Bradshaw, personal communication.
2 A presentation by a Tesco representative at the NRPF conference on Retail Planning Policy: The Next Ten Years, held in November 2005, consisted solely of descriptions of large-scale mixed-use schemes in town centres.
3 Although such schemes can also increase the incidence of walking trips (see Chapter Eight).

10 An evaluation of retail planning policy

1 Michael Bach (personal communication) has commented that the 'increasing detail is due to the resourceful approach of retailers/developers' in supporting their case at appeal inquiries etc.
2 Under which the detailed content of meetings are not made public, in order to encourage frankness in debate.
3 Some of the remaining 60 per cent of floorspace was located in centres too small to be included in the database concerned.
4 http://evidencenetwork.org/Bibliography.html, accessed 12 January 2006
5 I have argued elsewhere (Guy, 2006b) that assessment of 'quantitative need' in development control is unnecessary and could be omitted from government policy guidance.
6 The draft Scottish and revised Welsh advice mentioned in Table 10.2 could serve as examples.
7 It is tempting to suggest that these should be carried out by a neutral body of experts, as is the case in some western European countries. This would reduce the power of the private sector developer, save time and effort for the local authority and ensure some consistency in judgement.

Bibliography

Accessible Retail (2004) *Comments on Consultation Paper on Draft Planning Policy Statement 6*, http://www.accessibleretail.co.uk/press/2004/PPS6%20Final%20Signature%20Draft%2019%20March%202004.pdf.

Acheson, D. (1998) *Independent Inquiry Into Inequalities in Health*, London: TSO.

Action for Market Towns and Countryside Agency (n.d.), *Market Towns and Local Food*, http://www.countryside.gov.uk/Images/food_tcm2-15778.pdf.

Adair, A., Berry, J., McGreal, S., Poon, J., Hutchison, N., Watkins, C. and Gibb, K. (2005) 'Investment performance within urban regeneration locations', *Journal of Property Investment and Finance*, 23: 7–21.

Adams, D. and Hutchison, N. (2000) 'The urban task force report: reviewing land ownership constraints to brownfield redevelopment', *Regional Studies*, 34: 777–82.

Adams, D., Disberry, A., Hutchison, N. and Munjoma, T. (2002) 'Retail location, competition and urban redevelopment', *Services Industries Journal*, 22: 135–48.

Adlard, H. (2001) 'The "need" for retail development', *Journal of Planning and Environmental Law*, 522–34.

Ambrose, P.J. and Colenutt, R.J. (1975) *The Property Machine*, Harmondsworth: Penguin.

Anon. (1972) 'Comment by pragma: Planners versus shopping centres', *RTPI Journal*, 58: 244.

Anon. (1987) 'Comment', *Retail and Distribution Management*, 15 (2): 7.

Arnold, S. (1998) 'Proof that need is not an issue', *Planning*, 20 November: 10.

Asda (Associated Dairies Group plc) (1984) *Annual Report and Accounts*, Leeds.

Asda (1999) *Memorandum to the Select Committee on Environment, Transport and Regional Affairs: The Environmental Impact of Supermarket Competition*, London: TSO.

Asda (2005) *Asda and the Environment*, www.asda.co.uk/asda_corp/scripts/allaboutasda/aanewStores.

B and Q (2002) *Memorandum to the Select Committee on Office of the Deputy Prime Minister: Housing, Planning and Local Government and the Regions: Planning, Competitiveness and Productivity*, London: TSO.

Baker, N. (2002) *Retail Development and Regeneration: An Investigation into the Relationship Between Retail Planning Policy and Urban Regeneration*, Cardiff University: Dissertation for the Diploma in Town Planning.

Bamfield, J.A.N. (1980) 'The changing face of British retailing', *National Westminster Bank Quarterly Review*, May: 33–45.

Banister, D. (1994) 'Viewpoint: reducing the need to travel through planning', *Town Planning Review*, 65: 349–54.

Banister, D. (1997) 'Reducing the need to travel', *Environment and Planning B: Planning and Design*, 24: 437–49.

Banister, D. (1999) 'Planning more to travel less', *Town Planning Review*, 70: 313–38.

Barrett, G. (1996) 'The transport dimension', in Jenks, M., Burton, E. and Williams, K. (eds) *The Compact City: A Sustainable Urban Form?*, London: Chapman Hall / E and F N Spon, 171–80.

Bartlett School (2004) *Evidence from the University College London, Bartlett School of Planning, to the Environmental Planning Study*, London: Royal Commission on Environmental Pollution.

Bartlett, R. (2003) 'Testing the "popsicle test": realities of retail shopping in new "traditional neighbourhood developments"', *Urban Studies*, 40: 1471–85.

BDP Planning and Oxford Institute of Retail Management (1992) *The Effects of Major Out of Town Retail Development: A Literature Review for the Department of the Environment*, London: HMSO.

Beaumont, J., Lang, T., Leather, S. and Mucklow, C. (1995) *Report from the Policy Sub-Group to the Nutrition Task Force: Low Income Project Team*, Letchmore Heath: Institute of Grocery Distribution.

Bennison, D. and Davies, R.L. (1980) 'The impact of town centres shopping schemes in Britain: their impact on traditional retail environments', *Progress in Planning*, 14 (1).

Bennison, D., Byrom, J., Hogg, S. and Pal, J. (2000) *Linked Shopping Trips: A Report for Tesco Stores Ltd*, Manchester Metropolitan University, Department of Retailing and Marketing.

Bennison, D., Clarke, I. and Pal, J. (1995) 'Locational decision making in retailing: an exploratory framework for analysis', *International Review of Retail, Distribution and Consumer Research*, 5: 1–20.

Berry, B.J.L. (1967) *Geography of Market Centers and Retail Distribution*, Englewood Cliffs: Prentice-Hall.

Berry, B.J.L. and Parr, J.B. (1988) *Market Centers and Retail Location: Theory and Applications*, Englewood Cliffs: Prentice-Hall.

Birkin, M., Clarke, G. and Clarke, M. (2002) *Retail Geography and Intelligent Network Planning*, Chichester: Wiley.

Blake, J. (1976) 'Brent Cross: a regional shopping centre', *The Planner*, 62: 115–7.

Blythe, G. (1982) 'Relationships between the local authority and the private sector in the provision of retail facilities, using Swindon as a case study', *Proceedings of the PTRC Summer Annual Meeting*, C13.

Boddewyn, J.J. and Hollander, S.C. (1972) *Public Policy Toward Retailing*, Lexington, MA: Lexington Books.

Booth, P. (2003) *Planning by Consent: The Origins and Nature of British Development Control*, London: Routledge.

Bore, J. (2001) 'Planning Policy Guidance Note 6: An inspector's view', *Presentation to RTPI/Croner CCH Seminar on Planning and Retailing: PPG6 Five Years On*, London.

Bowhill, A. (2005) comment reported in http://seattlepi.nwsource.com/business/215272_costcouk10.html.

Bowhill, Anthony and Associates (2002) *BCOTR Newsletter Issue No 6*, London: British Council for Out-of-Town Retail.

Bowlby, S.R. (1984) 'Planning for women to shop in post-war Britain', *Environment and Planning D: Society and Space*, 2: 179–99.

Braithwaite, J. (1997) 'Scottish shopping guidance still wanting', *Town and Country Planning*, 66: 22–4.

Bray, M.E. (2003) *Retail Impact Assessment, Vitality and Viability and Future Planning Policy*, Cardiff University: Dissertation for the Diploma in Town Planning.

Breheny, M. (1995) 'The compact city and transport energy consumption', *Transactions of the Institute of British Geographers*, 20: 81–101.

British Council for Out of Town Retail (2002) *Research Report 2001–2002*, http://www.accessibleretail.co.uk/pdf/research/RESEARCH%20REPORT%2001-02.pdf.

British Council of Shopping Centres (1996) *Town Centre Futures: The Long-Term Impact of New Developments, Key Findings and Recommendations*, London: BCSC.

British Council of Shopping Centres (1997) *Public Transport and Town Centre Accessibility: Summary Report*, London: BCSC.

British Council of Shopping Centres (2004) *The Smaller Towns Report: Delivering Retail-led Renaissance in Towns and Smaller Cities*, London: BCSC.

British Council of Shopping Centres (2005) *Pipeline Development A1 Poster*, London: BCSC.

British Retail Consortium (2004) *Policies & Issues Content: Property & Regeneration*, http://www.brc.org.uk/policycontent04.asp?iCat=47&iSubCat=164&sPolicy=Property+%26+Regeneration&sSubPolicy=Regeneration.

British Retail Consortium (n.d.) *Towards Retail Sustainability: Protecting our Environment for the Future*, London: BRC.

Bromley, R.D.F. and Thomas, C.J. (1993) 'The retail revolution, the carless shopper and disadvantage', *Transactions of the Institute of British Geographers*, 18: 222–36.

Bromley, R.D.F. and Thomas, C.J. (1995) 'Small town shopping decline: dependence and inconvenience for the disadvantaged', *International Review of Retail, Distribution and Consumer Research*, 5: 433–55.

Bromley, R.D.F. and Thomas, C.J. (2002) 'Food shopping and town centre vitality: exploring the link', *International Review of Retail, Distribution and Consumer Research*, 12: 109–30.

Brown, C. (2003) 'Legal challenge to "town centre" plan for steel works site', *The Scotsman*, 2 September: 28.

Burns, W. (1959) *British Shopping Centres: New Trends in Layout and Distribution*, London: Leonard Hill.

Burt, S., Dawson, J.A. and Sparks, L. (1983) 'Structure Plans and retailing policies', *The Planner*, 69: 11–13.

Business in the Community (2004) *Under-served Markets: Preliminary Findings*, London: BITC.

Business in the Community (2005) *Tesco Regeneration Programme*, http://www.bitc. org.uk/resources/case_studies/tesco_regenerati.html.

Cabinet Office (1999) *Modernising Government*, London: HMSO.

Cabinet Office: Social Exclusion Unit (2001) *A New Commitment to Neighbourhood Renewal: A National Strategy Action Plan*, London: SEU.

Cabinet Office: Prime Minister's Strategy Unit, and Office of the Deputy Prime Minister (2005a) *Improving the Prospects of People Living in Areas of Multiple Deprivation in England*, London: Prime Minister's Strategy Unit.

Cabinet Office: Prime Minister's Strategy Unit (2005b) 'Government proposals aim to turn around deprived areas by 2021', *Press Release*, 31 January.

Caborn, R. (1999a) *Answer to Parliamentary Question in the House of Commons*, Hansard Col. 308, February.

Caborn, R. (1999b) *Answer to Parliamentary Question in the House of Commons*, Hansard Col. 138, June.

Cairns, S. (1995) 'Travel for food shopping: the fourth solution', *Traffic Engineering and Control*, 36: 411–18.

Cairns, S. (2005) 'Delivering supermarket shopping: more or less traffic?', *Transport Reviews*, 25: 51–84.

Campaign for the Protection of Rural England (1998) *Food Webs*, London: CPRE.

Campaign for the Protection of Rural England (2004) *Market Towns: Losing their Character?*, London: CPRE.

Campbell, H. and Henneberry, J. (2005) 'Planning obligations, the market orientation of planning and planning professionalism', *Journal of Property Research*, 22: 37–59.

Cannings, E. (2000) *District Centres and Food Retail Development: An Analysis of Superstores in District Centres*, Papers in Planning Research 179, Cardiff University: Department of City and Regional Planning.

Cannings, E. (2001) 'Planning out the food deserts', *Town and Country Planning*, 70: 303–4.

Carley, M., Kirk, K. and McIntosh, S. (2001) *Retailing, Sustainability and Neighbourhood Regeneration*, York: York Publishing Services.

CB Hillier Parker and Savell Bird Axon (1998) *The Impact of Large Foodstores on Market Towns and District Centres, Report for the Department of Environment, Transport and the Regions*, London: TSO.

CB Hillier Parker (2000) *The Sequential Approach to Retail Development*, London: National Retail Planning Forum.

CB Hillier Parker (2002) *B & Q Warehouse Research: Summary Report*, London: CBHP.

CB Hillier Parker and Cardiff University (2004) *Policy Evaluation of the Effectiveness of PPG6*, London: Office of the Deputy Prime Minister.

CB Richard Ellis (2003) *B & Q: The Implications of Retail Planning Policies for the DIY Sector*, London: CBRE.

CB Richard Ellis (2004a) *Retail Warehouse Parks in the Pipeline: Q4 2003*, London: CBRE.

CB Richard Ellis (2004b) *The Role and Vitality of Secondary Shopping – a New Direction*, London: National Retail Planning Forum.

CB Richard Ellis, University of Stirling and Colin Buchanan and Partners (2004c) *Research Study on the Effectiveness of NPPG8: Town Centres and Retailing, Report to the Scottish Executive Development Department*, Edinburgh: SEDD.

CB Richard Ellis (2005a) *Shopping Centres in the Pipeline: Q3 2005*, London: CBRE.

CB Richard Ellis (2005b) *UK Prime Rent & Yield Monitor: Q4 2005*, London: CBRE.

Centre for Advanced Spatial Analysis (2000) *Town Centre Vitality and Viability: A Review of the Health Check Methodology*, London: National Retail Planning Forum.

Chesters, L. (2004) 'Black Country blueprint', *Property Week*, 5 November: 85–7.

Clarke, G., Eyre, H. and Guy, C. (2002) 'Deriving indicators of access to food retail provision in British cities: studies of Cardiff, Leeds and Bradford', *Urban Studies*, 39: 2041–60.

Clarke, I. (2000) 'Retail power, competition and local consumer choice in the UK grocery sector', *European Journal of Marketing*, 34: 975–1002.

Clarke, I., Jackson, P., Hallsworth, A., de Kervenoael, R., Perez del Aguila, R. and Kirkup, M. (2004) *Retail Competition and Consumer Choice: Workshop Briefing Note*, Lancaster University Management School.

Clarke, R., Davies, S., Dobson, P. and Waterson, M. (2002) *Buyer Power and Competition in European Food Retailing*, Cheltenham: Edward Elgar.

Coca-Stefaniak, A., Hallsworth, A.G., Parker, C., Bainbridge, S. and Yuste, R. (2005)

'Decline in the British small shop independent retail sector: exploring European parallels', *Journal of Retailing and Consumer Services*, 12: 357–71.

Cockram, A. (2003) 'Sore point', *Estates Gazette*, 20 September: 58–9.

Commission for Architecture and the Built Environment (2004) *Design Reviewed: Town Centre Retail*, London: CABE.

Commission of the European Communities (1990) *Green Paper on the Urban Environment*, Brussels: European Commission.

Competition Commission (2000a) *Supermarkets: A Report on the Supply of Groceries from Multiple Stores in the United Kingdom*, London: TSO.

Competition Commission (2000b) *Supermarkets: Remedies Statement*, http://www.competition-commission.org.uk/inquiries/completed/2000/supermarkets/10-00rem.htm.

Competition Commission (2003) *Safeway plc and Asda Group Limited (owned by Wal-Mart Stores Inc); Wm Morrison Supermarkets plc; J Sainsbury plc; and Tesco plc: A Report on the Mergers in Contemplation*, London: TSO.

Corner, D.C. (1969) 'Recent trends in retail distribution', *National Westminster Bank Quarterly Review*, May: 22–32.

Costco (2005) http://www.costco.co.uk/what_is_costco/what_is_costco.htm, accessed 5.5.05.

Couper, M. and Barker, A. (1981) 'Joint and linked inquiries: the superstore experience', *Journal of Planning and Environment Law*, September: 631–55.

Cox, R.K. (1968) *Retail Site Assessment*, London: Business Books.

Crane, R. (1996) 'Cars and drivers in the new suburbs: linking access to travel in neotraditional planning', *Journal of the American Planning Association*, 62: 51–65.

Crow, S., Brown, A., Essex, S., Thomas, H. and Yewlett, C. (1997) *Slimmer and Swifter: a Critical Examination of District Wide Local Plans and UDPs*, London: Royal Town Planning Institute.

Cullingworth, J.B. and Nadin, V. (1997) *Town and Country Planning in the UK (12th edn)*, London: Routledge.

Cummins, S. and McIntyre, S. (1999) 'The location of food stores in urban areas: a case study in Glasgow', *British Food Journal*, 101: 545–53.

Cummins, S. and McIntyre, S. (2002a) 'A systematic study of an urban foodscape: the price and availability of food in Greater Glasgow', *Urban Studies*, 39: 2115–30.

Cummins, S. and McIntyre, S. (2002b) '"Food deserts" – evidence and assumption in health policy making', *British Medical Journal*, 325: 436–8.

Cummins, S., Findlay, A., Petticrew, M., and Sparks, L. (2005a) 'Healthy cities: the impact of food retail led regeneration on food access, choice and retail structure', *Built Environment*, 31: 288–301.

Cummins, S., Petticrew, M., Sparks, L. and Findlay, A. (2005b) 'Large scale food retail intervention and diet', *British Medical Journal*, 330: 683–4.

Davies, G. and Brooks, J.M. (1989) *Positioning Strategy in Retailing*, London: Chapman.

Davies, K. and Sparks, L. (1989) 'The development of superstore retailing in Great Britain 1960–1986: results from a new database', *Transactions of the Institute of British Geographers*, 14: 74–89.

Davies, R.L. (1976) *Marketing Geography – with Special Reference to Retailing*, Corbridge: Retailing and Planning Associates.

Davies, R.L. (1977) 'A framework for commercial planning policies', *Town Planning Review*, 48: 42–58.

Davies, R.L. (ed.) (1979) *Retail Planning in the European Community*, Farnborough: Saxon House.

Davies, R.L. (1984) *Retail and Commercial Planning*, Beckenham: Croom Helm.

Davies, R.L. (1985) 'The Gateshead Shopping and Information Service', *Environment and Planning B: Planning and Design*, 12: 209–20.

Davies, R.L. (ed.) (1995) *Retail Planning Policies in Western Europe*, London: Routledge.

Davies, R.L. (2004) 'Planning policy', in Reynolds, J. and Cuthbertson, C. (eds) *Retail Strategy: The View from the Bridge*, Oxford: Elsevier, 78–95.

Davies, R.L. and Champion, A.G. (1980) *Social Inequality in Shopping Opportunities: How the Private Sector Can Respond*, Cheshunt: Tesco Stores.

Davies, R.L. and Howard, E. (1989) 'Issues in retail planning within the United Kingdom', *Built Environment*, 14: 7–21.

Dawson, J. and Sparks, L. (1986) 'Information provision for retail planning', *The Planner*, 72 (7): 23–6.

Dawson, J.A. (1983a) *Public Policy Controls on Hypermarket Development*, University of Stirling, Department of Business Studies, Working Paper 8302.

Dawson, J.A. (1983b) *Shopping Centre Development*, London: Longman.

Dawson, J.A. and Broadbridge, A.M. (1988) *Retailing in Scotland 2005*, University of Stirling: Institute for Retail Studies.

Delafons, J. (1995) 'Policy forum: planning research and the policy process', *Town Planning Review*, 66: 83–95.

Department for Transport (2005a) *Focus on Personal Travel*, London: TSO.

Department for Transport (2005b) *National Travel Survey 2004*, London: TSO.

Department of Food and Rural Affairs (2003a) *Local Food – A Snapshot of the Sector*, London: DEFRA.

Department of Food and Rural Affairs (2003b) *Policy Paper on Local Food*, London: DEFRA.

Department of Health (1999a) *Improving Shopping Access for People Living in Deprived Neighbourhoods: Discussion Paper of Policy Action Team 13 of the National Strategy for Neighbourhood Renewal*, London: Department of Health.

Department of Health (1999b) *Reducing Inequalities in Health: An Action Report*, London: DoH.

Department of the Environment (1976) *The Eastleigh Carrefour: a Hypermarket and its Effects*, DoE Research Report 16, London: HMSO.

Department of the Environment (1978) *The Eastleigh Carrefour Hypermarket After Three Years*, DoE Research Report 27, London: HMSO.

Department of the Environment (1990a) *This Common Inheritance: Britain's Environmental Strategy*, London: HMSO.

Department of the Environment (1990b) *Planning Policy Guidance 15: Regional Planning Guidance, Structure Plans, and the Content of Development Plans*, London: HMSO.

Department of the Environment (1995a) *Shopping Centres and their Future: The Government's Response to the Fourth Report from the House of Commons Select Committee on the Environment*, London: HMSO.

Department of the Environment (1995b) *Revised PPG6: Consultation Draft*, London.

Department of the Environment (1996) *Planning Policy Guidance Note 6 (Revised): Town Centres and Retail Developments*, London: HMSO.

Department of the Environment (1997) *Planning Policy Guidance 1: General Policy and Principles*, London: TSO.

Department of the Environment and Welsh Office (1972a) *Out of Town Shops and Shopping Centres*, DoE Circular 17/72, WO Circular 48/72, London: HMSO.

Department of the Environment and Welsh Office (1972b) *Out of Town Shops and Shopping Centres*, Development Control Policy Note 13, London: HMSO.

Department of the Environment and Welsh Office (1974) *Warehouses – Wholesale, Cash and Carry, etc.*, Development Control Policy Note 14, London: HMSO.

Department of the Environment and Welsh Office (1976) *Large New Stores*, DoE Circular 71/76, WO Circular 98/76, London: HMSO.

Department of the Environment and Welsh Office (1977a) *Large New Stores*, Development Control Policy Note 13, London: HMSO.

Department of the Environment and Welsh Office (1977b) *Large New Stores*, DoE Circular 96/77, WO Circular 154/77, London: HMSO.

Department of the Environment and Welsh Office (1980) *Development Control – Policy and Practice*, DoE Circular 22/80, WO Circular 40/80, London: HMSO.

Department of the Environment and Welsh Office (1981) *Local Government, Planning and Land Act 1980. Town and Country Planning: Development Plans*, DoE Circular 23/81, WO Circular 34/81, London: HMSO.

Department of the Environment and Welsh Office (1984) *Memorandum on Structure and Local Plans*, DoE Circular 22/84, WO Circular 43/84, London: HMSO.

Department of the Environment and Welsh Office (1985) *Development and Employment*, DoE Circular 14/85, WO Circular 38/85, London: HMSO.

Department of the Environment and Welsh Office (1986) *Town and Country Planning (Shopping Development) (England and Wales) Direction 1986*, DoE Circular 21/86, WO Circular 54/86, London: HMSO.

Department of the Environment and Welsh Office (1988a) *Planning Policy Guidance Note 6: Major Retail Development*, London: HMSO.

Department of the Environment and Welsh Office (1988b) *Planning Policy Guidance Note 1: General Policy and Principles*, London: HMSO.

Department of the Environment and Welsh Office (1992) *Planning Policy Guidance Note 1: General Policy and Principles*, London: HMSO.

Department of the Environment and Welsh Office (1993) *Planning Policy Guidance Note 6 (Revised): Town Centres and Retail Developments*, London: HMSO.

Department of the Environment, Transport and the Regions (1997) *The Government's Response to the Fourth Report from the House of Commons Select Committee on the Environment: Shopping Centres*, London: TSO.

Department of the Environment, Transport and the Regions (1998) *Planning for Sustainable Development: Towards Better Practice*, London: TSO.

Department of the Environment, Transport and the Regions (1999) *A Better Quality of Life – Strategy for Sustainable Development for the United Kingdom*, London: TSO.

Department of the Environment, Transport and the Regions (2000) *Environmental Impact of Supermarket Competition, Response to Report of the House of Commons Select Committee*, London: TSO.

Department of Trade and Industry (2004) *Driving Change: The Retail Strategy Group Report*, London: DTI.

Department of Transport, Local Government and the Regions (2001) *Focus on Personal Travel*, London: TSO.

Departments of the Environment and Transport (1994) *Planning Policy Guidance 13: Transport*, London: HMSO.

Departments of the Environment and Transport (1995) *PPG13: A Guide to Better Practice*, London: HMSO.

Diamond, D.R. and Gibb, E.B. (1962) 'Development of new shopping centres: area estimation', *Scottish Journal of Political Economy*, 9: 130–46.

Dischkoff, N. (1979) 'Retail planning in West Germany', in Davies, R.L. (ed.) *Retail Planning in the European Community*, Farnborough: Saxon House.

Distributive Trades Economic Development Council (1970) *Urban Models in Shopping Studies*, London: HMSO.

Distributive Trades Economic Development Council (1971) *The Future Pattern of Shopping*, London: HMSO.

Distributive Trades Economic Development Council (1988) *The Future of the High Street*, London: HMSO.

Dixon, T.J. and Marston, A.D. (2002), 'UK retail estate and the effects of online shopping', *Journal of Urban Technology*, 9: 253–80.

Dixon, T.J. and Marston, A.D. (2003) *The Role of UK Retailing in Urban Regeneration*, Reading: College of Estate Management.

Donaldsons and Healey and Baker (1994) *The Effectiveness of Town Centre Management*, London: Association of Town Centre Management.

Donkin, A.J.M., Dowler, E.A., Stevenson, S.J. and Turner, S.A. (1999a) 'Mapping access to food at a local level', *British Food Journal*, 101: 554–64.

Donkin, A.J.M., Dowler, E.A., Stevenson, S.J. and Turner, S.A. (1999b) 'Mapping access to food in a deprived area: the development of price and availability indices', *Public Health Nutrition*, 3: 31–8.

Dowler, E., Blair, A., Rex, D. and Grundy, C. (2001) *Measuring access to Healthy Food in Sandwell: Final Report June 2001*, University of Warwick and Sandwell Health Action Zone.

Drivers Jonas (1992) *Retail Impact Assessment Methodologies: Research Study for the Scottish Office Environment Department*, Edinburgh: Scottish Office Central Research Unit.

Drivers Jonas (2003) *Analysis of Retail Planning Appeal Decisions*, London: Drivers Jonas.

DTZ Pieda Consulting (2000) *Retail Appeals Bulletin*, London.

DTZ Pieda Consulting (2004a) *National Retail Expenditure Growth Forecasts*, Information Brief 01/04, London: DTZ.

DTZ Pieda Consulting (2004b) *The Retail Development Process and Land Assembly, Report for DTI Retail Strategy Group*, London: DTZ Pieda Consulting.

Economic and Social Research Council (2005) *Society Today – The Digital Economy in the UK*, www.esrcsocietytoday.ac.uk/ESRCInfoCentre/facts/index48.aspx.

ECOTEC Research and Consulting Ltd (1993) *Reducing Transport Emissions Through Planning*, Department of the Environment Planning Research Programme and Department of Transport, London: HMSO.

Edwards, M. and Martin, J. (2005) 'Putting the spin into planning', *Estates Gazette*, Issue 511: 178.

England, J. (2000) *Retail Impact Assessment: A Guide to Best Practice*, London: Routledge.

Evans, R. (1997) *Regenerating Town Centres*, Manchester: Manchester University Press.

Evely, R. (1980) 'The impact of new developments: The Coatbridge Study', *Proceedings of the PTRC Summer Annual Meeting*, F7.

Evers, D.V.H. (2004) *Building for Consumption: An Institutional Analysis of Peripheral Shopping Center Development in Northwest Europe*, PhD Dissertation, University of Amsterdam.

Falconer, Lord (2002) *Speech to BURA/BRC Conference on Retail and Regeneration*, Birmingham, 14 May.

Farthing, S., Winter, J. and Coombes, T. (1996) 'Travel behaviour and local accessibility to services and facilities', in Jenks, M., Burton, E. and Williams, K. (eds) *The*

Compact City: A Sustainable Urban Form?, London: Chapman Hall/ E and F N Spon, 181–9.

Fell, D. (1999) *The Impact of Out-of-Town Food Superstores on Local Retail Employment: A Critique of the Boots Study*, London: National Retail Planning Forum.

Fernie, J. (1998) 'The breaking of the fourth wave: recent out-of-town retail developments in Britain', *International Review of Retail, Distribution and Consumer Research*, 8: 303–17.

Fernie, J. and Fernie, S. (1997) 'The development of a US retail format in Europe: the case of factory outlet centres', *International Journal of Retail and Distribution Management*, 25: 342–50.

Finch, J. (2006) 'Asda boss urges OFT to curb Tesco's growth', *The Guardian*, February 4.

Findlay, A.M. and Sparks, L. (2005) *Publications on Retail Planning in 2004*, University of Stirling: Institute for Retail Studies.

Finney, J.E. and Robinson, J. (1976) 'District shopping centres: some case studies', *Proceedings of the PTRC Summer Annual Meeting*, G16.

Fitch, D. (2004) 'Measuring convenience: Scots' perceptions of local food and retail provision', *International Journal of Retail and Distribution Management*, 32: 100–8.

Food Standards Agency (2004) *Results and Dissemination: Do Food Deserts Exist? A Multi-level, Geographical Analysis of the Relationship Between Retail Food Access, Socio-Economic Position and Dietary Intake (N09010)*, London: FSA.

Friends of the Earth (2004) *Press Release: Government Must Protect UK Town Centres*, London.

Friends of the Earth (2005) *Briefing: Good Neighbours? Community Impacts of Supermarkets*, London: FoE.

Friends of the Earth (2006a) *Calling the Shots: How Supermarkets Get Their Way in Planning Decisions*, London: FoE.

Friends of the Earth (2006b) *Press Release: Supermarket Heavyweights Trample Planning System*, London: FoE.

Garreau, J. (1991) *Edge City: Life on the New Frontier*, New York: Anchor Books.

Gayler, H.J. (1984) *Retail Innovation in Britain: The Problems of Out-of-Town Shopping Centre Development*, Norwich: Geo Books.

Gibbs, A. (1981) *An Analysis of Retail Warehouse Planning Inquiries*, Reading: Unit for Retail Planning Information, URPI U22.

Gibbs, A. (1986) *Retail Warehouse Planning Inquiries 1981–85*, Reading: Unit for Retail Planning Information, URPI U28.

Goddard, C. (2000) 'Consistency in retail decisions', *Planning Inspectorate Journal*, Issue 20: 14–15.

Gordon, P. and Richardson, H.W. (1997) 'Are compact cities a desirable planning goal?', *Journal of the American Planning Association*, 63: 95–106.

Goss, A. (1973) 'A better decision process', *Built Environment*, 2: 80–4.

Greater London Authority (2004) *Draft Best Practice Guidance: Making Better Use of Supermarket Sites*, London: GLA.

Greater London Authority (2005) *Retail in London: Working Paper B, Retail and Regeneration*, http://www.london.gov.uk/mayor/economic_unit/docs/retail_wpb_retail_and_regeneration.pdf.

Griffith, R. and Harmgart, H. (2005) 'Retail productivity', *International Review of Retail, Distribution and Consumer Research*, 15: 281–90.

Guariglia, A. (2002) 'Superstores and labour demand: evidence from Great Britain', *Journal of Applied Economics*, 5: 233–52.

Gummer, J. (1994) 'Planning for sustainable development', *Town and Country Planning*, 63: 78–9.

Guy, C.M. (1980) *Retail Location and Retail Planning in Britain*, Farnborough: Gower.

Guy, C.M. (1985) 'The food and grocery shopping behaviour of disadvantaged consumers: some results from the Cardiff Consumer Panel', *Transactions of the Institute of British Geographers*, 10: 181–90.

Guy, C.M. (1988) 'Retail planning policy and large store development: a case study in South Wales', *Land Development Studies*, 5: 31–45.

Guy, C.M. (1990) 'Outshopping from small towns', *International Journal of Retail and Distribution Management*, 18 (2): 3–14.

Guy, C.M. (1992) 'Estimating shopping centre turnover: a review of survey methods', *International Journal of Retail and Distribution Management*, 20 (4): 18–23.

Guy, C.M. (1994a) *The Retail Development Process*, London: Routledge.

Guy, C.M. (1994b) 'Whatever happened to regional shopping centres?', *Geography*, 79: 293–312.

Guy, C.M. (1994c) 'Grocery store saturation: has it arrived yet?', *International Journal of Retail and Distribution Management*, 22(1): 3–11.

Guy, C.M. (1995) 'Retail store development at the margin', *Journal of Retailing and Consumer Services*, 2: 25–32.

Guy, C.M. (1996a) 'Grocery store saturation in the UK – the continuing debate', *International Journal of Retail and Distribution Management*, 24 (6): 3–10.

Guy, C.M. (1996b) 'Corporate strategies in food retailing and their locational implications: a case study of Cardiff', *Environment and Planning A*, 28: 1575–602.

Guy, C.M. (1997) 'Fixed assets or sunk costs? An examination of retailers' land and property investment in the United Kingdom', *Environment and Planning A*, 29: 1449–64.

Guy, C.M. (1998a) 'Controlling new retail spaces: the impress of planning policies in western Europe', *Urban Studies*, 35: 953–79.

Guy, C.M. (1998b) '"High street" retailing in off-centre retail parks: a review of the effectiveness of land use planning policies', *Town Planning Review*, 69: 291–313.

Guy, C.M. (1998c) 'Alternative-use valuation, open A1 consent and the development of retail parks', *Environment and Planning A*, 30: 37–47.

Guy, C.M. (1999) 'Exit strategies and sunk costs: the implications for multiple retailers', *International Journal of Retail and Distribution Management*, 27: 237–45.

Guy, C.M. (2000) 'From crinkly sheds to fashion parks: the role of financial investment in the transformation of retail parks', *International Review of Retail, Distribution and Consumer Research*, 10: 389–400.

Guy, C.M. (2001) 'Internationalisation of large-format retailers and leisure providers in western Europe: planning and property impacts', *International Journal of Retail and Distribution Management*, 29: 452–61.

Guy, C.M. (2002a) 'Of outings and outlets', *Town and Country Planning*, 71: 4–5.

Guy, C.M. (2002b) 'Is retail planning policy effective? The case of very large store development in the UK', *Planning Theory and Practice*, 3: 319–30.

Guy, C.M. (2004a) 'A long road to retail revival', *Planning*, 21 May: 8.

Guy, C.M. (2004b) 'Neighbourhood retailing and food poverty: a case study in Cardiff', *International Journal of Retail and Distribution Management*, 32: 577–81.

Guy, C.M. (2004c) 'Game on!', *Town and Country Planning*, 73: 10–11.

Guy, C.M. (2006a, in press) 'Retail productivity and land use planning: negotiating "joined-up" retail planning policy', *Environment and Planning C: Government and Policy*, 24.

Guy, C.M. (2006b, in press) 'Is "demonstration of need" necessary in retail planning policy?', *Regional Studies*, 40.

Guy, C.M. and Bennison, D. (2002) 'Retail planning policy, superstore development and retailer competition', *International Journal of Retail and Distribution Management*, 30: 431–4.

Guy, C.M. and Bennison, D. (2006, in press) 'Planning guidance and large store development in the UK: the search for "flexibility"', *Environment and Planning A*, 38.

Guy, C.M. and David, G. (2002) 'Problems on the shop floor', *Planning*, 22 February: 19.

Guy, C.M. and David, G. (2004) 'Measuring physical access to "healthy foods" in areas of social deprivation: a case study in Cardiff', *International Journal of Consumer Studies*, 28: 222–34.

Guy, C.M., Bennison, D. and Clarke, R. (2005) 'Scale economies and superstore retailing: new evidence from the UK', *Journal of Retailing and Consumer Services*, 12: 73–81.

Guy, C.M., Clarke, G.P. and Eyre, H. (2004) 'Food retail change and the growth of food deserts: a case study of Cardiff', *International Journal of Retail and Distribution Management*, 32: 72–88.

Hallsworth, A.G. (1994) 'Decentralization of retailing in Britain: the breaking of the third wave', *Professional Geographer*, 46: 296–307.

Hallsworth, A.G. and Clarke, I. (2001) 'Further reflections on the arrival of Wal-Mart in the United Kingdom', *Environment and Planning A*, 33: 1709–16.

Hallsworth, A.G. and Evers, D. (2002) 'The steady advance of Wal-Mart across Europe and changing government attitudes towards planning and competition', *Environment and Planning C: Government and Policy*, 20: 297–309.

Hampson, S. (1987) 'Danger ahead without retail planning', *Town and Country Planning*, 57: 238–9.

Hass-Klau, C., Mobbs, I. and Crampton, G. (1998) *Accessibility, Walking and Linked Trips, A Report for the National Retail Planning Forum and the Department of the Environment, Transport and the Regions*, Brighton: Environment and Transport Planning.

Hay, A. (2005) 'The transport implications of Planning Policy Guidance on the location of superstores in England and Wales: simulations and case study', *Journal of Transport Geography*, 13: 13–22.

Healy, A. (2002) 'Commentary: Evidence-based policy – the latest form of inertia and control?', *Planning Theory and Practice*, 3: 97–8.

Heaps, P. (2005) 'Retail warehousing, shopping parks and leisure', *Journal of Retail and Leisure Property*, 4: 174–80.

Henley Centre for Forecasting (1988) *The Demand for Retail Space: A Survey of Major Retailers*, London: Hillier Parker.

Hernandez, T. and Bennison, D. (2000) 'The art and science of retail location decisions', *International Journal of Retail Distribution and Management*, 28: 357–67.

Hillier Parker (1987) *British Shopping Developments Master List*, London: Hillier Parker.

Hillier Parker (1989a) *British Shopping Developments 1988 Supplement*, London: Hillier Parker.

Hillier Parker (1989b) *Retail Parks*, London: Hillier Parker.

Hillier Parker (1991a) *Retail Warehouse Park Development Master List*, London: Hillier Parker.

Hillier Parker (1991b) *British Shopping Centre Developments 1990 Supplement*, London: Hillier Parker.

Hillier Parker (1994) *Retail Warehouse Park Development Master List*, London: Hillier Parker.

Hillman, M. (1973) 'The social costs of hypermarket developments', *Built Environment*, 2: 89–91.

Hitchman, C., Christie, I., Harrison, M. and Lang, T. (2002) *Inconvenience Food: The Struggle to Eat Well on a Low Income*, London: Demos.

HM Treasury (2000) *Productivity in the UK: The Evidence and the Government's Approach*, London: TSO.

Hogg, S., Medway, D. and Harvey, D. (2000) 'Measuring the effectiveness of town centre management', *Town and Country Planning*, 69: 177–9.

Hooper, G. (2002) *Retail-led Regeneration: An Examination of the Relationship between Retail Development and Regeneration*, Cardiff University: Dissertation for the MSc in City and Regional Planning.

House of Commons Environment Select Committee (1994) *Fourth Report: Shopping Centres and their Future*, London: HMSO.

House of Commons Environment Select Committee (1997) *Fourth Report: Shopping Centres*, London: TSO.

Howard, E. (1993) 'Assessing the impact of shopping centre development: the Meadowhall case', *Journal of Property Research*, 10: 97–119.

Howard, E.B. and Davies, R.L. (1993) 'The impact of regional out-of-town centres: the case of the Metro Centre', *Progress in Planning*, 40: 90–165.

Howard, M. (1990) 'Out of town shopping: is the revolution over?', *RSA Journal*, 138: 162–7.

Hughes, B. (2000) *Speech to the Third Annual Local Food Retailing Conference*, London.

Hunt Dobson (2002) *Brierley Hill Regeneration Partnership: Economic Impact Study*, http://www.brierleyhill.org/pdf%20downloads/EconomicImpactStudy.pdf.

Ibrahim, M.F. and McGoldrick, P.J. (2003) *Shopping Choices with Public Transport Options*, Aldershot: Ashgate.

Imrie, R. and Thomas, H. (eds) (1999) *British Urban Policy: An Evaluation of the Urban Development Corporations* (2nd edn), London: Sage.

Institute of Grocery Distribution (1989) *Food Retailing: A Review of Food Retailing Structure and Trends*, Watford.

Interactive Media in Retail Group (2005) *News Report: E-Christmas Internet Sales Soar 20%*, 17 January.

Jackson, C. and Watkins, C. (2005) 'Planning policy and retail property markets: measuring the dimensions of planning intervention', *Urban Studies*, 42: 1453–69.

Jackson, P., Perez-del-Aguila, R., Clarke, I., Hallsworth, A., De Kervenoael, R. and Kirkup, M. (2004) *Retail Restructuring and Consumer Choice 2: Understanding Consumer Choice at the Household Level*, Working Paper, Lancaster University Management School.

Jenks, M., Burton, E. and Williams, K., eds. (1996) *The Compact City: A Sustainable Urban Form?*, London: E and F N Spon.

Jones, P. (1983) 'DIY and home improvement centres: a growth area', *The Planner*, 69: 13–15.

Jones, P. (1984) 'Retail warehouse developments in Britain', *Area*, 16: 41–7.

Jones, P. (1989) 'The high street fights back', *Town and Country Planning*, 58: 43–5.

Jones, P. (1995) 'Factory outlet centres and planning issues', *International Journal of Retail and Distribution Management*, 23: 12–17.

Jones, P. and Vignali, C. (1993) 'Factory outlet shopping centres', *Town and Country Planning*, 62: 240–1.

Jones, P., Hillier, D. and Comfort, D. (2003) 'Urban regeneration companies and city centres', *Management Research News*, 26: 54–63.

Jones, P.M. (1978) *Trading Features of Hypermarkets and Superstores*, Reading: Unit for Retail Planning Information.

Journal of Planning and Environment Law (1999a) 'R. v. Hambleton District Council, ex parte Somerfield Stores Limited', B107–B109.

Journal of Planning and Environment Law (1999b) 'Need and the sequential test', 307–8.

Keeble, L. (1969) *Principles and Practice of Town and Country Planning* (4th edn), London: Estates Gazette.

Kingfisher plc (2002) *How Green is my Kitchen? Kingfisher's Update on the Social and Environmental Trends that Affect our Business*, http://www.kingfisher.com/files/english/environment/csrreport2002.pdf.

Kirby, D. and Holf, G. (1986) 'Planning responses to non-retail uses in shopping centres', *The Planner*, 72 (7): 28–30.

Kirkup, M., De Kervenoael, R., Hallsworth, A., Clarke, I., Jackson, P. and Perez-del-Aguila, R. (2004) 'Inequalities in consumer choice: exploring consumer experiences in suburban neighbourhoods', *International Journal of Retail and Distribution Management*, 32: 511–22.

Land Securities (2004) *Corporate Responsibility Report 2004*, http://www.investis.com/reports/land_csr_2004/report.php?type=1&zoom=1&page=20.

Land Use Consultants in association with Roger Tym and Partners and Oscar Faber TPA (1995) *Defining the Possible Effects of Draft PPG13: Transport, a Research Study for the Department of the Environment and the Department of Transport*, London.

Lang, T. and Caraher, M. (1998) 'Access to healthy foods: Part II. Food poverty and shopping deserts: what are the implications for health promotion and practice?', *Health Education Journal*, 57: 202–11.

Langston, P., Clarke, G.P. and Clarke, D.B. (1997) 'Retail saturation, retail location and retail competition: an analysis of British grocery retailing', *Environment and Planning A*, 29: 77–104.

Lee Donaldson Associates (1986a) *Superstore Appeals Review 1986*, London: Lee Donaldson Associates.

Lee Donaldson Associates (1986b) *Shopping Centre Appeals Review 1986*, London: Lee Donaldson Associates.

Lee Donaldson Associates (1987) *Retail Warehouse Appeals Review*, London: Lee Donaldson Associates.

Lee Donaldson Associates (1991) *Superstore Appeals Review Three*, London: Lee Donaldson Associates.

Lee, M. and Kent, E. (1975) *Caerphilly Hypermarket Study Year Two*, Donaldsons Research Report 2, London: Donaldsons.

Lee, M. and Kent, E. (1976) *Planning Inquiry Study*, Donaldsons Research Report 3, London: Donaldsons.

Lee, M. and Kent, E. (1978) *Planning Inquiry Study Two*, Donaldsons Research Report 5, London: Donaldsons.

Lee, M. and Kent, E. (1979) *Caerphilly Hypermarket Study: Year Five*, Donaldsons Research Report 6, London: Donaldsons.

Lee, M., Jones, P. and Leach, C. (1973) *Caerphilly Hypermarket Study*, Donaldsons Research Report, London: Donaldsons.

Lock, D. (1976) 'Small shop survival', *Built Environment Quarterly*, 2: 207–10.

Lockwood, J. (1999) *The Lockwood Survey 1999: Setting the Scene for the Next Century*, Armitage Bridge: Urban Management Initiatives.

London Development Agency (2005) *How London's Planners can Improve Access to Healthy and Affordable Food, Draft Guidance Notes from the Food Strategy Unit*, London: LDA.

Lord, J.D. (2000) 'Retail saturation: inevitable or irrelevant?', *Urban Geography*, 21: 342–60.

Low, N. (1975) 'Centrism and the provision of services in residential areas', *Urban Studies*, 12: 177–91.

Lowe, A. and Reeves, C. (2000) 'Contemporary issues in retailing: Tesco views on planning', *Proceedings of the 2000 Annual Manchester Conference for Contemporary Issues in Retail Marketing*, Manchester Metropolitan University Business School.

Lowe, M.S. (1998) 'The Merry Hill Regional Shopping Centre controversy: PPG6 and new urban geographies', *Built Environment*, 24: 57–69.

Lowe, M.S. (2000) 'Britain's regional shopping centres: new urban forms?', *Urban Studies*, 37: 261–74.

Lowe, M.S. (2005) 'The regional shopping centre in the inner city: a study of retail-led urban regeneration', *Urban Studies*, 42: 449–70.

Maat, K., van Wee, B. and Stead, D. (2005) 'Land use and travel behaviour: expected effects from the perspective of utility theory and activity-based theories', *Environment and Planning B: Planning and Design*, 32: 33–46.

Mackie, S. (1980) 'The impact of Central Milton Keynes', *Proceedings of the PTRC Summer Annual Meeting*.

Mahajan, V., Sharma, S. and Kerin, R. (1988) 'Assessing market penetration opportunities and saturation potential for multi-store, multi-market retailers', *Journal of Retailing*, 64: 315–33.

Manchester University (1964) *Regional Shopping Centres in North West England: Haydock Report*, Department of Town and Country Planning.

Manchester University (1966) *Regional Shopping Centres in North West England Part Two: a Retail Shopping Model*, Department of Town and Country Planning.

Marcus, M. (1973) 'The future of pedestrianised shopping precincts', *Retail Business*, no. 180, London: Economist Intelligence Unit.

Marriott, O. (1967) *The Property Boom*, London: Hamish Hamilton.

Marshall, S. (1999) 'Restraining mobility while maintaining accessibility: an impression of the "city of sustainable growth"', *Built Environment*, 25: 168–79.

McGlone, P., Dobson, B., Dowler, E. and Nelson, M. (1999) *Food Projects and How They Work*, York: York Publishing Services.

McIver, A. (1999a) 'Transportation impact assessment and trip-chaining behaviour', *Traffic and Engineering Control*, 40: 129–34.

McIver, A. (1999b) 'Transportation impact assessment: forecasting travel demand', *Traffic and Engineering Control*, 40: 262–6.

McKinsey Global Institute (1998): *Driving Productivity and Growth in the UK Economy*, Washington: McKinsey and Co.

McLaurin, I. (1976) 'A need for official policy', *Built Environment Quarterly*, 2: 193.

McLoughlin, J.B. (1969) *Urban and Regional Planning: A Systems Approach*, London: Faber and Faber.

McNair, D. (1999) 'Retailer case study: taking the Sainsbury's brand forward', *European Retail Digest*, Issue 21: 12–13.

McNulty, A. (2003) *Town Centre Planning: Written Ministerial Statement*, Hansard, 10 April.

Ministry of Housing and Local Government and Ministry of Transport (1962) *Town Centres: Approach to Renewal*, Planning Bulletin 1, London: HMSO.

Ministry of Housing and Local Government and Ministry of Transport (1963) *Town Centres: Current Practice*, Planning Bulletin 4, London: HMSO.

Ministry of Housing and Local Government and Welsh Office (1967) *The Needs of New Communities*, London: HMSO.

Ministry of Housing and Local Government and Welsh Office (1969) *The Development of District Centres in Towns with Central Area Traffic Congestion*, London: HMSO.

Ministry of Housing and Local Government and Welsh Office (1970) *Development Plans: A Manual on Form and Content*, London: HMSO.

Ministry of Town and Country Planning (1947) *The Redevelopment of Central Areas*, London: HMSO.

Ministry of Transport (1963) *Traffic in Towns*, London: HMSO.

Mitchell, A. and Kirkup, M. (2003) 'Retail development and urban regeneration: a case study of Castle Vale', *International Journal of Retail and Distribution Management*, 31: 451–8.

Moir, C. (1990) 'Competition in the UK grocery trades', in Moir, C. and Dawson, J. (eds) *Competition and Markets: Essays in Honour of Margaret Hall*, Basingstoke: Macmillan, 91–118.

Moir, C. and Dawson, J. (eds) (1990) *Competition and Markets: Essays in Honour of Margaret Hall*, Basingstoke: Macmillan.

MORI (2000) *Transport Preferences Among Out of Town Shoppers: Summary Report*, London: British Council for Out of Town Retail.

Moss, M. (2004) *Should Planning Policy be Used to Tackle Local Monopolies in the Supermarket Sector?*, Cardiff University: Dissertation for the Diploma in Town Planning.

Mynors, C. (1991) 'The Planning and Compensation Act 1991: (3) development plans, minerals and waste disposal', *The Planner*, 13 (September): 7–8.

National Assembly for Wales (2002) *Planning Policy Wales*, Cardiff: NAW.

National Assembly for Wales (2004) *Revised Initial Guidance Note - Implications for Development Plans in Wales of the Planning and Compulsory Purchase Act*, Cardiff: NAW.

National Assembly for Wales (2005) *Ministerial Interim Planning Policy Statement 02/2005: Planning for Retailing and Town Centres*, Cardiff: NAW.

Neuman, M. (2005) 'The compact city fallacy', *Journal of Planning Education and Research*. 25: 11–26.

New Economics Foundation (2002) *Ghost Town Britain*, London: NEF.

New Economics Foundation (2003) *Ghost Town Britain II: Death on the High Street*, London: NEF.

New Economics Foundation (2004) *Clone Town Britain*, London: NEF.

New Economics Foundation (2005) *Clone Town Britain: The Survey Results*, London: NEF.

Newman, P. and Kenworthy, J. (1989) 'Gasoline consumption and cities – a comparison of US cities with a global survey', *Journal of the American Planning Association*, 55: 24–37.

Nooteboom, B. (1980) *Retailing – Applied Economic Analysis in the Theory of the Firm*, Amsterdam: Gieben.

Norris, S. (1990) 'The return of impact assessment: Assessing the impact of regional shopping centre proposals in the United Kingdom', *Papers of the Regional Science Association*, 69: 101–19.

Oc, T. and Tiesdell, S. (eds) (1997) *Safer City Centres: Reviving the Public Realm*, London: Paul Chapman.

Office of the Deputy Prime Minister (2003) *Consultation on Draft Planning Policy Statement 6: Planning for Town Centres*, London: ODPM.

Office of the Deputy Prime Minister (2004) *Tackling Social Exclusion: Taking Stock and Looking to the Future: Emerging Findings*, London: ODPM.

Office of the Deputy Prime Minister (2005a) *Planning Policy Statement 6: Planning for Town Centres*, London: TSO.

Office of the Deputy Prime Minister (2005b) *Planning Policy Statement 1: Delivering Sustainable Development*, London: TSO.

Office of the Deputy Prime Minister (2005c) *Planning for Town Centres: Guidance on Design and Implementation Tools*, London: ODPM.

Office of the Deputy Prime Minister (2005d) *Technical Report: Using Town Centres Statistics to Indicate the Broad Location of Retail Development – Initial Analysis*, London: ODPM.

Office of the Deputy Prime Minister (n.d.) *What is Social Exclusion?* http://www.socialexclusion.gov.uk/page.asp?id=213.

Office of the Deputy Prime Minister and British Retail Consortium (2003) *Research Report 6: Changing Practices. A Good Practice Guide for Businesses Locating in Deprived Areas*, London: ODPM.

O'Kelly, M. (2001) 'Retail market share and saturation', *Journal of Retailing and Consumer Services*, 8: 37–45.

Oxford Institute of Retail Management (2004) *NRPF Scoping Paper: Linked Trips and the Viability and Vitality of Centres of Retail Activity*, Oxford: Templeton College.

Oxford Retail Group (1989) *Planning for Major Retail Development*, Oxford: Templeton College.

Pain, G.M. (1967) *Planning and the Shopkeeper*, London: Barrie and Rockliffe.

Pal, J., Bennison, D., Clarke, I. and Byrom, J. (2001) 'Power, policy networks and planning: the involvement of major grocery retailers in the formulation of Planning Policy Guidance Note 6 since 1988', *International Review of Retail, Distribution and Consumer Research*, 11: 225–46.

Peters, T. and Lang, T. (2000) *The Crisis in UK Local Food Retailing*, Thames Valley University, Centre for Food Policy Discussion paper 11.

Piachaud, D. and Webb, J. (1996) *The Price of Food: Missing Out on Mass Consumption*, STICERD, London School of Economics and Political Science.

Pickering, J.F. (1972) 'Economic implications of hypermarkets in Britain', *European Journal of Marketing*, 6: 257–69.

Pilat, D. (2005) 'Assessing the productivity of the UK retail sector: some further reflections', *International Review of Retail, Distribution and Consumer Research*, 15: 291–6.

Planner (1988) 'Shopping provision cannot be left to market forces', *The Planner*, 74 (February): vi.

Planner (1989) 'Ridley awards costs in "Golden Triangle" decision', *The Planner*, 75 (Mid-month Supplement, March): 3.

Planning (2000) 'Council rejects call to give mall district centre status', *Planning*, 21 July: 1.

Planning Officers' Society (2004) *Policies for Spatial Plans: Consultation Draft*, http://www.planningofficers.org.uk/documents/spatialpolicies0704.pdf.

Porter, S. and Raistrick P. (1998) *The Impact of Out-of-Town Superstores on Local Retail Employment*, London: National Retail Planning Forum.

Price, D.G. (1985) 'Data bases and superstore development: a comment', *Transactions of the Institute of British Geographers*, 10: 377–9.

Rawcliffe, P. and Roberts, J. (1991) 'The art of shortening trip lengths', *Town and Country Planning*, 60: 310–11.

Raynsford, N. (1997) 'Out of town supermarkets', *Parliamentary Answer*, Hansard Vol. 302, Cols. 401–2.

Raynsford, N. (2000) *Speech to National Retail Planning Forum Conference on 'Town centres: turning the lights on'*, http://www.nrpf.org/speech.pdf.

Raynsford, N. (2001) *Speech to the Retail Week Property Forum*.

Reisig, V. and Hobbiss, A. (2000) 'Food deserts and how to tackle them: a study of one city's approach', *Health Education Journal*, 59: 137–49.

Reynolds, J., Howard, E., Dragun, D., Rosewell, B. and Ormerod, P. (2005) 'Assessing the productivity of the UK retail sector', *International Review of Retail, Distribution and Consumer Research*, 15: 237–80.

Rhodes, J. (2000) 'What is the policy on retail development?', *Planning*, 27 October: 20.

Ridgway, J.D. (1976) 'The future of district shopping centres – a retailer's view', *Proceedings of the PTRC Summer Annual Meeting*, G16.

Roberts, P. and Sykes, H. (eds) (1999) *Urban Regeneration: A Handbook*, London: Sage.

Robinson, N., Caraher, M. and Lang, T. (2000) 'Access to shops: the views of low-income shoppers', *Health Education Journal*, 59: 121–36.

Rogers, D.S. (1979) 'Evaluating the business and planning impacts of suburban shopping developments: a proposed framework of analysis', *Regional Studies*, 13: 395–408.

Rooker, Lord (2004) *Speech to the British Urban Regeneration Association Conference 'Deprived or Under-served?'*, http://www.societyandbusiness.gov.uk/pdf/f31rooker0104.pdf.

Royal Town Planning Institute (1988) *Planning for Shopping into the 21st Century*, London: RTPI.

Rubin, E. (2005) *A Study into the Effects of Poor Food Access Experienced by Residents of a Food Desert and the Coping Mechanisms they Employ*, Cardiff University: Dissertation for MSc in City and Regional Planning.

Sainsbury, Lord (1989a) 'New attitudes for better decisions: a business view of the planning system', *The Planner*, 75 (10 November), 16–19.

Sainsbury, J., plc (1989b) *Local Attitudes to Central Advice: A Survey of the Response of Planning Authorities to Government Planning Guidance*, London: J Sainsbury.

Sainsbury, J., plc (1993) *Food Shopping and the Car: Findings from a Survey of Car Users*, London.

Sainsbury, T. (1973) 'Success and survival in retailing', *Built Environment*, 2: 85–8.

Sainsbury's Supermarkets Ltd (1999) *Memorandum to the Select Committee on Environment, Transport and Regional Affairs: The Environmental Impact of Supermarket Competition*, London: TSO.

Sampson, S.D. and Tigert, D.J. (1994) 'The impact of warehouse membership clubs: the wheel of retailing turns one more time', *International Review of Retail, Distribution and Consumer Research*, 4: 33–60.

Schiller, R. (1986) 'Retail decentralisation: the coming of the third wave', *The Planner*, 72 (7): 13–15.

Scotsman, The (2000) 'Tesco true to Jack's wishes', *The Scotsman*, 20 September.

Scott, N.K. (1989) *Shopping Centre Design*, London: Van Nostrand Reinhold.

Scottish Development Department (1978) *National Planning Guidelines on the Location of Major Shopping Development*, Circular 63/1978, Edinburgh: SDD.

Scottish Development Department (1986) *National Planning Guidelines: Location of Major Retail Developments*, Edinburgh: SDD.

Scottish Executive Development Department (2000) *1998 Retail Development Survey*, Edinburgh: SEDD.

Scottish Executive Development Department (2002) *Scottish Planning Policy 1: The Planning System*, Edinburgh: SEDD.

Scottish Executive Development Department (2004) *2002 Retail Development Survey*, Edinburgh: SEDD.

Scottish Executive Development Department (2005) *Scottish Planning Policy SPP8: Town Centres: Consultation Draft*, Edinburgh: SEDD.

Scottish Office Development Department (1996) *National Planning Policy Guideline 8: Retailing*, Edinburgh: SODD.

Scottish Office Development Department (1998) *National Planning Policy Guideline 8 (Revised 1998): Town Centres and Retailing*, Edinburgh: SODD.

Scottish Office Development Department (1999) *Planning Advice Note 59: Improving Town Centres*, Edinburgh: SODD.

Simmonds, D. and Coombe, D. (2000) 'The transport implications of alternative urban forms', in Williams, K., Burton, E. and Jenks, M. (eds) *Achieving Sustainable Urban Form*, London: E and F N Spon, 121–30.

Skerratt, S. (1999) 'Food availability and choice in rural Scotland: the impact of "place"', *British Food Journal*, 101: 537–44.

Smith, G. (1994) 'Vitality and viability of town centres', *Journal of Planning and Environment Law*, Special Issue on 'Planning Icons: Myth and Practice', 91–106.

Social Exclusion Unit (2003) *Making the Connections: Final Report on Transport and Social Exclusion*, London: ODPM.

Social Exclusion Unit (2005) *Inclusion Through Innovation: Tackling Social Exclusion Through New Technologies, A Social Exclusion Unit Final Report*, London: ODPM.

Solesbury, W. (2002) 'The ascendancy of evidence', *Planning Theory and Practice*, 3: 90–6.

Sparks, L. (2000) *Employment Effects of Food Superstores: Who is Right and Who Cares?*, Institute for Retail Studies, University of Stirling, Research Paper 0003.

Sparks, L. (2005) 'Special issue: assessing retail productivity', *International Review of Retail, Distribution and Consumer Research*, 15: 227–36.

Sparks, L. and Aitken, P. (1986) 'Retail planning policies in Scottish structure plans', *Land Development Studies*, 3: 59–75.

Speak, S. and Graham, S. (2000) *Service Not Included: Social Implications of Private Sector Restructuring in Marginalised Neighbourhoods*, Bristol: Policy Press.

Spriddell, P.H. (1980) 'Retailing – town centres in the 1980s', in Unit for Retail Planning Information, *Town Centres of the Future*, Reading: URPI U17: 33–40.

Stead, D. (2001) 'Relationships between land use, socioeconomic factors, and travel patterns in Britain', *Environment and Planning B: Planning and Design*, 28: 499–528.

Stocks, N. (1989) 'The Greater Manchester Shopping Inquiry, a case study of strategic retail planning', *Land Development Studies*, 6: 57–83.

Sumner, J. and Davies, K. (1978) 'Hypermarkets and superstores: what do the planning authorities really think?', *Retail and Distribution Management*, 6(4): 8–15.

Sustain (2000) *A Battle in Store? A Discussion of the Social Impact of the Major UK Supermarkets*, London: Sustain.

Templeton College (2004) *Assessing the Productivity of the UK Retail Sector, Report for DTI Retail Strategy Group*, Oxford Institute of Retail Management, Templeton College, University of Oxford.

Tesco (2004) *Tesco plc Annual Review and Summary Financial Statement 2004*, Cheshunt.

Tesco Stores Ltd (2005) *Tesco Regeneration Partnerships: The Story so far ...*, http://www.tesco.com/everylittlehelps/downloads/TescoCR_Regeneration.pdf.

Tewdwr-Jones, M. (1997) 'Plans, policies and inter-governmental relations: assessing the role of national planning guidance in England and Wales', *Urban Studies*, 34: 141–62.

The Mall Cribbs Causeway (2003) *Information Pack*, http://www.mallcribbs.com/downloads/mall_information_pack.pdf.

Thomas, C. and Bromley, R. (2003) 'Retail revitalization and small town centres: the contribution of shopping linkages', *Applied Geography*, 23: 47–71.

Thomas, M. (1976) 'Planners outdistanced by retailers' speed of change', *Built Environment Quarterly*, 2: 194–7.

Thomas, R. (1983) 'Milton Keynes: city of the future?', *Built Environment*, 9: 245–54.

Thorncroft, M. (1976) 'Dynamics of the market place', *Built Environment Quarterly*, 2: 203–6.

Thornley, A. (1991) *Urban Planning Under Thatcherism: The Challenge of the Market*, London: Routledge.

Thorpe, D. (1974) 'Locating retail outlets', in Thorpe, D. (ed.) *Research into Retailing and Distribution*, Farnborough: Saxon House.

Thorpe, D. (1975) *Town Planning for Retailing*, Retail Outlets Research Unit, Research Report no. 20, Manchester.

Thorpe, D. (1990) 'Economic theory, retail output and capacity in British retailing', in Moir, C. and Dawson, J. (eds) *Competition and Markets: Essays in Honour of Margaret Hall*, London: Macmillan, 153–206.

Thorpe, D. (1991) 'The development of British superstore retailing – further comments on Davies and Sparks', *Transactions of the Institute of British Geographers*, 16: 354–67.

Thorpe, D. (1999) *Superstores and Employment in Retailing*, London: National Retail Planning Forum.

Thorpe, D., Bates, P. and Shepherd, P. (1976) 'Retail structure and town planning: superstore impact and long term trends', *Proceedings of the PTRC Summer Annual Meeting*, G14.

Thrall, G.I. and Del Valle, J.C. (1997) 'Applied geography antecedents: marketing geography', *Applied Geographic Studies*, 1: 207–14.

Treadgold, A.D. and Reynolds, J. (1989) *Retail Saturation: Examining the Evidence*, London: Longman.

Tucker, P. (2000) 'Finding a way around the site selection test', *Planning*, 21 April: 18.

Turner, A. (2003) 'What's wrong with Europe's economy?', *Lecture given to London School of Economics*, 5 February, http://cep.lse.ac.uk/queens/Adair_Turner_Transcript.pdf.

Turok, I. (1992) 'Property-led urban regeneration: panacea or placebo?', *Environment and Planning A*, 24: 361–79.

Tym, Roger and Partners (1993) *Merry Hill Impact Study*, London: HMSO.

Unit for Retail Planning Information (1977) *District Shopping Centres: Report of an URPI Workshop*, Reading.

Unit for Retail Planning Information (1982) *Trading Characteristics of Retail Warehouse Operators*, Reading.

Unit for Retail Planning Information (1990) *Planned Inquiries for Proposed Regional Shopping Schemes 1987–1990*, URPI Information Brief 90/5, Reading.

URBED (1994) *Vital and Viable Town Centres: Meeting the Challenge*, Research Report for the Department of the Environment, London: HMSO.

Van, U.-P. and Senior, M. (2000) 'The contribution of mixed land uses to sustainable travel in cities', in Williams, K., Burton, E. and Jenks, M. (eds) *Achieving Sustainable Urban Form*, London: E and F N Spon, 139–48.

Wade, B. (1979) 'Retail planning in Britain', in Davies, R.L. (ed.) *Retail Planning in the European Community*, Farnborough: Saxon House.

Wade, B. (1983a) 'Retail planning without data', *The Planner*, 69: 26–8.

Wade, B. (ed.) (1983b) *Superstore Appeals: Alternative Impact Assessment Methods*, Reading: Unit for Retail Planning Information.

Wade, B. (1985) 'From lifeline to leisure', *Town and Country Planning*, 54: 215–16.

Walker, B. (2005) 'Lost in translation', *Regeneration and Renewal*, 4 November: 20–2.

Warren, G. and Taylor, D. (1991) 'The big shop – carless in Camden?', *Town and Country Planning*, 60: 206–7.

Webber, R. (2004) *Tracking Retail Trends in London – Linking the 1971 Census of Distribution to ODPM's New Town Centre Statistical Series: a Revised Report*, University College London: Centre for Advanced Statistical Analysis, Working Paper 91.

Welsh Office (1996a) *Planning Guidance (Wales): Planning Policy*, Cardiff: WO.

Welsh Office (1996b) *Technical Advice Note (Wales) 4: Retailing and Town Centres*, Cardiff: WO.

Welsh Office (1999) *Planning Guidance: Planning Policy Wales First Revision*, Cardiff: WO.

Westlake, T. (1993) 'The disadvantaged consumer: problems and policies', in Bromley, R.D.F. and Thomas, C.J. (eds) *Retail Change: Contemporary Issues*, London: UCL Press.

Westlake, T. and Smith, M. (1994) 'Facing the fourth wave of retail development?', *Town and Country Planning*, 63: 334–5.

Whelan, A., Wrigley, N., Warm, D. and Cannings, E. (2002) 'Life in a "Food Desert"', *Urban Studies*, 39: 2083–100.

Whysall, P. (1995) 'Regenerating inner city shopping centres: the British experience', *Journal of Retailing and Consumer Services*, 2: 3–13.

Whysall, P. (1999) 'Revisiting the first wave of retail decentralisation: Britain's first out-of-town store', *Proceedings of the 10th International Conference on Research in the Distributive Trades, University of Stirling*, 462–71.

Williams, C.C. (1996) 'Rethinking the role of retailing and consumer services in local economic development: a British perspective', *Journal of Retailing and Consumer Services*, 3: 53–6.

Williams, C.C. (1997) 'Rethinking the role of the retail sector in economic development', *Service Industries Journal*, 17: 205–20.

Williams, C.C. and Windebank, J. (2000) 'Modes of goods acquisition in deprived neighbourhoods', *International Review of Retail, Distribution and Consumer Research*, 10: 73–94.

Williams, C.C. and Windebank, J. (2002) 'The "excluded consumer": a neglected aspect of social exclusion?', *Policy and Politics*, 30: 501–13.

Williams, H. and Baker, T. (1998) 'Town centre management: a retailer's perspective', *Proceedings of the 1998 Annual Manchester Conference for Contemporary Issues in Retailing and Marketing*, Manchester Metropolitan University.

Williams, J.J. (1991) 'Meadowhall: its impact on Sheffield city centre and Rotherham', *International Journal of Retail Distribution and Management*, 19(1): 29–37.

Williams, K., Burton, E. and Jenks, M. (eds) (2000) *Achieving Sustainable Urban Form*, London: E and F N Spon.

Williams, P. and Hubbard, P. (2001) 'Who is disadvantaged? Retail change and social exclusion', *International Review of Retail, Distribution and Consumer Research*, 11: 267–86.

Wilson, L.C., Alexander, A. and Lumbers, M. (2004) 'Food access and dietary variety among older people', *International Journal of Retail and Distribution Management*, 32: 109–22.

Winter, J. and Farthing, S. (1997) 'Coordinating facility provision and new housing development: impacts on car and local facility use', in Farthing, S.M. (ed.), *Evaluating Local Environmental Policy*, Aldershot: Avebury, 159–79.

Wood, S., Lowe, M. and Wrigley, N. (2006) 'Life after PPG6: recent food retailer responses to planning regulation tightening', *International Review of Retail, Distribution and Consumer Research*, 16: 23–41.

World Commission on Environment and Development (1987) *Our Common Future*, Oxford: Oxford University Press.

Wrigley, N. (1991) 'Is the "golden age" of British grocery retailing at a watershed?', *Environment and Planning A*, 23: 1537–44.

Wrigley, N. (1992) 'Sunk capital, the property crisis, and the restructuring of British food retailing', *Environment and Planning A*, 24: 1521–7.

Wrigley, N. (1994) 'After the store wars: towards a new era of competition in UK food retailing?', *Journal of Retailing and Consumer Services*, 1: 5–20.

Wrigley, N. (1996) 'Sunk costs and corporate restructuring: British food retailing and the property crisis', in Wrigley, N. and Lowe, M. (eds) *Retailing, Consumption and Capital: Towards the New Retail Geography*, Harlow: Longman, 116–36.

Wrigley, N. (1998a) 'Understanding store development programmes in post-property-crisis UK food retailing', *Environment and Planning A*, 30: 15–35.

Wrigley, N. (1998b) 'PPG6 and the contemporary UK food store development dynamic', *British Food Journal*, 100: 154–61.

Wrigley, N. (2001) 'Local spatial monopoly and competition regulation: reflections on recent UK and US rulings', *Environment and Planning A*, 33: 189–94.

Wrigley, N. (2002) '"Food deserts" in British cities: policy context and research priorities', *Urban Studies*, 39: 2029–40.

Wrigley, N., Guy, C. and Lowe, M. (2002a) 'Urban regeneration, social inclusion and large store development: the Seacroft development in context', *Urban Studies*, 39: 2101–14.

Wrigley, N., Warm, D., Margetts, B. and Whelan, A. (2002b) 'Assessing the impact of improved retail access on diet in a "food desert": a preliminary report', *Urban Studies*, 39: 2061–82.

Wrigley, N., Warm, D. and Margetts, B. (2003) 'Deprivation, diet and food-retail access: findings from the Leeds "food deserts" study', *Environment and Planning A*, 35: 151–88.

Wrigley, N., Warm, D., Margetts, B. and Lowe, M. (2004) 'The Leeds "food deserts" intervention study: what the focus groups reveal', *International Journal of Retail and Distribution Management*, 32: 123–36.

Index